PLAYS OF LOVE AND RAGE

by

Mark Lee

California Dog Fight

Rebel Armies Deep Into Chad

Pirates

An American Romance

&

notes by the playwright

@ Copyright, 2020, by Mark W. Lee

Both theater professionals and amateurs are hereby warned that the author notes, poems and plays found in PLAYS OF LOVE AND RAGE are fully protected under the copyright laws of the United States of America and of all other countries covered by the Pan-American Copyright Convention and the Universal Copyright Convention.

The stage performance rights of REBEL ARMIES DEEP INTO CHAD are controlled exclusively by Dramatists Play Service, Inc. in New York City.

Contact: https://www.dramatists.com/text/rights.asp

The stage performance rights of CALIFORNIA DOG FIGHT, PIRATES and AN AMERICAN ROMANCE are controlled exclusively by the playwright.

Contact: http://www.markwlee.com/

The author acknowledges the "Fair Use" doctrine in US copyright law: i.e. that brief excerpts of copyright material may, under certain circumstances, be quoted verbatim for purposes such as criticism, news reporting, teaching, and research, without the need for permission from or payment to the copyright holder.

This edition published by Brook Farm Books
Paperback Edition ISBN: 978-1-947635-30-2
Eboook Edition ISBN: 978-1-947635-31-9

For

Gilbert Parker

&

Peter Hagan

CONTENTS

INTRODUCTION: FOUR POEMS AND A PLAY

NOTES: CALIFORNIA DOG FIGHT

CALIFORNIA DOG FIGHT

NOTES: REBEL ARMES DEEP INTO CHAD

REBEL ARMIES DEEP INTO CHAD

NOTES: PIRATES

PIRATES

NOTES: AN AMERICAN ROMANCE

AN AMERICAN ROMANCE

INTRODUCTION: FOUR POEMS AND A PLAY

In the summer of 1969, I visited London for the first time and saw the musical, *Hair*. I was a long-haired eighteen-year-old watching actors who were supposedly speaking for my generation, but I thought that the musical's Summer of Love plot and faux rock songs were already past their sell date. Naked hippies dancing on stage were just an amusement for old people. But a few days later I took the tube to Sloane Square and watched a play that changed my view of what could be dramatized on the stage.

Saved by Edward Bond, was set in the shabby council estates of outer London. It was originally performed for private audiences after the Lord Chamberlain refused to give the play a performance license. London theater censorship was abolished in 1968 and I saw the play's first public run at the Royal Court Theatre.

Saved is notorious for the scene in which a group of young men kill a baby in a perambulator. But that shocking death wasn't as important to me as the feeling that I was seeing an intensification of reality on stage. I realized that "theatrical" didn't have to mean false or mannered. A playwright could create a world that could show both love – and rage.

In my senior year of high school I met a college admissions officer that decided to play God and offered me a full scholarship to Yale University. Sitting at seminar tables in oak-paneled rooms, I felt a painful awareness of my own ignorance, but I read constantly and began to attend the plays produced by the drama school and Yale Repertory Theatre. If I walked two miles down empty streets and under a freeway, I could buy discount tickets at New Haven's Long Wharf Theatre.

The Long Wharf was where I saw the American premiere of *The Changing Room* by British playwright David Storey. The play was set in the locker room of a North England rugby team. During the play, you watched the team assemble before the game, gather their courage during halftime and celebrate a victory afterwards. *The Changing Room* didn't have a conventional plot and character development, but the playwright made you care about the weary athletes that fought for victory on a frozen battlefield.

I was inspired and entertained by the theater, but the idea of becoming a playwright never occurred to me. During my final year at Yale, I become friends with the author Robert Penn Warren. I wanted to be like my mentor: a poet who also wrote popular novels. Working as a night time security guard, I read the *Oxford Anthology of English Literature* multiple times. My first published poem in *The Atlantic Monthly* had a fictional character and story, and was written in a traditional form.

JIMMY BIGNELL'S SONNET

The basket of my cuts creaks down the stairs
These caulking days, don't require much these days
My stomach, lungs, all sold to some squeak doctor to obey
The rest propped like a kewpie on this chair
I swear to Christ I once had teeth to tear
The salt meat, nibble on the breasts along the way
Lost, all lost, for some slow reason, until my death plays
Like a cat beside the door; guess I should care
Where the next shipping's going to be
And pray to find a captain who's a gentleman
Like sailor's wives who blubber hymns for waveless seas
Remember riding Baja when a downward Santa Ana ran
And squeezed us in her arms until the winch rope snapped on free
I grabbed it, felt the singing in my hands

Moving down to New York City after graduation, I went to almost every production of Joe Papp's Public Theater, including David Rabe's electrifying trilogy of plays inspired by the Vietnam War. I was working as taxi driver and could barely pay my rent so I would sneak into Broadway plays during the intermission and watch the second act. Although I admired plays and playwrights, I was still exploring the traditional forms of poetry. The *Times Literary Supplement* published one of my poems that was influenced by Dylan Thomas and Gerard Manley Hopkins.

MAY DEATH NOT BE THE FALL

May death not be the fall that takes you in
That lures you from the midway to his tent
All Holly Molly for a squeeze
Of majesty of end of everything and known
The slither feather of his name

May death not kiss you to the darkness and the freaks
Avoiding all the hot exhaustion of the room
The breath and bootlegs prismed by the light
That blue calf slippering the womb
Below the pig gun, ripper knife and tongue

May death fail to amuse you with his show
That naked dancer with her lips upon the snake
Forgetting grace, the morning by the sun
When down I touched the stomach of a dead
And held it there
And it was cold and concave, smooth and whole

So how does a writer create a distinctive voice? While living in New York, I came up with the idea of writing a long poem about the last voyage of Henry Hudson. After wintering on the shore of Hudson Bay, the English sea captain continued his search for the Northwest Passage, but his crew mutinied and left him in a rowboat with his son. Inspired by the story, I visited Hudson Bay at the beginning of winter, paid two Crees to take me across the bay, and then ran out of food exploring the cold landscape. The poem that was published in *The Sewanee Review* was a theatrical monologue in a poetical form. I tried to imagine was Hudson was thinking as he remembered his past three voyages and contemplated his own death.

HUDSON BAY 1611

On the two and twentieth of June
Four days from our wintering
On fish and scurvy grass beside a frozen sea,
William Wilson – the boatswain –
Bennett and the others,
Bound my arms and forced me
With my son and seven of the sick
Into the open shallop –
Cut us from the stern alone
Upon black water.

> Remembering The Desolations:
> Whales rolled and steamed beside us,
> Shuddering beneath the hull,
> Its wet wood, pitch, and man smell,
> Cold grey bottom clay that dripped
> Onto the deck from hand on hand of fathom rope.
> The wheel set north-northwest,
> A snow land glowing ghost at night
> I gave the name: Desire Provokes.

I cannot find that way again.
All sightings lost, as if each island
Cut its anchor, perished in the fog.
The stars are blind,
The mountains pressed away,
Our small boat bumping ice to ice
With two oars cracked and spray
On the three sick shivering the bow.
I cat the bandage,
Scratched my knife upon my son's white hand.

> I fixed my senses on the wind,
> And thought of voyages past:
> A summer river and the savages
> With black paste slashed across their cheeks,
> Their women naked to our eyes
> As we gave wine for otter skins
> And watched the young men dance upon the deck.
> Then there were knifes and treachery,
> A brown hand hammered on the mast,
> And blood that spread its dark smoke through the water.

Death knelt down quietly
And cupped his leech upon the carpenter
Until his legs drained cold;
His loins, my hand upon his stomach cold,
And knew his end
And stripped him for his clothes
To cast him naked in the sea.
I prayed, then rowed against the wind
With two men pulling on each oar;
In time we could not find him there.

> In memory we traveled North from Gravesend,
> Ran the wind past Blackwall where
> The water transformed green and dark and then was clear,
> Splattered with the roll and plunging of our fall.
> Then cold came hard,

And ice chewed hungry at the sleep
That sealed me in my parents' bed.
All warm and waking to an old man's bones –
The slap of wave and lamp swing in a little room.

I am a prisoner upon this water;
Captive to the fog grown in its government of white,
The rush and wood creak of the ice released
With birds like women keening for a lost son
And the failure of the wind.
Failure of the man who lay down on the bottom of a boat,
And felt the darkness cover him.
The moon destroyed, the stars consumed in night.

    For I was falling sightless on a constant edge of wave,
    Until the sun burned through the clouds and from the water rose Cathay.
    I immediately proceeded with my proper command:
    Obtained the tea and clove, the beggar's root still wet with clay.
    The turmeric and gold, a black stone born of alchemy.
    We saw the worship of strange gods,
    And women moving gracefully beside the Royal Gates.
    The soft and yellow of their faces beckoning
    That endless slide down dark green valleys,
    Endless climb up mountains of the sea.

God's Mercy for Temptation,
Pride born Pride,
This Vanity of Days,
The night sky torn
To strips of fire twisted north.
Our way is clear,
Our sail a white curve to the wind.
I touch the coldness,
Lift the skim of water to my lips.
I hold the tiller
North.

After a stint teaching at shabby private school, I moved to Paris where I worked at the Shakespeare and Company bookstore and slept in the bookstore attic every night. A few years later I returned to California where I roofed houses and wrote unproduced film scripts. It was clear that my life – and career as a writer – was going nowhere. But there were occasional moments of clarity among the confusion. Watching a scratchy home movie in a friend's bedroom inspired a poem published in the *Vanderbilt Poetry Review*.

ALBERT EINSTEIN IN CALIFORNIA

With a crack running down through his nose
And a coat hook set in his knees,
Albert Einstein appears on the wall
Of a kitchenette on Cortez Street.

Home movies. Fragile heirlooms
Of a cousin's lover's Great Aunt's friend,
Who drove the Great Man to the beach
And led him, like a child, to the sand.

He walks. He talks. (though we can't hear him)
The wind explores his famous tufts of hair.
In saggy pants he stands upon the limit of the west
And stares and shields his eyes and stares.

His head is split apart
And light appears as brilliant as the sun.
The broken film slaps time until
The plug is pulled and darkness comes.

In the early 1980's I became a foreign correspondent in East Africa and, for a time, was the only western journalist living in Uganda during a genocidal civil war. After the Ugandan government kicked me out of the country, I returned to the United States, got married and moved to Sacramento where my wife had a job with the phone company. I had left the war zone, but for several years I dealt with the symptoms of stress disorder. In restaurants, I had to sit with my back against the wall and I couldn't fall asleep without placing a knife under my pillow.

I stopped writing poetry. The compression of poetical language didn't allow me to fully express the chaos and destruction I had witnessed in Uganda. I struggled to write a novel set in Africa, but that didn't seem to go anywhere. I had survived soldiers shooting at me, but I couldn't express these experiences in fiction.

One night my wife and I attended a local production of *Buried Child,* Sam Shepard's Pulitzer Prize winning play. Years later, I realized that *Buried Child* is a difficult work to direct and perform. But that amateur production made the play seem like a meandering collection of unconnected scenes.

On the way back to our apartment I turned to my wife and announced "I could write something better than that."

She smiled and shrugged her shoulders. "So why don't you."

CALIFORNIA DOG FIGHT

The next morning I sat for several hours with a pad of paper on my lap. I had once written a *North American Review* article about illegal dog fighting and knew that it was a violent and highly dramatic world. So I scrawled *California Dog Fight* at the top of the page and wrote the following stage directions:

> *Darkness. Skip, a young man wearing cowboy boots, jeans and a leather jacket, walks out onto a bare stage. He reaches beneath his jacket, pulls out a revolver and fires it point blank at the audience. Lights up.*

These words written for a play set me free. I realized that I didn't have to write directly about my past. These painful experiences could power my fiction. An illegal dog fight at an abandoned farm reflected the violence I witnessed in Africa.

The world of *California Dog Fight* was also shaped by people I had met living in Sacramento. I'd become friends with two brothers who raised a small herd of cattle and supported their families cutting down timber. I branded and castrated yearling cattle with these ranchers and even went logging with them on several occasions. The tension between the tough-edged morality of these real-life cowboys and the compromises and corruption of the world that surrounded them was expressed in their attitudes toward animals - and women. It's no coincidence that two crucial scenes in the play involve the death of a dog and a man manipulated into wearing a woman's high-heel shoes.

When I finished writing the play my wife informed me that she was pregnant and that she wanted to quit her job. With a few thousand dollars in our bank account, we tossed our furniture into a rental truck, drove south to Los Angeles and moved into a shabby apartment on Hollywood Boulevard.

While hustling for work as a screenwriter, I sent *California Dog Fight* to a film director I knew named Lamont Johnson. After showing the play to a few actor friends, Lamont offered to direct a workshop production of the play if I rented a small theater and found two pit bulls. By now, my wife was six months pregnant. We only owned one car so I brought her along when we met a teenage pit bull owner who also owned pet rattlesnakes. A few days later, I negotiated with a Latino gang leader whose friend covered us with a shotgun while we inspected his kennel of fighting dogs.

Charles Durning, the great theater and film actor, had agreed to play Vern and suddenly our workshop production in the San Fernando Valley became the hottest theater ticket in town. Using highly aggressive pit bulls in a 99-seat theater was mesmerizing. When both dogs appeared on stage it was obvious that they wanted to attack each other.

While all this was going on, Gilbert Parker, the legendary theater agent, and read my play. Gilbert called me up from New York City and asked me one crucial question:

"What do you think about rewrites?"

"I love them if they improve the play."

"Good. I'd like to be your agent."

Gilbert sent the play to Lynne Meadow, the Artistic Director of the Manhattan Theatre Club, who decided to premiere it on the main stage of her theater. She forwarded the play to Bill Bryden, a British theater director who had recently had a hit at the Royal National Theatre. Bryden decided that *California Dog Fight* would be the first play he directed in the United States.

Up until this point, I had simply tried to write a good play. But now I began to receive a series of real-life lessons on what it means to be a playwright.

As *California Dog Fight* moved toward its New York City premiere, I was hired to write a feature film for a Hollywood studio. A screenwriter is usually a hired employee writing a script for a production company or a studio that is listed at the legal author. In contrast, a playwright owns the copyright to his work and the play's director and cast can't change lines without the author's permission.

The copyright issue shaped my daily experiences as a writer. Both Bill Bryden and the theater's literary manager were respectful and supportive when they gave their suggestions about the play. Meanwhile the studio executive in charge of developing my project yelled at me during meetings and once told me that my script needed to be "twenty percent funnier."

When I flew to New York to cast the play and meet the brilliant set designer Santo Loquasto, I realized that every theatrical production is a group effort. When writing a novel, you create a fictional world on the page. When you write a play, you create a fictional world that's expressed by human beings performing in a theatrical reality. At the Manhattan Theater Club, tons of real dirt and a rusty pick-up truck were being placed on stage.

Lynne Meadow, the MTC's Artistic Director, was pregnant during this time and rarely appeared at rehearsals. I missed her support. As a first-time playwright, I didn't feel confident about challenging Bill Bryden's decisions. Growing up in Scotland, the director had fallen in love with Hollywood movies and he had decided that my play was a Western - with pit bulls. Now that he was in New York for his first American play, he wanted everyone in the cast to be a movie star, including some actors who had never appeared in a play.

As we stumbled through rehearsals with an odd cast of semi-famous film actors, it was clear that several people involved with the play had addiction problems. The 1980's were the cocaine era in New York City and this malevolent drug seemed to poison the entire production.

A MTC employee who had seen me sitting in the lobby during a preview said that I looked sad and dazed - like someone who had just been in a car accident. When the play opened, the reviews were savage and all the blame was placed on my shoulders. One of the first lessons I learned about the theater was that writing a play could cause pain and public humiliation.

But sometimes the same play with the same characters offers you pleasure and a feeling of triumph. I was just about to experience this dramatic reversal.

A few weeks after the MTC production of *California Dog Fight* closed, I got a phone call from Simon Stokes, a director connected to the Bush Theatre in London. Simon had read my play and wanted to put it on stage.

I swallowed hard and decided to be honest. "Have you read the New York reviews?"

"A few of them." Simon laughed. "I'm not worried about that. Everything is going to be different...except for your play."

I flew to London a few months later where it immediately became clear that Simon was right: everything would be different. The theater's artistic manager Jenny Topper and its literary manager Sebastian Born worked in a basement office a short distance away from the theater.

They believed in the play and knew about every element of the production. The London theater world is dominated by personal connections. Jenny told agents about the play and we quickly signed a cast of highly talented actors that included John Shrapnel, Stuart Wilson and Deborah Norton. At the time, there weren't many pit bulls in London so we used Staffordshire Terriers.

Because of the influence of" method acting," most American actors approach their roles from the inside to the outside. The actors involved in the New York production of my play asked detailed questions about their character's personal history A few of them even created journals where they wrote complex descriptions of their character's emotions and motivations.

But the British actors I met during rehearsal approached their roles from the outside to the inside. When John Shrapnel accidentally stumbled and dropped a dog carrier, he smiled and said: "First rule of acting... don't lose your prop." John and the rest of the play's cast were focused on getting the right accent and wearing clothes appropriate for their character. They learned their lines early, but easily adjusted to changes. Once the mechanics of the performance were right, they filled out their characters and brought them to life.

California Dog Fight received positive reviews from the London critics and had sold-out audiences throughout its run. I had survived a painful - and exhilarating - introduction to the theater. Now I was ready to write another play.

***

CALIFORNIA DOG FIGHT was given its London premiere by the Bush Theatre (Jenny Topper, Artistic Director) on July 15, 1985. It was directed Simon Stokes. The set design was by Grant Hicks. The cast was as follows:

Skip......Jimmy Chisholm

Peter......Daniel Webb

Sarah......Lizzy McInnerny

Vern..... .John Shrapnel

Rawley......Stuart Wilson

Lillian.....Deborah Norton

CALIFORNIA DOG FIGHT won the "Best New Play of the Year" award given by the *London Tribune.*

CALIFORNIA DOG FIGHT

A Play

by

Mark Lee

CALIFORNIA DOG FIGHT

The top of a low hill at an abandoned pear orchard on the Sacramento delta. It's about one o'clock in the afternoon and very hot. Anyone looking down the hill can see a line of parked cars, a growing crowd of spectators, and the sixteen square foot "pit" where the dogs will fight.

The stage is bare except for a few old fruit crates. Some rusty farm equipment could be placed in the background. The set should help concentrate the play's energy rather than dissipating it with an unlimited panorama.

When lights come up we see Skip pacing at the edge of the stage. Skip is in his twenties. He wears a jacket, jeans, and cowboy boots.

A Beat. Skip stops and tries to make a confident smile, then gives up and resumes pacing. He stops again, bounces on his toes like a boxer, and throws a few quick punches at the air. He takes a deep breath, smoothes down his jacket, and then tries to pick up an imaginary girl.

            SKIP
    How you doing, baby? Nice dress you go
    on. Very nice. You...you got nice
    hair, too. Like your hair that way...
    long...very nice.
            (pretends to listen)
    Me? My name's Skip. Like the stone.
            (pantomimes throwing
             a stone)
    You know...skip...the stone.
            (losing confidence)
    Like your dress. Like your shoes.
    Like your eyes. Like your...shit!

He paces back and forth, then composes his face and tries to speak with a deep voice.

            SKIP
    How you doing? The name's Skip. You
    come around here much? A little?

He jerks his head towards something behind him.

                    SKIP
          That's my car out there. It's a
          Trans Am. Five liter engine. Four
          barrel carb. Dual exhaust. It's
          mine.
                (pretends to listen)
          What do I do? I'm a professional
          gambler and I ahhh I repair televisions on
          the side as a...kind...of...hobby. Damn!

He sits down on one of the fruit crates A Beat, then stands up and tries one last time.

                    SKIP
          My name's Skip. Skip! What's it to you?
          Want to get in my car? Want to go home
          with me? No?
                  (A Beat)
          No?

He reaches beneath his jacket, pulls a .38 revolver out of a shoulder holster, and fires it. A Beat, then he fires two more times as Pete and Sarah walk onstage.

                    PETE
          Hey, what's going on? What are you
          doing uphere?

Pete is in his late twenties. He's wearing jeans and is carrying a black medical bag. Sarah is twenty-one years old. She wears white "painter's pants" and carries a large shoulder bag. Pete looks annoyed as Skip lowers the gun and turns around.

                    PETE
          Christ, I should have figured it
          was you who was shooting.

                    SKIP
          Yeah.

                    PETE
          What the hell for?

                    SKIP
          Practice.

Skip stuffs the gun back in his shoulder holster as Pete looks down the hill.

                    SKIP
          Where's your belt, Pete? You're not
          wearing that belt today.

                    PETE
There are about a hundred people down there.

                    SKIP
I liked that belt. I really did. I thought it was cute.

                    PETE
Skip, that joke was funny a year ago. Don't you ever think of new ones?

                    SKIP
I'm just asking about the belt. I just wanted to know.

                    PETE
Why are you going around shooting guns? The farmyard's filling up. You could have hit somebody.

                    SKIP
Forget it. I was pointing this way. There's nothing out there but a bunch of dried-up pear trees.

Skip stares at Sarah.

    Who's she?   SKIP

                    SARAH
               (stepping forward)
I'm--
                    PETE
Her name's Sarah. She's a friend of mine.

                    SKIP
What do you mean...a friend?

                    PETE
What the hell do you think? Look, just go tell Rawley I'm here. Vern's going to be showing up in a few minutes.

Skip begins to exit stage left.

                    SKIP
Vern bring the money?

PETE
That's his business.

SKIP
If he's betting with Rawley, it's my business.

PETE
Just go tell him we're here, all right? And don't go shoot your prick off by mistake.

Skip shrugs and exits stage left.

PETE
If you got one.

Pete sits down on a fruit crate. He opens the medical bag, takes out a towel, and spreads it out on another crate.

SARAH
Now he was pleasant. A real cheerful personality. Is everybody around here going to be that way?

PETE
Not everybody. Skip is a bodyguard for this guy named Rawley. He lives in Sacramento, but he grew up here on the delta.

SARAH
What does that mean?

PETE
Most people around here are a little bent. You've got cousins marrying cousins. Stuff like that.

SARAH
Come on.

PETE
I'm not making it up. It gives you a whole new idea about "brotherly love."

Sarah laughs and walks over to Pete.

SARAH
You know, half the time I can't tell if you're joking or serious.

PETE
Good. That makes us even.

Pete begins to take syringes, bandages and bottles of medicine out of the bag.

                    SARAH
What's this about your belt? What was he talking about?

                    PETE
It's no big deal. Just something an old girlfriend made for me.

                    SARAH
Which one? Dee Dee? Annette? Was it the girl who tattooed your name on her hip?

                    PETE
You jealous?

                    SARAH
No. It's just that you talk more about your old girlfriends than about anything else in your past.

                    PETE
If you don't want to hear about them, then I won't tell you.

                    SARAH
I'm not saying that.

                    PETE
If it makes you jealous...

                    SARAH
                (exaggerated)
Peter, please. Tell me about the belt.

Pete shrugs and continues to take out medical equipment.

                    PETE
This girl named Terri made it for me at adult ed. It was an all right belt...good leather...but she put both our names on the back.

                    SARAH
Kind of like a brand, huh?

Pete glares at her, then looks back down at the bag.

PETE
Anyway, she kept bugging me to wear it so I did. A couple weeks later, I was handling a dog in the pit. Skip saw the belt and he started saying things like: "Pete, don't get that belt dirty. Terri wouldn't like that." Pretty soon everybody started laughing and there I am in the pit with blood on my hands and I can't take the belt off because that would make me look bad and I can't leave it on because --

SARAH
That would make you look bad.

PETE
Right.

He takes an ice pick out of the bag and jabs it into the crate.

PETE
Swear to god, I would have killed him if Rawley hadn't told him to shut up.

SARAH
Well, that tells me a lot, Peter. It really does. Remind me not to knit you a sweater.

PETE
Knit me anything you want. Just don't put your name on it. All right?

Sarah begins to walk away from him.

PETE
All right?

SARAH
That's an awful lot of bandages. Are you really going to need that many?

PETE
Maybe. Maybe not. It depends which dog wins.

He stands up and looks down the hill.

PETE
Listen, if you've changed your mind about the fight, you don't have to see it. The pit's at the bottom of the hill. You can wait here until it's done.

SARAH
No, I want to see it. You know, all the time I was living at home I felt like I was asleep. It was only when I got to college that I started to wake up and see things.

PETE
I don't know about that, but I do know about the law. You can go to prison for matching dogs.

SARAH
So why do people do it?

PETE
Money.

SARAH
Seems like a difficult way to earn it.

PETE
Don't talk about money. You don't know anything about it.

SARAH
Peter, we've already had this conversation.

PETE
People who've got it, don't know how important it is. Money's your life blood. It's --

Sarah walks over to Pete and touches him.

SARAH
No argument. No disagreement. You're ab-so-lute-ly cor-rect.

She links arms with Pete and guides him downstage.

SARAH
This is a pear farm, right? So how come all the trees are dead?

PETE
Nobody's watering them. The old man who owned this place went broke and his son started running these conventions.

SARAH
That's what these things are called? Conventions?

PETE
(nods)
We'll be the first match today if Vern shows up with the dog.

Pete breaks away from Sarah and moves upstage. As he peers down the hill --- searching for Vern --- Sarah takes a camera out of her shoulder bag. Pete looks startled when he sees her taking a photograph.

PETE
What are you doing?

SARAH
Taking a picture. I like the shadows on the trees. The juxtaposition of the light and the dark.

Pete looks down the hill, trying to see if anyone's coming.

PETE
Put it away.

SARAH
Why?

PETE
Put it away!

He moves towards her as she continues taking pictures.

PETE
There are some tough people around here. Not like that asshole, Skip. Everybody's worried about the sheriff, the feds, the goddamn humane society.

SARAH
Nobody's coming, Peter. You can see all the way down the hill.

PETE
I told you --

He grabs at the camera, but she avoids him.

>   SARAH
> Don't order me around.

>   PETE
> Put it away!

She takes one last picture of his anger, then drops the camera into her bag.

>   SARAH
> All right. I'll put it away.

>   PETE
> Goddamn you.

>   SARAH
> I'm sorry.

>   PETE
> You're always pushing me.

Pete turns and walks away. Sarah follows -- trying to tease him into a good mood.

>   SARAH
> That's not true. I'm just a simple, honest, All-American college girl.

>   PETE
> Oh, yeah.

>   SARAH
> I like pep rallies, peanut butter...

She caresses him, but he doesn't respond.

>   SARAH
> Ping-Pong, pickles...

Pete turns and smiles.

>   PETE
> What else?

>   SARAH
> Pork roast, popcorn, prunes...

>   PETE
> What else?

They kiss, then Sarah pulls away.

                    SARAH
          You mad at me?

                    PETE
          Yeah.

She kisses him again.

                    SARAH
          Still mad?

                    PETE
          I'll talk to Vern. Maybe you can
          take some pictures of the dog if
          nobody else is around.

                    SARAH
          Thanks. When are you --

                    VERN (offstage)
          Anybody up there?

                    PETE
          That's Vern.

                    VERN (offstage)
          Give me a hand, will you? I'm
          getting a heart attack!

Pete walks offstage, then helps Vern bring on an animal carrying box. Vern is in his fifties. He wears work boots and khaki pants.

                    PETE
          Over here, Vern. Put it right here.

The two men place the box downstage right.

                    PETE
          There you go.

Vern straightens up and stares at Pete.

                    VERN
          What's your name, son?

                    PETE
          Come on, Vern.

                    VERN
          Wait a minute...you look like a boy I
          knew once, used to come up to my ranch,
          sit out on the porch.

                    PETE
          That's me, all right.

                    VERN
          Well, I do believe it is.

Vern smiles and touches Pete.

                    PETE
          Good to see you, Vern.

                    VERN
          Where you been?

Pete turns towards Sarah.

                    PETE
          Vern, this is the girl I told you about...
          the one who goes to the university. Sarah,
          this is Vern Christiansen. Vern...Sarah
          Preminger.

Vern walks over to Sarah as Pete puts away the medical supplies.
He smiles and extends his hand.

                    VERN
          Pleased to meet you, Sarah.

He remembers something and pulls his hand back.

                    VERN
          Sorry, but I got dog spit on that one.

He wipes off his hand, extends it, then hesitates again.

                    VERN
          I guess that's not so good either.

Sarah smiles and shakes Vern's hand.

                    SARAH
          Glad to meet you, Vern.

                    VERN
          Well now, you ever been to a
          convention before?

                    SARAH
          This is my first time.

                    PETE
          She's never seen a pit bull, Vern.

                    VERN
          I guess she's going to see one now.

Vern walks over to the carrying box. He opens it, lifts out his pit bull, and snaps a leash onto its body harness.

                    SARAH
          He's beautiful.

                    VERN
          Isn't he now?

Vern leads the dog over to Sarah. Feeling cautious about this "fighting dog," she backs away.

                    VERN
          The miners in England bred them for
          fighting hundreds of years ago.
          It's in their blood.
               (notices her fear)
          What's the matter, Sarah?

                    SARAH
          Can I pet him?

                    VERN
          Sure. They love people. They just
          can't stand other dogs.

                    PETE
          Cats, too.

                    VERN
          Cats. Birds. Coyotes. I had one a
          couple of years ago that like to
          fight horses.

                    SARAH
          Can I take his picture?

Surprised, Vern glances at Pete.

                    PETE
          She brought her camera along, Vern. She
          wants to take a picture of Big Boy, not the
          fight.

                    VERN
          Fine...Fine..Take all you want as
          long as those rounders don't see you.

Sarah takes out her camera while Pete makes sure that no one is coming up the hill.

                              SARAH
                    Okay, smile.

Vern smiles, posing with the dog. Sarah takes a picture and he starts to walk away.

                              SARAH
                    Could I take one more, please?

Vern stops and poses again.

                              SARAH
                    That looks good...great...great!

She takes a few more pictures. Vern shakes his head.

                              VERN
                    Never could smile too long.

                              RAWLEY (offstage)
                    Is he up there? You see him?

                              PETE
                    Here comes Rawley.

                              VERN
                    Put the camera away, Sarah.

                              PETE
                    Come on! Hurry up!

Sarah shoves the camera into her bag. Pete walks back to Vern and takes the dog's leash.

                              RAWLEY
                    There he is! Scared to show his face!

Everyone looks stage left as Skip, Rawley, and Lillian appear. Rawley is in his late forties. He wears expensive cowboy boots, a sport coat, and western tie.

Lillian is about the same age as Rawley, but is trying to divert attention from that fact. She is overdressed for the delta: wearing jewelry, an attractive dress, and high-heeled shoes. Skip is carrying a hand scale similar to the device used to weigh fish.

                              RAWLEY
                    Why you hiding up here, Vern? I was
                    starting to think that you'd backed out
                    on me.

                    VERN
          I put the money up, Rawley. That meant I
          wanted to fight.

Vern smiles and walks over to Lillian.

                    VERN
          Why, Lillian. I didn't know you
          were coming today.

                    LILLIAN
          Good to see you, Vern.

                    VERN
          How you doing? You look...you look
          just fine.

                    LILLIAN
          I'm not complaining. Where you been,
          Vern? I haven't seen you for awhile.

Rawley and Skip walk over to Pete and check out the dog.

                    RAWLEY
          Vern's not going to conventions
          these days. He got tired of losing.

Lillian notices Sarah and gives Vern a teasing smile.

                    LILLIAN
          Who's your friend, Vern?

                    VERN
          No...no...she came with Pete.

Vern glances at Pete as if to say: "be a gentleman."

                    PETE
          Right. Sarah, this is Rawley Bates and
          Lillian...Lillian...

                    VERN
          Bettencourt.

                    SKIP
          Maybe she should put it on a belt.

                    LILLIAN
                (nodding to Sarah)
          That's all right, Pete. I've never been
          big on last names. Not with friends.

                    RAWLEY
          So Pete, what are you doing these days?
          Still roofing houses?

                    PETE
          Part time.

                    RAWLEY
          Part time at that job would be too
          long for me. You keep mopping hot tar
          and you're going to fry your brains
          for breakfast.

Irritated, Vern walks over to the dog.

                    VERN
          Come on, Rawley. Let's get going.

                    RAWLEY
          Hey, I've been waiting here for three
          hours. You're the one who's been holding
          up the show.
                    (turns to Skip)
          All right, Skip. Let's see if we can
          make some forfeit money.

Skip pushes the stick through a ring at the top of the hand scale. Pete takes the leash off the dog and attaches the other end of the scale to the harness ring.

                    RAWLEY
          It had better be forty-four pounds
          ...give or take two pounds. If it's
          not, I get your money.
                    (watching the dog)
          He looks trembly, Vern. A little
          nervous.

                    PETE
          He's all right.

                    RAWLEY
          He was a good dog a couple years
          ago. He could grab onto something and
          not let go.

Pete and Skip grab the stick and pull the dog off the ground.

                    VERN
          Forty-four and a half. That's good.

The two handlers lower the dog down. Pete detaches the hand scale and clips the leash back onto the harness.

> RAWLEY
> Hector is 44 pounds. I weighed him this morning.

> VERN
> Is that so? Maybe I'll just check him to be sure.

> RAWLEY
> Don't you trust me, Vern? Won't you take my word?

Vern begins to lead Skip and Rawley offstage, then walks back to Pete and speaks softly.

> VERN
> Take Big Boy behind that old barn. Water him and walk him for awhile.

> PETE
> Right now?

> VERN
> He hasn't had any water since last night. I didn't think he'd make weight.

> LILLIAN
> I need a shot of air conditioning, honey. Give me the keys to the car.

> RAWLEY
> The car is locked and it's staying locked. You wait right here and we'll be right back.

> LILLIAN
> Okay, but don't take too long.

> RAWLEY
> Come on, Vern. You wanted to weigh him. Let's do it.

Vern, Rawley, and Skip exit.

> RAWLEY
> Now you're going to see a real dog, Vern. A real fighter.

Pete watches the men exit, then turns to Sarah.

> PETE
> Watch the medical bag.

                    SARAH
          Okay.

                    PETE
          Don't put anything in it. Don't
          take anything out. All right?

                    SARAH
          I think I can handle it.

Pete exits with the dog. Sarah sits down on the carrying box. She stares at the medical bag while Lillian wanders around the stage. Both women glance at each other and smile. No one speaks. Lillian stops to adjust her bra and slip.

                    LILLIAN
          Hot, isn't it?

                    SARAH
          Sure is.

                    LILLIAN
          The delta just gets hot and stays hot all
          summer long. It's God's crock pot and
          we're what's cooking.

She takes a few steps towards Sarah, then stops to adjust her hose.

                    LILLIAN
          Shouldn't have worn my pantyhose.
          That's for sure.

                    SARAH
          Take them off. Nobody's around.

                    LILLIAN
          Well, I don't know about that. In the
          last couple of years, I've started to
          think that all this stuff holds me
          together. If I didn't have it on, I'd
          probably fall apart.

                    SARAH
          Come on.

                    LILLIAN
          Well, almost. In an air conditioned place
          I can pretty well get away with
          anything, but not on the delta.

Lillian looks around her.

                    LILLIAN
God, I hate it.

                    SARAH
Why are you here?

                    LILLIAN
Rawley wanted me to come. He likes having a
woman with him when he's around a lot of
men. Usually, I can wiggle out of it, but
not this time. Why are you here?

                    SARAH
I asked Pete if I could come along.

                    LILLIAN
You ever seen a dog fight?

                    SARAH
No.

                    LILLIAN
But you wanted to?

                    SARAH
It's an experience.

                    LILLIAN
Oh, I'll grant you that.

Curious, she moves closer to Sarah.

                    LILLIAN
What are those loops on your pants for?
I've never seen those on a woman's pants.

                    SARAH
They're called painter's pants. You hang
tools on them.

                    LILLIAN
You're a painter?

                    SARAH
No, it's just clothes. You don't have
to be a painter to wear the pants.

                    LILLIAN
I guess you're right. Look at me.
          (shows her rings)
I'm not married, but I'm wearing all
this junk.

Slowly, she walks over to the carrying box.

                    LILLIAN
Let me tell you, Sarah? There are a lot of little steps along the way. First bra. First boy. First man. But the one thing they never tell you about is when you walk into a jewelry store... alone...and buy your own diamond ring.

                    SARAH
That's independence.

                    LILLIAN
That's expensive. Especially if you had to shuffle a million cards to get the money.

                    SARAH
You're a dealer? In Nevada?

                    LILLIAN
I lived there for a couple years. Now I work at a poker room in Sacramento...the Hi-Low Club.

She sits down beside Sarah, takes a compact out of her purse, and starts to inspect her makeup.

                    LILLIAN
What do you do?

                    SARAH
I'm going to college, majoring in anthropology. You know, primitive cultures and things like that.

                    LILLIAN
You ought to come down to The High-Low Club. That's primitive culture. How long have you been going with Pete?

                    SARAH
About five months.

                    LILLIAN
That Pete's really something. He's always strutting around.

                    SARAH
I kind of like him that way.

LILLIAN
Oh, I'm not knocking him. Pete's good looking. It's just that it makes me smile to see a man doing something he thinks a woman wants to see.

SARAH
Like showing his muscles?

LILLIAN
That's one way.

SARAH
At college, some of the men try to show how much they know. I prefer muscles.

Lillian stands up and imitates a cowboy.

LILLIAN
Now if you meet some cowboy and he's interested in you, he's going to stick his thumbs in his belt and rock in his boots and stare at you like you got a wart on your nose.

SARAH
Pete does that a little. He likes to stare. You know, it's funny, but the times I've really liked him he wasn't doing anything in particular.

LILLIAN
Just scratching himself, huh?

SARAH
Not exactly. Things like jump starting my car.

LILLIAN
Yeah, that can be pretty sexy.

SARAH
It's not... It's just...

Lillian takes a cigarette out of her purse. She lights it and starts moving around the crate.

LILLIAN
What do you feel about him?

SARAH
I'm not quite sure. If I analyze the situation

LILLIAN
You can't "analyze" it. Love is like jumping off a cliff in the dark. You're falling, flapping your arms around, but you just don't care.

SARAH
Are you in love with Rawley?

LILLIAN
Rawley? Do I look that dumb? I mean I like having a good looking man take me out, but I've only been in love one time for real...for really real. He was a cowboy. A rodeo rider named T.C. Holmes.

SARAH
What happened?

LILLIAN
It was real good for awhile, but my timing was wrong I caught him when he was just coming off being Grand National Champion. He could get on the bulls, but he couldn't hold tight anymore. Pretty soon he started breaking bones and breaking and breaking. When he got out of bed in the morning you could hear him creak and crack like a busted up chair.

SARAH
Why didn't he quit?

LILLIAN
He was something...he had been something ...and that was all he could see. We had some good years together, but then he started drinking and going at me with words. Each time it was like a little knife going cut...cut...leaving scars.

SARAH
People hurt each other.

LILLIAN
Yeah. Well, there's hurting and
then there's blood on the floor.

She shakes her head and walks back over to Sarah.

LILLIAN
You've got to understand that
women, most women, we know we're
women. But men, most men...they
don't know who they are.

SARAH
But they got the power.

LILLIAN
You think so?

SARAH
They control the government, the
media, the economy --

LILLIAN
I guess you're right. They do have
all that blow-up-the-world power,
but I can still get most men to do
anything I want.

SARAH
You think you can control them?

LILLIAN
If I want to.

SARAH
I heard my mother say that lots of
times. But she couldn't get my father to
turn off the television set.

LILLIAN
I could.

SARAH
It's not true.

SKIP (offstage)
Did you see that guy with the van?
He's got a machine gun in the back.
Swear to god.

VERN (offstage)
Must be hunting some pretty big
rabbits.

                    LILLIAN
          They're coming back. They must have
          weighed the dog.

Lillian smiles and steps on her cigarette.

                    LILLIAN
          Look, Sarah, you pick anything and
          I'll make them do it. All of them.

                    SARAH
          What are you saying?

                    LILLIAN
          You know what I'm saying.

                    SKIP (offstage)
          You see Nathan's dog? The long-
          eared brindle?

                    RAWLEY (offstage)
          I watched him at a roll down in
          Fresno. Looked pretty good.

                    LILLIAN
          They're coming. Pick anything.
          Anything!

Sarah nods at Lillian's high-heeled shoes.

                    SARAH
          Make them wear your shoes.

Lillian nods, then turns left as Rawley, Skip, and Vern enter. Vern is carrying a five gallon jerry can full of water and an empty bucket.

                    LILLIAN
          How'd it go boys?

                    VERN
          Did Pete come back?

                    LILLIAN
          Not yet.

Vern places the jerry can and the bucket beside the carrying box. He walks upstage looking for Pete.

                    LILLIAN
          So...did you get rich quick, Vern?

                    RAWLEY
          No, Hector made weight. Vern was praying.
          Oh, he was praying, but it looks like his
          dog's going to have to fight.

                    LILLIAN
          You going to wash your dog, Vern?

                    VERN
          Pete'll wash him when he gets back. I've
          got to see Skip wash Rawley's dog.

                    LILLIAN
          You guys really trust each other,
          don't you?

                    SKIP
          There's a lot of money riding on this,
          Lillian. Can't trust anybody.

                    LILLIAN
          That's right. I guess you're right. Got to
          watch out or somebody will make you do
          something you don't want to do.

Vern returns to the carrying box and begins to inspect the supplies inside the medical bag.

                    LILLIAN
          God, you got big feet, Vern.

                    VERN
          Big enough to hold me up.

                    LILLIAN
          I mean, they're big next to mine.

                    SKIP
          Old Vern's got frog feet.

Lillian walks over to Vern and takes off one of her shoes.

                    LILLIAN
          I bet your shoes are twice as big.

                    VERN
          Probably.
                    LILLIAN

          Let's see.

She pulls up one of Vern's feet and he balances himself on the carrying box.

                VERN
Yeah, it's about twice as big.

              LILLIAN
But do you know...

                VERN
I'll take your word on it, Lillian. It's twice as big.

Frustrated, Lillian puts on the shoe. She glances at Sarah, then wanders across the stage as Rawley approaches Vern.

              RAWLEY
So Vern, you going to be worrying about your dog? Sweating over him like you aways do?

                VERN
I want to win, Rawley.

              RAWLEY
Me, too. But not the same way. Christ, when you've got a dog in the pit, you look like you're about to die.

Skip laughs. Irritated, Vern turns towards Rawley.

                VERN
Rawley, you talk too much.

                SKIP
Whoa. Vern's acting tough today.

              RAWLEY
Easy, Vern. No need to get angry. You and I go back a long time. I match dogs. You match dogs. But with me, it's different.

                VERN
It's a business with you. That's all it's ever been.

              RAWLEY
Look, I lived on a ranch when I was a kid. I know what your job's like. If you're raising sheep, you've got to crop their tails and cut off their balls, then send them to the butcher at slaughtering time.   (MORE)

                    RAWLEY
          An animal's just a animal.
                (smiling)
          Hell, a woman's just a woman, but
          that's another story.

Vern walks away from Rawley.

                    VERN
          I can't talk to you.

                    RAWLEY
          I just want to know why you can't see the
          truth. A dog is just something to handle. No
          more. No less.

Vern looks down the hill A BEAT, then he turns to Rawley.

                    VERN
          If you care about something, you just
          care. You can't help it.

Skip laughs. Rawley and Vern stare at each other.

                    RAWLEY
          "I can't help it. I can't help it!"
                (shakes his head)
          Christ, you sound like some little slut
          in the back seat of a car.

Lillian walks over to the jerry can. She picks it up and begins to carry it stage left.

                    VERN
          Don't do that, Lillian.

                    LILLIAN
          Why not?

                    VERN
          It's too heavy.

                    LILLIAN
          Come on, Vern, who do you think is always
          lugging the babies around? Who's
          chopping the wood on a ranch?

She sets the jerry can down on the ground and faces the men.

                    LILLIAN
          One thing you men won't face up to is that
          women are stronger and tougher than you.

                    SKIP
          Oh, yeah?

                    LILLIAN
          You don't believe me?

                    SKIP
          There ain't no women in the Super Bowl.

                    LILLIAN
          That's because we're too smart to
          get our heads bashed in.

She lifts up one foot.

                    LILLIAN
          Look, see these shoes? I bet none of
          you men could walk twenty feet
          wearing them.

                    RAWLEY
          Why would we want to?

Skip laughs while Lillian rummages through her purse.

                    LILLIAN
          I bet you twenty, thirty...damn,
          where is that? Fifty dollars.

She holds up a wad of bills and waves it at Skip.

                    LILLIAN
          Bet you can't walk over to Sarah
          there.

Sarah smiles and stands up. She moves to a spot about twenty-five feet away from Lillian.

                    SKIP
          Forget that.

                    LILLIAN
          See, you're chicken. All that big talk and
          you won't even take this fifty dollars
          right out of my hand.

SKIP
I couldn't even fit in those shoes.

LILLIAN
That's right. But I know you men are such big athletes. You've got such perfect balance. I'm sure you could handle it.

She kicks off her shoes and they land at Skip's feet.

LILLIAN
Go ahead, Skip. Give it a try.

Skip looks at the shoes, then turns to Rawley.

SKIP
She's crazy.

RAWLEY
I guess so, but her money's not crazy. Go ahead. Take it.

SKIP
(to Lillian)
Fifty bucks.

Lillian rummages through her purse and finds another bill.

LILLIAN
Sixty.

SKIP
Shit. I'd be crazy not to take it.

Skip unties his shoes. Lillian glances at Sarah.

SKIP
I once ate a can of Jalapeno peppers for five bucks...and that was hard.

LILLIAN
This is hard, too.

SKIP
That's bullshit. You women are all bullshit. Everything's always a big deal with you. A big production.

LILLIAN
If you say so, Skip.

SKIP
I'm not going to say anything. I'm going to show you.

Skip stands up wearing Lillian's shoes.

SKIP
Just watch this It's easy.

He begins to walk towards Sarah.

SKIP
You just take one step...then another step.

RAWLEY
Looking good, Skip.

SKIP
Then another one and...damn!

Skip stumbles and falls on the ground.

LILLIAN
See, I told you. I told you that you couldn't do it.

She flutters the money through the air.

LILLIAN
I think your sixty dollars just flew away.

Skip pulls off the shoes and throws them on the floor.

SKIP
They're too damn small.

VERN
You're walking too far forward, Skip. You've got to sit back on them like stirrups.

LILLIAN
How do you know, Vern?

Rawley and Skip laugh.

RAWLEY
Yeah, do you know? You got some little secrets we should hear about?

VERN
I've seen my wife walking in them.

                    LILLIAN
          Think you could do any better, Vern?

     Lillian picks up the shoes and walks over to Vern.

                    VERN
          I'm not going to try.

                    LILLIAN
          Come on, Vern. It's just for fun. You
          might even win sixty dollars.

                    VERN
          My feet are too big, Lillian. You said
          that yourself.

                    LILLIAN
          It won't hurt you.

                    VERN
          I'm not saying that it'll hurt me.

     Lillian stands next to Vern, flirting with him.

                    LILLIAN
          Then what are you saying? We're friends,
          right? I've known you for a couple years.

                    RAWLEY
          Oh-oh. Watch out, Vern.

                    LILLIAN
          Ease off. Vern's a friend. And he's
          going to do it because he's a
          friend. Aren't you, Vern?

     Vern glances at Lillian, then examines the shoes.

                    VERN
          Well, I know I could do better than
          Skip.

                    SKIP
          No way.   No way.

                    RAWLEY
          You're crazy, Vern. You're going to
          fall on your ass.

                    VERN
          We'll see about that.

>   Vern picks up the shoes and walks over to the jerry can. He sits down
>   and begins to take off his boots.

                    LILLIAN
          It's sixty dollars. An eeeeasy
          sixty dollars.

                    SKIP
          No way!

                    VERN
          It's just like anything else. You've
          got to set it up right.

He forces on Lillian's shoes and stares at his feet.

                    VERN
          Then think about it awhile. Plan what
          you're going to do.

Vern tries to stand up, then sits back down.

                    VERN
          Give me a hand, Lillian.

She helps him stand up. Vern gets his balance, then starts to walk towards Sarah. Lillian follows him clutching the money.

                    LILLIAN
          You got it, Vern. Looking good. Looking
          real good.

Vern starts to lose his balance.

                    LILLIAN
          Shift to your left! Get your --

Vern falls on the ground. He shakes his head and removes the shoes.

                    VERN
          Guess I didn't think that one out.

                    LILLIAN
          No, that was good. Good enough
          for me. Sixty dollars. There you go.

Vern stands up and walks back to his boots.

                    VERN
          I don't want it, Lillian.

                    LILLIAN
          Come on!

                    RAWLEY
          Don't give it to him. He didn't win the
          bet!

                    LILLIAN
          Think you could do better?

                    RAWLEY
          Of course, but I'm not going to try.

  Lillian picks up the shoes and walks over to him.

                    LILLIAN
          Why not?

                    RAWLEY
          Forget it, Lillian.

                    LILLIAN
          Think you're going to lose?

                    RAWLEY
          I know I wouldn't lose.

                    LILLIAN
          Scared of having Vern beat you?

                    RAWLEY
          I'm not scared of anybody. I always
          win.

                    VERN
          You haven't always beat me, Rawley. We've had two
          dog fights together. The score is one to one.

                    RAWLEY
          The first time was a joke.

                    VERN
          I don't recall you laughing.

Lillian turns away from Rawley. She walks back to Vern
swinging the shoes in her hand.

                    LILLIAN
          No need to argue about it. If
          Rawley doesn't want to put on the
          shoes, that's fine. Rawley does win,
          Vern. He always wins...usually.

Rawley glares at Lillian.

                    RAWLEY
            Give me the shoes.

                    LILLIAN
            What?

                    RAWLEY
            Give me the shoes.

Rawley walks over to Lillian. He takes the shoes, hands his jacket to Skip and sits down on a fruit crate

                    RAWLEY
                (to Sarah)
            The only problem with winning is that
            you have to keep on doing it just to
            show that you can.

Rawley pulls off his cowboy boots.

                    LILLIAN
            Don't look at me, Rawley. I'm not
            arguing with you.

                    RAWLEY
            I've won playing poker. I've won at
            the track. I've won with my dogs.

Rawley stares at his feet, then forces on the shoes.

                    VERN
            Those are some dogs you've got
            there, Rawley.

                    RAWLEY
            Help me up, Skip.

Skip pulls Rawley up and he starts to shuffle towards Sarah.

                    RAWLEY
            I got it...I got it...
                (smiles at Sarah)
            Come here, baby.

Pete enters with the dog. Startled, Rawley looks up and falls to the ground.

                    PETE
            What's going on? Rawley, how come
            you're wearing Lillian's shoes?

                    RAWLEY
            None of your goddamn business!

Furious, Rawley stands up and walks back to his boots.

                    VERN
We're just having a little fun, Pete. Lillian's been making bets.

                    LILLIAN
Now, Pete... I know Pete can do it. You played football in high school, didn't you?

                    PETE
A little.

                    SKIP
Third string.

                    PETE
I was varsity. Everybody knows that.

                    LILLIAN
What do you think, Sarah? Could he do it?

                    SARAH
It's not necessary.

                    PETE
Do what?

                    LILLIAN
Walk in my shoes for sixty dollars.

                    PETE
That's easy.

                    SARAH
Not necessary.

Lillian smiles at Sarah, then nods. Rawley stands up and puts on his jacket.

                    RAWLEY
Let's get moving. We're wasting time. Skip, you go back and wash Hector. Pete, start washing that mutt of yours.

Lillian sits down on the carrying case and puts on her shoes. Pete takes a towel and a sponge out of the medical bag, then places them in the bucket. He walks over to the jerry can with the dog and Sarah follows him. Vern begins to exit with Skip.

                        VERN
          Too bad you tripped, Rawley.
                    (walks like a woman)
          Maybe if you practiced.

                        RAWLEY
          I'm going to beat you.

                        VERN
          Uh huh.

                        RAWLEY
          Remember that.

Vern and Skip exit stage left. Pete pours water into the bucket and starts to wash the dog with the sponge.

                        PETE
          What happened with the shoes? What
          was that all about?

                        SARAH
          It was nothing, Peter. Just a
          little experiment.

                        PETE
          What experiment?

Still angry, Rawley walks over to Lillian.

                        RAWLEY
          You know, when I first met you I just thought
          you had a **big** mouth. Nowadays, I think you're
          crazy.

                        LILLIAN
          I'm sorry, honey. I really am. You **got**
          your **pants** all dirty and everything.

Lillian tries to brush the dirt off Rawley's pants. He stops her.

                        RAWLEY
          I don't like getting messed up.

                        LILLIAN
          Of course not, Rawley.

                        RAWLEY
          Vern doesn't **give** a damn what he looks
          like, but I got...

                        LILLIAN
          ...clothes.

RAWLEY
Everybody's got clothes.

LILLIAN
An appearance.

RAWLEY
Right. When people look at me, they know I'm not kicking cows for a living.

LILLIAN
It was just an accident. That's all. You would have beat Vern if Pete hadn't come back like that.

RAWLEY
Damn right.

LILLIAN
You want the sixty dollars?

RAWLEY
Of course not.

Rawley starts to walk over to Pete.

LILLIAN
You won it. You went the farthest.

RAWLEY
Don't try to handle me.

LILLIAN
I'm not doing anything.

RAWLEY
You're not stupid. I like that about you. Just don't be too smart.

PETE
Okay, Rawley. I've just got to dry him.

Pete starts to dry the dog with the towel. Sarah moves away from the dog as Rawley walks over to Pete.

RAWLEY
Pete, I like you. I really do. I just don't know why you're working for an old piece of meat like Vern.

PETE
He's all right

                    RAWLEY
          You know, Skip's always knocking you and
          that's kind of my fault. He knows I want you
          to be my handler.

                    PETE
          Come on.

                    RAWLEY
          It's true. Skip might be a good
          handler in a couple of years, but
          you're good right now. Don't you
          want to make some money?

                    PETE
          Sure I do. A lot of money. But I'm working
          for Vern.

                    RAWLEY
          What work? How many conventions have you
          gone to this year? Two? Three? If you joined
          up with me, you'd be working every weekend.
          Each Spring we take the dogs east to Texas,
          Arkansas, Missouri. There's a big country
          out there.

                    PETE
          I've heard about it.

                    RAWLEY
          You'd get the chance to see some new towns.
          New people. You'd get the chance to see
          what's going on beneath the surface. That's
          what this country is: a big ocean with a lot
          of things swimming underneath.

                    PETE
          I'll think it over.

                    RAWLEY
          Come on, Pete. When a woman says she's
          going to think it over, that means you're
          not getting inside.

Rawley leans over the dog and licks the skin on its neck.

                    SARAH
          What are you doing?

                    RAWLEY
          What do you think I'm doing? Drying him?

PETE
He's checking for poison or drugs. If someone puts it on the skin, you can taste it.

Rawley stands up and spits.

RAWLEY
Maybe you can taste it. Maybe you can't. I just want to cover all the angles.

PETE
You always do, Rawley.

RAWLEY
I'm glad somebody knows it. A man's got to be appreciated in his own time.

Rawley starts to leave the area.

RAWLEY
Come on, Lillian.

Lillian follows after him.

LILLIAN
Bye, Sarah. See you.

RAWLEY
Let's go!

Rawley exits stage left.

LILLIAN
See you a little later. Remember what I said now.

RAWLEY (offstage)
Lillian!

Lillian exits. Still holding the dog, Pete looks at Sarah.

PETE
What'd she say?

SARAH
Everything. Nothing.

She drifts away from Pete.

PETE
Come on, what'd she say?

SARAH
We talked about men and women.
Shoes. Love.

PETE
What about it?

SARAH
It's not that easy to summarize. I mean, she doesn't have a systematic philosophy or anything.

PETE
I ask a simple question and I get educational TV.

Sarah walks over to Pete. She kneels down and pets the dog.

SARAH
Peter, what did you think about me when we first met?

PETE
I was wondering if you had a bra on. You didn't.

SARAH
What else?

PETE
I don't know. You looked pretty good. What'd you think about me?

SARAH
You were different. That was the main thing. I thought I could learn from you. Learn about the world.

PETE
So did you?

SARAH
Not exactly. You want all these things. Things in advertisements. On television.

PETE
What's wrong with that? Your family's got that stuff already. Couple cars. Big house. Goddamn money in the goddamn bank.

Sarah stands and moves away from him.

                    SARAH
          Let's not talk about it.

                    PETE
          Why not? What if I want to?

Pete stands up and points to a spot next to the dog.

                    PETE
          Come here.

                    SARAH
          No.

                    PETE
          Come here!

Pete steps towards her dragging the dog as Vern enters.

                    VERN
          Pete, don't drag the dog on the leash.

                    PETE
          I'm not dragging him!

                    VERN
          He doesn't like being pulled around.

Vern takes the leash from Pete and guides Big Boy over to the carrying box. Watching them, Sarah moves away.

                    PETE
          What took you so long?

                    VERN
          I was checking Rawley's dog.

                    PETE
          How's he look? I've never seen him
          fight before.

Vern lifts up the dog and places him on top of the box.

                    PETE
          Vern?

                    VERN
          Rawley's dog is strong. Real strong.

PETE
Big Boy is a good dog. He's got lots of heart. You're always saying that.

Vern starts to check the dog's left hind leg.

VERN
He was a good dog until he broke that hind leg.

PETE
The leg's better, isn't it?

VERN
No. It's not better.

PETE
What are you telling me?

VERN
I thought it was healed, but the vet called up yesterday and said he'd found a hairline fracture in the last X-ray.

PETE
So why didn't you call off the match?

VERN
I gave them my word.

PETE
You gave them you...damn!

VERN
The front money was already up. I can't afford to lose it. Last month, the well pump burned out on me, the truck broke its axle...

PETE
Why didn't you tell me about this? You never mentioned anything on the phone.

VERN
If you had come out to the ranch, you could have seen what was going on.

PETE
I don't have to see it, Vern. Just tell me. Send me a postcard if you want.

VERN
I don't tell my troubles over the phone.

PETE
Great. I've got to play detective. Is something wrong, Vern? No, wait... wait...don't tell me.

Looking disappointed, Vern turns away.

PETE
Well, that's what you're saying. Isn't it? Vern?

VERN
I don't tell my troubles over the phone. Just leave it at that.

PETE
All right.
(slowly)
All right. All right. All right.

Pete checks the dog.

PETE
So you're going to fight him?

VERN
Yeah. I'm going to fight him.

PETE
We're...we're low on disinfectant.

Vern looks surprised for a moment, then he shrugs.

VERN
There's some in the pickup. Near the toolbox.

PETE
I better go get it.

Pete starts to walk away, then he stops and faces Vern.

PETE
Listen, anything can happen. You're always saying that. It can go any way.

VERN
He's a brave dog.

                    PETE
        You know he is. We can do it. We just got
        to believe.

                    VERN
        All right.

                    PETE
        Not all right...all right!
                (slaps Vern's shoulder)
        I'll be back.

Pete takes the dog off the box and exits with him stage left.

                    VERN
                (still smiling)
        All right.
                (worried again)
        All right.

He glances at Sarah, then crosses the stage to the jerry can.

                    VERN
        Everything okay, Sarah?

                    SARAH
        Yeah. No problem.

                    VERN
        You thirsty? Want something to drink?

                    SARAH
        I'm fine.

                    VERN
        They're selling beer down the hill. I
        could go and --

                    SARAH
        I'm fine, Vern. Really.

Vern nods. He picks up the bucket and jerry can, then brings them over to the carrying box.

                    SARAH
        Is the dog going to be okay?

                    VERN
        He's got as much chance as anybody. He
        just has to go fast. Get the other
        dog early. You going to be watching
        him, Sarah?

SARAH
I guess so.

VERN
Good. He'll try harder if you're around.

SARAH
I don't think he cares.

VERN
Oh, he cares. He doesn't like to look bad in front of pretty girls.

Vern puts the sponge and towel back in the medical bag. Slowly, Sarah walks over to him.

SARAH
You know, I was really looking forward to meeting you today.

VERN
Me?

SARAH
Pete's told me a lot about you. You're the only man he ever talks about.

VERN
I like having Pete around. He's still young enough to be sure about everything.
    (watching her)
What about you, Sarah? Do you like having him around?

SARAH
Pete's different from anyone I've ever known. It's been fun going out with him, but then one of us --

VERN
Acts human.

SARAH
Right.

VERN
The only thing harder than being alone is being with someone...even if you love them.

SARAH
Are you married?

                    VERN
          I was married. My wife died about a
          year ago.
                    (smiles)
          She was a good woman.

                    SARAH
          What's a good woman?

                    VERN
          Somebody that knows every stupid thing
          you've ever done, but doesn't go around
          reminding you of them.

Vern walks upstage looking for Pete. Sarah watches him.

                    SARAH
          Vern, why do you do this?

                    VERN
          I don't know. You do this, you do that,
          and all of a sudden you find yourself
          in a place you never planned. Funny
          thing is, I always kind of hated dogs.

He walks back to her.

                    VERN
          See, I'm a sheep man. Always have been.
          Now when you own sheep you always got
          coyotes sniffing around your flock, but
          the main thing you've got to watch out for
          is dogs. Your common everyday house dog.

                    SARAH
          They'll kill the sheep?

                    VERN
          If they're in a pack, they'll kill them
          and keep killing. They don't even want
          to eat them...just kill.

                    SARAH
          Dogs.

                    VERN
          Uh-huh. Some kid's Airedale or some
          old lady's pet poodle. Those goddamn
          poodles, they're the worst.

                    SARAH
          You've seen this?

VERN
A couple times. Once, really bad. I was about fifteen then. Working for some sheep men up North. We grazed the flock in the mountains for the summer and when we brought them back down these two men decided to go to a dance in Susanville.

SARAH
They left you alone? And you were 15?

VERN
What could happen? The sheep were in a pen. They weren't going anywhere. And if there was trouble with coyotes we always had a rifle in the tent.

He shrugs and begins to move nervously around the stage.

VERN
Anyway, they left camp around eight o'clock...already half drunk and trying for the second half...and about two hours later I heard the sheep bleating and running around. I ran out with a flashlight and there were five dogs in the pen and they'd killed a sheep, bit into her neck, and they were barking and the flock was trying *to* get out.

He walks to the edge of the stage -- consumed by the memory.

VERN
So...so I ran back to the tent to get the rifle, but it wasn't there! Those bastards had put it behind the seat of the pickup and forgotten all about it and now the sheep were sounding again...almost screaming like scared children. So I grabbed a stick and ran back out. The dogs had killed three more and now they're on the other side of the pen and the sheep kept running, spinning around. I tried to fight, I tried to do something, but then the sheep cracked the pen and they were out and it was dark...too dark...and the dogs were killing them...killing them all.

Vern turns away from Sarah. A Beat, then he forces a smile.

       VERN
  So you see, I never was a big fan of
  Lassie. All that man's best friend
  stuff.

Sarah stands up and walks over to Vern.

       SARAH
  Vern, don't make your dog fight. Not
  if he can't win.

       VERN
  I told you, Sarah. Big Boy might win.
  It's possible.

       SARAH
  But his leg...

       VERN
  I already put the money up.

       SARAH
  But what if he dies? What if Rawley's
  dog kills him?

       VERN
  That won't happen. I'll make sure of
  that.

Pete runs onstage with the dog.

       PETE
  We got to get going! Rawley wants to
  tease the dogs. He's bringing Hector
  up the hill.

       VERN
  What's the point? They'll meet each
  other in the pit.

       PETE
  Vern, there're almost two hundred
  people down there. They want to see a
  good fight.

       VERN
  They'll see one.

       SARAH
  What's going to happen?

                    PETE
          Don't worry about it. Just keep out of
          the way.

Sarah moves quickly upstage. Vern and Pete turn to the left.

                    PETE
          They're coming! Rawley's got the dog
          with him!

                    VERN
          All right, Big Boy! You gotta show
          them some heart!

                    PETE
          You can do it! You can get him!

Skip enters leading another pit bull. Rawley and Lillian follow a few steps behind him. When the dogs see each other, they jerk forward and tighten their leashes.

                    RAWLEY
          All right! Your dog's gonna get
          whipped, Vern! I'm gonna beat you bad!

                    VERN
          Looking strong now! Looking real
          strong!

The dogs strain to get at each other as we hear the sound of a crowd shouting. Pete and Skip let the dogs get closer and closer. BLACKOUT as Skip begins to howl.

The crowd sound continues for about thirty seconds, then spotlights appear on the six characters arranged in a wide semicircle. Pete and Vern stand close to each other on the downstage right side. Sarah and Lillian are both upstage: each woman standing within her own circle of light. Rawley and Skip stand close together on the downstage left side.

There are no dogs on stage, but Pete and Skip pantomime handling them. Lillian steps slightly forward when she plays the character of the referee while Sarah, Vern, and Rawley generally stay within their spotlights.

The characters don't attempt to recreate all the activities of a dog fight. They address each other and the unseen members of the crowd, but on the whole their movements are stylized and not specific. Whenever possible the scene should resemble a dream – easily moving from dialogue to spoken thoughts.

LILLIAN
So all the men just stood there, sniffing and howling at each other like a bunch of mutts at the pound. Looking at them, I wanted to laugh and tell them to get rabies shots or something, but the dogs scared me. Both of them were barking, digging their paws in the dirt, pulling out their leashes into two tight lines.

RAWLEY
Then I get Hector around. Get him around and I hand the leash to Skip.

Rawley turns to Skip and holds out his hand.

RAWLEY
Take it. Come on. Take it.

SKIP
I feel Rawley's hand first, then the leash, then Hector snaps forward and I feel the power there.

Skip's hand goes forward.

SKIP
It's like revving up a cycle or shooting a gun. You can feel that power. Melting into your hand. Burning up your arm.

PETE
And Vern says --

VERN
You got the medical bag, Pete? The cotton? The tape?

PETE
I got it.

VERN
What about the stitching needles? Did you put the thread in?

PETE
Everything's set.

The characters start walking in place.

SARAH
Then we turn around and follow Rawley down the hill. Vern is walking with his leg spread wide so the dog won't pull him over and the dog is walking the same way...stocky-legged and big-shouldered, snorting through his little black nose.

VERN
Watch the crowd. Watch the dog. He's watered. His stomach is empty.

SARAH
I see some parked cars and pickups, a clapboard house and some old sheds too tired to fall down. There's a clump of trees beyond that, then the dark brown line of the river.

PETE
There's my truck. Vern's truck. There's Rawley's Cadillac.

RAWLEY
How you doing, Nathan? You betting on us today?
          (nods)
Damn right. You know who's going to win.

SKIP
Hey, stand back from the dog! Get away!

PETE
Where's Michael? Where'd he go? Wonder if you placed that bet.

SKIP
The power. Feeling that power.

SARAH
Feeling alert to every sound...like somebody slapped me awake.

LILLIAN
Feeling itchy. But I'm not going to scratch myself in front of this crowd.

                    VERN
Good to see you, Nathan. How's your
boy? Sure. What do you think? You
know he's going to win.

                    LILLIAN
Lot of farm workers with dirty
jeans and tractor caps. Some older
men. One or two women. A lot of
cowboys, spitting snuff and holding
onto their belts.

                    RAWLEY
          (looks right)
Is that Buddy Dawson? God, he looks
like hell.
          (smiling)
Hey, Buddy, looking good!
          (looks left)
There's that Mexican...Carlos
Whatshisname. Fights red dogs.
Carries a knife.
          (nods)
Hey, Carlos! How's it going, amigo?
          (to himself)
Little bastard owes me forty bucks.

                    SARAH
And then into the crowd. The smell of
sweat and spilled beer. All the men
staring at me. Their eyes bright.

                    PETE
Where's Mike? There...there he is.
Just nod at me. That's right. You placed
the bet. Don't nod again. Vern's going
to see you. Don't nod again.

                    VERN
What's he nodding at Pete for? That's
Mike Dawson, Buddy Dawson's boy. He's a
little wild. Always betting.

                    LILLIAN
Billy Crawford, the referee, is
standing in the pit. Bandy legs and
black snake eyes. Mean little mouth.
Licking his lips.

                    RAWLEY
          Hey, Billy! How you doing? You betting
          on us? Come on, you can tell me!

Skip steps over the three foot barrier into the pit. He begins
to pick up the dog.

                    RAWLEY
          Get him over the wall, Skip. Put him
          in the near corner. Steady, Hector.
          Yeah, you'll get him.

Vern, Pete, and Sarah stop walking. Vern pulls on the leash.

                    VERN
          Hold up now. Pete, get into the pit.

                    SARAH
          Vern steadies the dog while Pete steps
          into a pen with a low plywood wall.
          The crowd moves closer, gathering
          around to get a good view.

   Pete steps into the pit and nods to the referee.

                    PETE
          I thought you were dead, Billy. Well, you
          look dead. Yeah, I remember the rules.
          Who you think you're talking to?

                    VERN
          Easy now, Big Boy. Hold his front
          legs, Pete. Get him around. Don't let
          him see Hector.

                    PETE
          I got him, Vern. Got it!

                    SARAH
          People making bets. Rawley shouting...

                    RAWLEY
               (waving money)
          Two hundred on the Cajun dog! Two hundred!

                    SARAH
          And now I'm looking down into the pen at an
          old green carpet hammered to the ground.
          Scuff marks. Stains. Dried blood.

Both Pete and Skip crouch down holding the dogs so that they can't see each other.

                    SKIP
          Pull Hector around. Get him so his
          head's facing the corner. I can
          feel him breathe. Hear him panting.

                    PETE
          I can feel his heart beat and his muscles
          tighten while his tongue goes in and out.

                    SKIP
          Rawley's watching me.

                    PETE
          Vern's talking.

                    SKIP
          How much did he bet today? How much
          would he lose?

                    PETE
          Look up. See everybody's eyes. Vern's
          still talking.

                    VERN
          Let him go quick. Don't hold him back.

                    PETE
          I know.

                    VERN
          Make sure you --

                    PETE
          I know!

                    LILLIAN
          And Billy Crawford stands in a side corner
          and yells: "This is it! Get them ready!"

                    RAWLEY
          All the money's out. Betting. I can see
          twenties. Hundreds. Held within the
          fingers. Crunched inside a fist.

                    LILLIAN
          "Everybody ready?"

                    SKIP
          Any time.

                    PETE
          Let's do it.

                    LILLIAN
          "Face your dogs!"

Pete and Skip face each other. They're crouched down with
their feet spread wide, holding the dogs' front legs.

                    SARAH
          And both handlers pull them around so
          they can see each other and Big Boy
          strains forward...almost ripping out
          of Pete's hands.

                    VERN
          Hold him, Pete! Don't let go!

                    PETE
          Big Boy is pulling hard. Trying to get
          across the pit.

                    VERN
          Come on. Come on. Come on.

                    LILLIAN
          "Let 'em loose!"

Pete and Skip raise their hands, palms open, in a slow stylized
motion.

                    SARAH
          No sound. No shouting. And the dogs run
          across that dirty green carpet and slam
          together into a snapping ball of rage.

                    RAWLEY
          Get him, Hector! Kill that bastard!

                    VERN
          Head down, Big Boy! Head down!

Skip and Pete follow the dogs -- occasionally crouching down to
see what's happening.

                    SKIP
          Shake him hard! That's it! Just shake
          him!

                    PETE
          You got him, Big Boy! Get...get up! Now
          hold him!

                    SARAH
Watch it. Make yourself watch it. The dogs
tearing at each other's lip. Their eyes
rolling. The first red cut of blood on Big
Boy's neck. You wanted to come here. You
wanted to see this.

She looks down for A Beat, then jerks her head back up.

                    SARAH
Watch it!

                    VERN
Watch it, Big Boy! Watch it! Watch it!

                    RAWLEY
Right now is when you feel it. Right
now is when it's good. When you first get
your cards. When you make the first bet.
When you first see a woman. First touch
her. First stand by the bed and make her
pull her dress high, high over her head.
And that's it. That's the feeling.
Everything else is just loose change.
Dead cards. Passing the time.

                    SKIP
Don't look at me, Hector. I can help
you. Watch...watch out. Here he comes!

                    PETE
You got him. Now, down! Put him
down!

                    SARAH
And the dogs come close, closer, and they
smash together against the plywood wall.
I can feel the vibration in my hands.
Hear the quick gasps as their ribs
move in and out.

                    PETE
That's it! Looking good!

                    SKIP
Roll off him, Hector! Just...roll him!

                    LILLIAN
          Look away. Look around the pit. Rawley's
          on the other side. Hands in his pockets,
          jiggling his change. Vern stands a little
          closer. His eyes on the dogs.

                    VERN
          If he gets a good hold, if he stays on
          top --

                    RAWLEY
          Fourteen hundred, fifteen hundred,
          sixteen hundred dollars --

                    VERN
          If he goes too long, if he starts
          to get tired --

Rawley holds up some money.

                    RAWLEY
          Who's got their money out? Who wants
          to bet?

                    SKIP
               (glances at Rawley)
          He's always pressing me. Always
          putting up more money.
               (to dog)
          Come on!

                    PETE
          Rawley's betting.

                    VERN
          Rawley's...betting.

                    PETE
          Looking cool and clean. Looking like
          he knows.

                    RAWLEY
          One hundred on my Cajun dog! Even odds!

                    VERN
          Why's he doing that? Why? Big Boy
          looks strong. Pretty strong.

                    SARAH
          Now they break apart...circling...circling.

                    PETE
          Then they slam back together with a thump
          and a cracking sound!

                    SKIP
          Did he break a bone?

                    VERN
          Did he break that leg?

                    PETE
          Rawley's dog bites hard, trying to get a
          hold behind Big Boy's ear. Pull apart.
          Pull...apart.

                    RAWLEY
          Cracked it.

                    SARAH
          A white tooth lying on the dark green
          rug.

                    PETE
          Stay with him, Big Boy! You got it!

                    SKIP
          Get...get...kill him!

                    SARAH
          Step back. Take a deep breath. Make
          yourself look at everything. Pete's shirt.
          Skip's hands. The dog's skin shiny,
          flecked with blood.

                    SKIP
          Don't back off, Hector! Get on him!

                    VERN
          Both dogs have their first wounds and
          now and they're shaky-legged and wary.

                    RAWLEY
          Vern's dog comes closer, a little
          closer --

                    VERN
          And Rawley's dog jerks back so the
          referee shouts --

In the character of the referee, Lillian points at Rawley's dog and
clicks an imaginary stopwatch (there is a thirty second interval
between each scratch).

                    LILLIAN
          "Turn! Turn on the Cajun dog! Pick
          'em up and hold 'em for the scratch."

                    SKIP
          Got to pick Hector up, drag him back
          to the corner, see if he wants to keep
          fighting.

Rawley leans over the barrier as Skip checks the dog.

                    RAWLEY
          How's it going, Skip?

                    SKIP
          He's okay. Nothing to worry about. He just
          got a little surprised so he turned.

                    RAWLEY
          Look at him. He's still ready to fight.

                    VERN
          What about the ear?

                    PETE
          It's ripped a little. Nothing much.

                    VERN
          Look at his mouth. I think he lost a
          tooth.

                    PETE
          I got it.
                    (to himself)
          Lean over. Feel the wet fur. The dog's
          all shaky. Shivering beneath my hands.
                    (to Vern)
          Yeah, he cracked it right out.

                    LILLIAN
          "Face your dogs! Get 'em ready!"

The handlers turn the dogs towards each other.

                    SKIP
          So I pull Hector around and he
          jerks forward --

                    LILLIAN
          "Let him loose!"

Skip lets go of Hector first --- showing that the dog still wants to fight.

                    RAWLEY
          And Hector runs across the pit still
          ready to fight --

                    VERN
          So Pete lets go of Big Boy and the dogs --

                    SKIP
          Hit hard! Hard!

                    LILLIAN
          And the crowd's yelling and clapping
          and pressing against the plywood.

                    PETE
           Come on, Big Boy! You got it!

                    SKIP
          Don't let him catch you, Hector! Watch
          out!

                    LILLIAN
          And Big Boy bites into Hector's nose
          and holds it tight while Hector shakes
          like something caught in a trap.

                    RAWLEY
          That'll kill him quick. He'll choke on
          his own spit.

                    SARAH
          Jerking back and forth. He can't breathe!

                    PETE
          Got him! Caught him good!

                    SKIP
          Pull it out! You've got to pull it out!

                    SARAH
          Can't...breathe...

                    VERN
          What's Rawley doing? He's going to lose
          his dog.

                    RAWLEY
          Too weak. Shouldn't have bought him.
          No guts.

                    SARAH
          His head jerking back and forth. His eyes
          pleading to Skip...to anyone. He's
          going to die.

                    SKIP
                (glances at Rawley)
          Rawley?

                    RAWLEY
          Keep off him, Skip.

                    LILLIAN
          It's like you're sleeping and someone
          pushes his hand over your mouth and you
          wake up and you're fighting and you
          can't --

                    SKIP
          Free! Pulled free!

                    SARAH
          Blood on the dog's muzzle. Blood trickling
          down the jaw to his teeth and now they're
          fighting again, going forward. Their red
          blood smearing on the green.

                    RAWLEY
          Now we got it. No problem.

                    VERN
          Big Boy should have won it there. He's
          going to get tired. Weak.

                    PETE
          Come on, Big Boy! Get him again!

                    SKIP
          Looking strong!

                    LILLIAN
          Something's gotta die. That's what
          they want to see.

                    SKIP
          Strong! Strong!

                        PETE
          Now Hector turns quick and bites Big
          Boy on the back leg. He's caught...
          caught bad...and Hector won't let go.

                        VERN
          That's the bad leg. The one that
          was hurt.
                    (leans forward)
          Roll him now, Big Boy! Roll him off!

                        SARAH
          The dog's legs pushing. The sound of
          his nails scratching on the carpet.

                        SKIP
          Hold onto him! That's it!

                        LILLIAN
          Think of something. Think of
          anything good.

Pete and Skip kneel and shout at the dogs.

                        PETE
          Get up!

                        SKIP
          Hold him!

                        PETE
          Get up!

                        SKIP
          Hold him!

                        LILLIAN
          I remember driving back from a dance
          with T.C. Holmes and there was snow all
          over the mountains. It was cold... cold as
          death outside the truck...but all of a
          sudden T.C. parked by a meadow and said:
          "Let me show you summer."

                        RAWLEY
          You're gone, Vern! You're dead!

                        VERN
          Come on, Big Boy! Come on!

                    LILLIAN
          "Let me show you summer." And I was still
          enough in love to follow him across the
          meadow to this haystack covered with snow.
          And he bent down and he brushed away the
          snow and pulled out some grass and little
          yellow flowers, still smelling sweet.
          Still summer.

Lillian turns away as Rawley glances at her.

                    RAWLEY
          What's she thinking about? Why's she --
                    (looks at dogs)
          Goddamn it, Skip! Stay with him!
          Keep him on the hold!

                    VERN
          Pete. Over here.

Keeping his eyes on the dog, Pete steps closer to Vern.

                    VERN
          How's it look?

                    PETE
          He's got a damn good hold. Big Boy can't
          break it.

                    VERN
          He getting weak?

                    PETE
          I don't think so. Not yet.

                    VERN
          He bleeding?

                    PETE
          A little. It's a good hold.

                    VERN
               (leaning forward)
          Let's go, Big Boy. You can do it. Come to
          me, fella. Come to me.

                    SARAH
          And the dog tries... <u>tries</u>. His legs
          pushing on the carpet. His eyes
          watching Vern. Don't love him.
          Don't love him... you dumb dog!

                        PETE
          He's up! Now, watch it!

                        SKIP
          Hector's circling. Going for the throat
          and --

                        LILLIAN
          "Turn! Turn on the red dog!"

Pete and Skip drag the dogs back to their corners. Skip kneels and checks Hector while Rawley watches him.

                        RAWLEY
          Looking good.

                        SKIP
          Yeah, he's real strong. Vern's dog was
          twitching like a frog on a knife.

                        RAWLEY
          I got no more money. I bet all my
          wallet and my clip, too.

Pete bends over and checks the dog.

                        PETE
          Got to hold the dog. Wipe off the blood.
          Turn around and there's Sarah looking
          like she's been kicked in the gut.

                        SARAH
          He doesn't care about the dog. He just
          wants to win.

                        VERN
          How's the leg, Pete?

                        PETE
          Bleeding.

                        VERN
          Did he crack the bone?

                        PETE
          It's just ripped up, that's all.

                        VERN
          Look at him. He thinks he's going to lose.
          You can see that in his eyes.

                    PETE
          He's just a dog, Vern. He doesn't think
          about anything.

                    VERN
          He knows!
                    (bends down)
          You got to beat him on this scratch, Big
          Boy. You got to try.

                    LILLIAN
          Face your dogs!

   The two handlers pull the dogs around.

                    PETE
          He can't even see colors. Just black
          and --

                    LILLIAN
          "Turn 'em loose!"

   Pete lets go of his dog first.

                    SARAH
          And Big Boy runs forward, still ready to
          fight and Rawley's dog is let go and they
          meet, their sharp teeth biting, trying
          to find a week point in the skin.

                    VERN
           And Hector keeps going for the bad
           leg while Big Boy keeps dragging it
           slow.

                    RAWLEY
          Look at him, just nipping at that back
          leg, wearing him down.

                    SKIP
          Raw meat! Chew him up!

                    SARAH
          Hector's biting at Vern's dog,
          spinning him around. But the dog keeps
          trying, fighting helplessly.

                    SKIP
          Raw meat!

                    VERN
These dogs got courage. Heart. Every
damn thing a man should have in this
world. I tried to explain that to Mary
the first time I brought one home...
ripped up and bleeding bad.

                    SKIP
Where's your good luck belt, Pete?
Should have worn that belt!

                    PETE
Rawley...

                    SKIP
What'd you bet, Pete? How much are you
gonna lose?

                    PETE
It's not over!

                    VERN
I talked to her, tried to explain, but
every time I brought a dog home I knew
what she was thinking: "Do I really
love this man?

                    RAWLEY
Hector's got him now. Biting hard and --

                    LILLIAN
Pulling him. Twisting him around and --

                    PETE
Crack! You can hear that back leg go.

                    SARAH
Like a stick of firewood snapping only
It's a leg with blood and bone. Oh, god.

                    SKIP
Broke it. Cracked it. Forced them down.

                    SARAH
God.

                    RAWLEY
And Hector lets go and Vern's dog
backs off so Billy Crawford shouts:

                    LILLIAN
          "That's a turn! Turn on the red dog!"

Pete and Skip drag the dogs back to their corner.

                    PETE
          It's almost over now. Just don't let
          Vern see your face.

                    VERN
          He broke the leg. Didn't he?

                    PETE
          Maybe. I think so.

                    VERN
          Pete, you're the handler. You're
          Supposed to know.

                    SARAH
          What else do they want? Why isn't it
          over?

                    RAWLEY
          Looking good, Skip. No problem.

                    SKIP
          I'm lucky for you. Aren't I, Rawley?

                    PETE
          It's not my fault, Vern. I did
          everything I could.

                    LILLIAN
          And Billy Crawford just keeps
          grinning and shouts: "Face your dogs!"

                    SARAH
          What are they doing?

                    LILLIAN
          "Face them up!"

                    SARAH
          They can't put him back in. They can't.
          Peter!

                    SKIP
                (imitating Sarah)
          Peter! Oh, Peter!

                    PETE
                (to Sarah)
          Just shut up! All right!
                (to crowd)
          This dog's going to make scratch!

                    LILLIAN
          "Let 'em loose!"

Pete releases his dog first, then Skip lets go of Hector.

                    RAWLEY
          And Hector runs across that pit as Big Boy
          moves forward, dragging that back leg.

                    SARAH
          Kill them. Make the earth clean. Start over.

                    RAWLEY
          Hector's on him now. Going for the throat.

                    SKIP
          Tearing him. Shaking him like a
          bloody little rag.

                    VERN
          Pete! That's enough. Pull him off.

Pete and Skip move forward to grab the dogs as we hear the sound of the crowd whistling and shouting.

                    LILLIAN
          And everybody's shouting and laughing and --

                    SARAH
          Kill them! Kill them all!

BLACKOUT and everyone exits. About five seconds pass, then the crowd sound fades. The lights rise as Pete runs on stage carrying the medical bag.

                    VERN (offstage)
          Pete, get the box!

                    PETE
          I got it!

Pete sets down the medical bag. He places the carrying box on top of two crates, then opens the top.

                    VERN
          Give me a hand! Hurry up!

Vern enters carrying the dog in a bloody towel.

                    PETE
          It's all set. Just lay him down.

The two men gently place the dog inside the carrying box. Vern grabs a fruit crate and sits beside the box while Pete pulls some sterile cotton out of the bag. Looking stunned, Sarah enters.

                    VERN
          Easy, Big Boy. I know it hurts,
          baby. I know that. Just take it easy.
          We're going to make you feel better.

                    PETE
          He's cut bad, Vern. He's really bleeding.

                    VERN
          Let's have some cotton.

Pete rips off a wad of cotton and hands it to Vern.

                    PETE
          Jesus, look at that. He's going to
          bleed to death.

                    VERN
          Not if we do something. Give me some
          more cotton and get the blood stopper.

Pete hands another wad of cotton to Vern.

                    PETE
          Get what?

                    VERN
          The blood stopper! Goddamn it, Pete!
          What's your problem? Wake up!

Sarah hurries over to Pete as he rummages through the medical bag.

SARAH
Can I help?

PETE
No.

SARAH
Maybe I can find it. Is it a coagulant? What's it look --

PETE
Get the hell out of our way, all right? Just get away!

Sarah backs away from Pete and walks stage left. Pete finds a plastic syringe and a small bottle of coagulant. Moving quickly, he fills the syringe.

VERN
Easy now. I know it hurts, baby. I know that.

Pete hands the syringe to Vern.

VERN
Now get me the small stitching needle. We'll sew the neck wound first. Put bandages on the rest.

PETE
What about the leg?

VERN
Forget that now. It's not making him bleed.

He bends over the dog.

VERN
We've got to stop the blood first or he'll get too weak. Easy, Big Boy.

He injects the coagulant, then hands the syringe to Pete.

PETE
It was the leg that got him. He could have won if it wasn't for the leg.

VERN
That's right.

Pete takes a threaded surgical needle out of the bag.

                    PETE
          He almost had Rawley's dog, then that
          leg had to --

                    VERN
                (takes needle)
          Yeah, he's a good dog. He's got a lot
          of heart.

Sarah takes the camera out of her shoulder bag.

                    VERN
          Now this is going to hurt, baby, but
          it'll make you feel better. Pete, get
          rid of that blood.

Pete dabs with the cotton as Vern sews up the wound.

                    PETE
          Where?

                    VERN
          Right. You got it.

                    PETE
          He really got cut.

                    VERN
          It's not that bad.

                    PETE
          Look at that...near the jaw. Jesus,
          that's the bone.

                    VERN
          It's not that bad! Just...yeah, right
          there.

Sarah walks over to the men and raises the camera.

                    PETE
          He's taking it good. He's not crying.

                    VERN
          Yeah, he's a brave dog.

Sarah takes the picture. The men hear the shutter click and look up. Furious, Pete jumps to his feet and walks over to her.

                    PETE
           You bitch!

Sarah backs away from him and pushes the camera into her bag.

                    SARAH
        I'm sorry, Peter. I shouldn't have
        done that. I just thought it was a
        good shot and --

Pete slaps her - leaving a smear of dog blood across her cheek.

                    VERN
        Pete.

                    PETE
        Do you think we're a goddamn picture? Is
        that it?

                    VERN
        Pete!

Pete stops and turns towards Vern.

                    VERN
        You don't hit a woman.

                    PETE
        Some people do.

                    VERN
        Some people do a lot of things!

                    PETE
        Did you see what she did?

                    VERN
        She made a mistake. Now get over
        here. Help me with the dog.

                    PETE
        She's a --

                    VERN
        I said, get over here! Right now!

A Beat, then Pete walks back over to the carrying box. Dazed, Sarah walks to downstage left and sits on the ground.

                    VERN
        Sop that blood up. I can't see what I'm
        doing.

                    PETE
        I got it.

                    VERN
          The dog is hurting. You've got to --

                    PETE
          All right!

                    VERN
          Now I'm going to tie it. With your
          finger...yeah...just like a package.

                    PETE
          That'll hold.

Sarah touches her cheek, feels something, and looks in horror at the blood. Pete and Vern start bandaging the dog.

                    PETE
          That left ear looks bad. I think Hector
          took off about a half inch.

                    VERN
          Won't hurt him.

                    PETE
          What about the hind leg?

                    VERN
          Can't do anything about that.

                    PETE
          It's broken.

                    VERN
          I _know_ it's broken, but that's all
          we _can_ do.

Vern stands up and looks at the dog.

                    VERN
          We'll let him rest for awhile, then
          take him back to town.

                    PETE
          You want me to go and call the vet?

                    VERN
          There's no need. Somebody will be there.
          We've just got to wait a little, that's
          all. Give me the bottle.

Pete reaches into the bag and pulls out a bottle of tequila. He walks over to Vern and pours a little on Vern's hands.

PETE
He wanted to make scratch.

VERN
Yeah. He wouldn't give up.

Vern dries his hands, then drinks from the bottle.

VERN
He would have kept on fighting forever, but he couldn't move that leg.

Vern glances at Sarah, then offers the bottle to Pete.

VERN
Pete, go over there and talk to Sarah.

PETE
What?

VERN
Go over and talk to her. Apologize.

Pete takes the bottle.

PETE
After what she did?

VERN
She made a mistake. So what? If everybody in this world got whipped for their mistakes, nobody could sit down.

Pete drinks some tequila, then hands the bottle to Vern.

PETE
I'm not crawling to her.

VERN
Why not? When my wife was alive, half the time she was crawling to me and half the time I was crawling to her. After awhile, you get callouses on your knees.

PETE
We're not married.

VERN
So practice.

Pete takes a step towards Sarah, then hesitates.

>   VERN
>   Go on. Do it.

Slowly, Pete walks over to Sarah. He stands beside her for a few seconds, but she doesn't look around.

>   PETE
>   Sarah?

She doesn't acknowledge him.

>   PETE
>   Sarah?

He touches her shoulder, but she brushes his hand away.

>   SARAH
>   Don't touch me.

>   PETE
>   What's your problem?

>   SARAH
>   My problem? Five minutes ago, you
>   attacked me and now you want to
>   make up. Am I supposed to be happy
>   about that? Am I supposed to smile?

>   PETE
>   Come on, I didn't really hurt you.

>   SARAH
>   Don't you understand anything?

>   PETE
>   Yeah, I understand. Stuck up college
>   bitch.

Pete walks back to Vern and sits down on a fruit crate. Vern shakes his head.

>   VERN
>   That didn't look too successful.

>   PETE
>   I knew it wouldn't work.

>   VERN
>   You didn't say the right things.

>   PETE
>   You can't say anything to her!

							VERN
				You didn't go at it right.

							PETE
				You try.

							VERN
				She's not my girl.

							PETE
				You try. She's all yours.

A Beat. Vern reaches inside the box and touches the dog.

							VERN
				How you feeling, Big Boy? Yeah, I know
				it hurts. We'll be going in awhile.
				Won't be too long.

He turns and walks over to Sarah.

							VERN
				Sarah?

							SARAH
				I want to get out of here.

							VERN
				All right, I'll take you back to the
				city in a little while. I just got to --

							SARAH
				I want to go home, back to my apartment.
				I want to take a shower and have some ice
				tea and get a book, a good book, and --

							VERN
				I'll take you home. Promise.

She twists around and faces him.

							SARAH
				Vern, I thought you loved your dog
				and then you made him suffer.

							VERN
				At least I didn't take pictures of
				him when he was hurting. I'm not
				yelling at you because of that, all
				right? So you owe me one.

							SARAH
				What do I owe you?

Vern sits down beside Sarah. He takes out a bandanna and helps wipe the blood off her face.

>							VERN
>	You know, when I was a kid growing up in Jackson, my parents used to take me with them to the dances in town.

>							SARAH
>	What's that got to do with anything?

>							VERN
>	Just listen. When I was a kid and watching them dancing I thought they were all so graceful. It was only when I got older and walked out on the dance floor myself, that I realized that everybody was drunk and stepping all over everybody else's toes.

Sarah doesn't react.

>							VERN
>	That's how it is between men and women. Most of the time you're just stumbling around, but sometimes you get together and then...then it's all right.

Vern smiles and stands up.

>							VERN
>	Now come on over. Have a drink.

>							SARAH
>	No.

>							VERN
>	Come on. You don't have to marry Pete or anything. Just show him you're not scared.

>							SARAH
>	Who said I was scared?

She lets Vern guide her over to Pete.

>							VERN
>	I wasn't saying that.

>							SARAH
>	I'm not scared. Not of him.

They reach the carrying box and Vern lets go of Sarah.

                        VERN
Now Pete, if you were a gentleman, you'd wipe off that bottle before you handed it to Sarah.

A BEAT, then Pete wipes off the mouth of the bottle and hands it to Sarah. She drinks some of the tequila, then stops and starts coughing. She laughs at herself. Vern laughs and Pete joins in.

                        SARAH
Strong stuff.

                        VERN
Sometimes, we've used it for disinfectant.

Sarah turns and offers Pete the bottle.

                        PETE
What's this?

                        SARAH
Something to drink. If you can.

Pete takes the bottle and begins to drink. Suddenly, Sarah tips the bottom of the bottle and forces him to drink even more. Pete swallows a cup of tequila, then pulls his mouth away --- coughing and sputtering.

                        VERN
Not bad, Pete. I think you've been practicing.

Pete raises the bottle and smiles at Sarah.

                        PETE
Again?

                        SARAH
That'll do. For now.

Pete nods, then turns to Vern.

                        PETE
Let's get out of here. All right?

                        VERN
Not yet. The dog's got to rest a while and I got to give Rawley his money.

PETE
I'm sorry, Vern.

VERN
Nothing to be sorry about.

PETE
I know you needed --

VERN
It's done. You make a decision and then it's over.

Looking tired, Vern bends back over the dog.

PETE
Have some more tequila.

VERN
No. That's enough.

PETE
He'll be okay. Remember that black dog...Little Kelly? Remember how bad he was cut?
            (A Beat)
Vern?

VERN
Yeah.

Pete glances at Sarah, determined to cheer Vern up.

PETE
Listen, we'll just...we'll take Big Boy to the vet and then we'll go over to Ray's bar and...
            (to Sarah)
And then Vern can show you how to do the Slippery Duck.

SARAH
What's the Slippery Duck?

VERN
Come on, Pete. This isn't the time for that.

PETE
The Slippery Duck's this dance that Vern thought up.

VERN
I didn't think it up. They were doing up in Jackson when I was a boy.

PETE
It's quite a dance. I've seen people run for cover when Vern --

VERN
I've only done it once in the last twenty years and Pete's been teasing me about it ever since.

Sarah walks over to Vern and tries to dance with him.

SARAH
How do you do it, Vern? Show me.

PETE
All right. Now we're going to see it. Ladies and Gentlemen, The Slippery Duck!

Vern pulls away from Sarah.

VERN
I'm not doing The Slippery Duck on the dirt at a busted-out farm. You've got to have a smooth floor and --

SARAH
Come on, Vern. Please. Show me the steps.

PETE
Be a gentleman, Vern. You're always telling me to be one.

Vern smiles, then gives up and faces Sarah.

VERN
Well, it's like you're a duck.
(A beat)
And you've come back north in the Spring, but all the lakes are still frozen. So you're slipping...slipping on the ice.

SARAH
So you --

Vern begins to show Sarah the dance. He takes two steps to the left and shuffles his feet twice.

                    VERN
          You take two step to the left and slip-
          slip, then two steps right and slip-slip...

Sarah imitates Vern, then reaches out and takes his hand. They begin to dance.

                    VERN
          Then you go back two steps and then
          You do...the duck.

He steps back, then steps forward, flapping his elbows like wings.

                    PETE
          All right! They're doing The Slippery
          Duck!

Pete stands up and walks over to Vern and Sarah.

                    PETE
                 (singing)
          They're doing it...doing it. The
          Slippery Duck!

Pete bows and cuts in on Vern. Sarah and Pete start to dance.

                    VERN
          You're looking good, Sarah.

                    SARAH
          One, two...slip-slip...one, two...

                    VERN
          Come on, Pete. Move with her. Watch what
          she's doing.

                    RAWLEY
          I can't believe it! They've gone crazy!

Rawley, Lillian, and Skip enter. Lillian looks hot and rumpled. Rawley and Skip have been drinking.

                    RAWLEY
          I think they've been out in the sun too
          long, Skip. Here they are, dancing
          with no music.

Rawley walks over to the carrying box and peers inside.

                    RAWLEY
          And their dog's dead!

Vern hurries over to the box. He examines the dog, then glares at Rawley.

                    VERN
          You know he's not dead, Rawley.

                    RAWLEY
          Maybe he should be dead the way Hector cut
          into him.

                    SKIP
          He was crying. Your little bitty dog
          was crying.

Pete and Sarah move over to the carrying box with Vern. Skip and Rawley stand center stage while Lillian moves away from them.

                    PETE
          Shut up, Skip.

                    SKIP
          Why? We're just stating the facts.

                    RAWLEY
          That's right. Vern's dog just laid
          right down on the ground and --

                    VERN
          He wasn't crying. He's got heart.

                    RAWLEY
          Maybe he's got heart, but he's got no
          more blood.

Skip laughs and tries to look inside the carrying box.

                    SKIP
          I think you should kill him, Vern. Put
          him out of his misery.

                    LILLIAN
          Rawley, tell Skip to shut up.

                    RAWLEY
          What's it to you? Maybe Vern should
          kill him.

                    LILLIAN
          It's been a long day, all right?
          Everybody's tired.

                    RAWLEY
          Vern's got an ice pick. I've seen that
          little ice pick he carries around in
          his bag. You've just got to press it
          against the soft spot on the back of
          the skull. One little push and --

                    VERN
          That's enough, Rawley.

                    RAWLEY
          You got an ice pick. Admit that.

                    VERN
          I've never used it. I've only got it
          for the bad pain.

Triumphant, Rawley turns to Lillian.

                    RAWLEY
          See? What'd I tell you? And all
          this time you've been telling me
          what a good man Vern is.

                    LILLIAN
          All right, he's got an ice pick. You
          know what? I don't care. It's hot. My
          feet hurt. Let's just call it a day and
          get out of here.

                    RAWLEY
          We'll go when I want to go.

                    LILLIAN
          When's that?

                    RAWLEY
          A couple minutes. Not too long. First,
          I've got to get my fifteen hundred dollars.

Vern takes bills out of his pocket and hands them to Rawley.

                    VERN
          There you are...fifteen hundred
          dollars. Now go back to town.

Rawley counts off $200 as Vern walks back to the dog.

                    RAWLEY
          Hold it. I've got to pay Skip here
          for being my handler.

Grinning, Skip takes the money. Rawley counts off another $200 and offers it to Lillian.

>   RAWLEY
>   And here's something to Lillian for
>   handling something else.

Skip laughs. Lillian stares at the money, then glances at Sarah.

>   LILLIAN
>   I don't want it, Rawley.

>   RAWLEY
>   Hey, it's money! Real money!

>   LILLIAN
>   I've got my own job and my own money.
>   Keep it.

>   RAWLEY
>   Well, now. That is a surprise. After
>   two years of take and take, you don't
>   want this.

>   SKIP
>   I'll take it, Rawley.

>   LILLIAN
>   Let's go.

>   SKIP
>   I'll take it.

Rawley turns away from Lillian. He starts to give Skip the money, then pulls back his hand.

>   RAWLEY
>   Tell you what. Maybe we should give it
>   to Vern. Help him put Big Boy in an
>   animal hospital.

>   SKIP
>   Yeah. Buy him some little crutches. You
>   know...

Skip limps a few feet across the stage.

>   SKIP
>   Put him in the crippled dog's home.

>   PETE
>   Get out of here, Skip!

Skip turns and faces Pete.

                    SKIP
          Forget that. You're losers and we're
          winners. We won today and you lost.

                    PETE
          You're not a winner, Skip. Rawley doesn't
          even want you as his handler. You know
          that? He asked me to work for him today.

                    SKIP
          Bullshit.

                    PETE
          Talk to him. He doesn't want you.

                    SKIP
          Rawley --

Rawley smiles confidently.

                    RAWLEY
          It's not true, Skip. Ask Lillian.

Skip turns to Lillian as she watches Rawley.

                    RAWLEY
          Go ahead. Ask her.

                    SKIP
          Lillian?

                    LILLIAN
          Yeah, it's true. He asked Pete to be
          his handler.

                    RAWLEY
          That's not what I said!

He walks over to Skip and puts his arm around him.

                    RAWLEY
          I just thought that you could be a kind
          of assistant...sometimes.

                    SKIP
          I'm not going to be an assistant.

                    RAWLEY
          All right. Fine.

Skip pulls away from Rawley.

SKIP
I'm not a goddamn assistant!

RAWLEY
I said, all right. We're friends.
We trust each other.
       (looks at Lillian)
But I don't know if we can trust this whore.

VERN
Rawley...

Vern steps towards Rawley, but Pete stops him. Controlling her emotions, Lillian turns towards Rawley.

LILLIAN
Please, let's go.

RAWLEY
Go where?

LILLIAN
Go...go to a bar.

RAWLEY
What'll we do?

LILLIAN
Have a drink.

RAWLEY
Then what?

LILLIAN
Have another drink.

RAWLEY
Then what'll we do?

Lillian hesitates.

RAWLEY
Then I'll fuck you any way I want.

VERN
That's it, Rawley.

Vern walks towards Rawley. Frantic, Skip pulls out his gun and points it at Vern.

SKIP
Stop! You stop right there!

                    VERN
          Put that thing away.

                    SKIP
          Don't talk like that to me!

                    VERN
          You tell him to heel, Rawley. Do you
          hear me? I want him to heel right now!

                    SKIP
          I could blow you away.

                    VERN
          Listen, I've put just about every-
          thing on the line today and I don't
          mind losing the rest. So don't give
          me your cheap talk because I won't
          take it!

He steps forward and Skip cocks the gun.

                    SKIP
          You're dead, Vern.

                    LILLIAN
          Rawley!

                    RAWLEY
          Put it away, Skip.

Skip's head jerks around. He stares at Rawley.

                    SKIP
          But he was going to --

                    RAWLEY
          Don't worry. I'll handle it.
                    (A Beat)
          Put it away!

Skip lowers the gun. Vern walks back to the carrying box.

                    SKIP
          I was just trying to protect you,
          Rawley. That's my job.

                    RAWLEY
          I know. I know. I'm not knocking you. Look,
          why don't you go down to the car and watch
          Hector. I don't want anybody fooling with
          him.

Still holding the gun, Skip walks over to Rawley.

      SKIP
  I'm sorry, Rawley.

      RAWLEY
  There's nothing to be sorry about.
  You were great. You were backing me up.

      SKIP
  I'll go down and guard Hector.
  Somebody might do something.

      RAWLEY
  Right. Good idea. I'll be down in a
  second.

      SKIP
  Rawley, I'm not an assistant. Right?

      RAWLEY
  Don't worry. We'll talk about it.

Skip hesitates, then puts the gun back in his holster and exits. Vern shakes his head.

      VERN
  I knew you talked too much, Rawley. But
  I never thought you were stupid.

      RAWLEY
  Is that so?

      VERN
  You better keep that boy on a short
  chain...real short...or he's going to
  get you in a lot of trouble.

      RAWLEY
  Maybe. Sometimes, he comes in handy.

      LILLIAN
  Comes in handy? Rawley, he almost killed
  Vern!

Rawley walks away from Lillian.

      RAWLEY
  You're gone, Lillian. I don't see you
  anymore.

                    LILLIAN
          I don't disappear that easy.

                    RAWLEY
          I said you're gone! You're a cheap
          dress with nothing in it!

                    LILLIAN
          Nothing? I'm nothing? Now that's a
          laugh. I know that I'm strong. I
          don't have to put some dogs in a pit
          and watch them bleed just to prove it.
          You want to think you're tough, but if
          they took away your money and your
          guns you'd just stand there shivering,
          holding onto your little dick like it
          might fall off.

Furious, Rawley steps towards Lillian.

                    VERN
          Rawley!

Rawley stops as Vern approaches him.

                    RAWLEY
          Don't play hero, Vern. You don't owe
          her anything.

                    VERN
          I care about Lillian.

                    LILLIAN
          Vern, you don't have to --

                    VERN
          Maybe you don't know about caring,
          Rawley. You don't have any friends.
          You don't have anything, but your
          goddamn Cadillac.

Rawley hesitates A Beat. He smooths out a wrinkle in his jacket and faces Vern.

                    RAWLEY
          Vern, I've known you a long time,
          but we've never had a fight. I
          always figured that, if we did,
          somebody would have to die.

                    VERN
          If you say so, Rawley.

The two men stare at each other, the Rawley smiles.

>   RAWLEY
>   Yeah, we could have a fight, just like
>   the dogs. But first, you better cover
>   your ass.
>
>   VERN
>   What are you talking about?
>
>   RAWLEY
>   Nothing. I just ran into Mike Dawson
>   before we came up here. He said that Pete
>   put a bet down on your dog.
>
>   VERN
>   So?
>
>   RAWLEY
>   Pete bet on him to lose.
>
>   VERN
>   Don't make up stories, Rawley.
>
>   RAWLEY
>   I'm not making up anything. You're the
>   one believing this big dream...that
>   everyone cares about you.

Uneasy, Vern walks over to Pete.

>   VERN
>   Pete, is he telling the truth?
>
>   PETE
>   I didn't think --
>
>   VERN
>   Is it true?
>
>   PETE
>   You said the dog had a bad leg. You
>   said that yourself.
>
>   VERN
>   Did you bet against me?

A Beat, then Pete nods. Vern almost slaps him, then he turns and walks away.

PETE
I helped you, Vern! I helped you in the pit! I just needed the money!

SARAH
So you bet against your friend.

PETE
What do you know? The fact is, I won today. The fact is, I doubled my money. You two can talk about whatever you want, but you can't get around that.

Vern turns and faces Pete.

VERN
That doesn't mean anything! I've been trying to show you!

PETE
Show me what? That if I'm lucky I can end up with a beat-up truck and a half-dead dog? Oh, that sounds great! That's what I want!

VERN
I've tried to make the right choices, Pete. That's all a man can do.

PETE
You guessed wrong.

VERN
I wasn't guessing.

LILLIAN
Listen to him, Pete.

PETE
Listen to what?

RAWLEY
(laughs)
Oh, I love this.

PETE
Rawley!

                    RAWLEY
          I'm not jumping on you, Pete. For years,
          I've been listening to people make up
          excuses for why they bet and lost. But it
          doesn't make any difference because the
          money's in my hand.

Rawley takes a few steps left. He stops and looks back at Pete.

                    RAWLEY
          I'm going now. You coming with me, Pete?
          My offer's still good.

                    PETE
          Skip will kill me.

                    RAWLEY
          I can handle him. It's easy. I'll show you
          how to handle anybody.

Sarah walks over to Pete.

                    SARAH
          Peter, don't go with him.

                    PETE
          I'll do what I want to do.

                    VERN
          Pete...

                    PETE
          Don't order me around! I'm not going
          to be a loser, with nothing, for the
          rest of my life.

                    VERN
          I'm not asking for that.

                    PETE
          You're asking for everything. Don't you
          see that? You're asking for things I
          can't give.

                    RAWLEY
          All right, Pete. Let's go.

Rawley exits. Pete takes a step left, then stops.

                    PETE
          I'll be back. I'll come up to the ranch.
          All right? I just want to win a little.

He starts to walk left, and then stops in front of Sarah. He pauses and looks at her.

>PETE
>I've got to win.

He runs after Rawley.

>PETE
>I'm coming, Rawley! Wait up!

Pete exits. The two women and Vern stare at the ground for a few seconds, then Lillian looks up.

>LILLIAN
>Vern...

>VERN
>I can't talk to you, Lillian. I've got to check the dog.

Vern walks over to the carrying box.

>VERN
>How you feeling, Big Boy? A little better?

He takes some tape out of the medical bag and starts to bandage the dog. Lillian walks over to Sarah and touches her shoulder.

>LILLIAN
>That's all right, Sarah. It's all right.

>SARAH
>I hate him. I think. I don't know. I feel angry and sad and confused. All at the same time.

>LILLIAN
>Stay angry. Sometimes you learn more that way. Meanwhile, let's go find someone to take us home.

>SARAH
>What about Vern?

>LILLIAN
>He doesn't want us acting sorry for him. It would only make things worse.

Lillian walks over to Vern as Sarah picks up her bag.

> LILLIAN
> Vern, we're going now. I think Nathan Williams will give us a ride home.

> VERN
> Yeah, I'm sure he will.

They watch each other for a few seconds. Lillian extends her hand.

> LILLIAN
> Now I want you to promise that you'll come down to the club and see me.

> VERN
> I'm not a very lucky man, Lillian.

> LILLIAN
> I'm not too lucky myself, but you could give it a try. Vern?

Vern takes her hand and they smile at each other. Lillian begins to exit as Sarah walks over to Vern.

> LILLIAN
> Come on, Sarah. We've got to get going.

> SARAH
> Goodbye, Vern.

> VERN
> Bye, Sarah.

> SARAH
> I'll try to remember what you said About the dancing.

> VERN
> Good.

Sarah turns away, then steps back and embraces Vern. At first, he doesn't respond, then he pats her shoulder. Sarah breaks away and exits with Lillian. Alone, Vern paces on the stage.

                    VERN
          Pete's gone, Big Boy. Everyone's gone.

Vern walks back to the dog and picks up the bottle.

                    VERN
          But I'm still here and you're still
          hurting. And you'll be hurting tonight
          and tomorrow and next week. And you're
          not going to understand why because you're
          just a dog.

He takes a drink and sits down beside the carrying box.

                    VERN
          Listen, Big Boy, I'm sorry about what
          happened. I put you in the pit...I know
          I did that...but I had to. Everything
          you do is some kind of risk. Even if you
          love someone, they might hurt you or leave
          you or die.

Vern stares at the dog, then he makes a decision. He stands up and reaches into the medical bag.

                    VERN
          Yeah, you're hurting...I know
          you're hurting...but don't you
          worry. 'Cause I'm your daddy and I'm
          not going to let you feel bad.

He takes the ice pick out of the bag, then hides it behind his leg. Slowly, he leans over the dog.

                    VERN
          I love you, baby. Love you.

Vern stabs the dog --- killing it. Vern stands, closes the box, and walks to the edge of the stage. Alone, he stares out at the trees.

FADE TO BLACKOUT.

A DOG FIGHT GLOSSARY

PIT BULL - The commonly used name for an American Staffordshire Terrier. Adult pit bulls weigh between thirty and sixty pounds. They are often identified by their color (a red dog) or their breeding (a Cajun dog comes from Louisiana).

ROLL - A practice dog fight with little or no betting.

CONVENTION - An organized meeting where a series of dog fights are held. Before the gathering, opposing dog owners agree on a weight for their dogs and a side bet. If one of the dogs doesn't make weight, his owner forfeits the money.

THE PIT - A sixteen-foot square surrounded by a three-foot high barrier. Only the two dogs, their handlers, and a referee are allowed inside the pit during a match.

FACE YOUR DOGS - The command to ready the dogs for fighting.

TURNING - If any dog shows fear in the pit be is considered to have "turned." The two dogs are pulled apart and returned to their handlers for a thirty second interval.

MAKING SCRATCH - The dog that has turned must continue to show his desire to fight. At the end of the interval, he is released first and encouraged to cross the pit. The fight is over only when a dog refuses to make scratch or if his owner pulls him out of the pit.

REBEL ARMIES DEEP INTO CHAD

My next play was strongly influenced by the director and actors involved in the play's workshop production and its premiere performance. Although the playwright creates a play's characters and dialogue, he or she must listen closely to the reactions of the performers who say those lines on stage.

This time, I was writing about a life experience. When I was a journalist in Uganda, a young reporter working for BBC radio had gone into the war zone north of the capital and interviewed Yoweri Museveni, the head of the guerrilla group fighting the army. The reporter casually mentioned the name of the area during his radio interviews. Two days after that broadcast, I visited the area for a follow-up story and discovered that every man, woman and child in a nearby village had been murdered. I had no way to prove that the BBC reporter's radio broadcast had innocently caused these deaths, but the experience made me sensitive to the destruction caused by self-centered foreigners in Africa.

Family friends who lived in Santa Cruz, California wanted to see an event in Los Angeles so we traded homes for a week. While my wife took our two children to the beach, I sat on the coach in our friends' living room and thought about my time in Uganda. I had been expelled from the country because I had written about the soldiers who tortured and killed civilians. The day I returned to Kenya, I spent the night writing a final article at a wire service editor's home outside the city.

I had met a number of professional British journalists during this period and was aware of their extreme cynicism. Although they were constantly complaining about Africa, they didn't want to go back to England. From these real-life examples, I created a wire service editor named

Dove who wanted to discover why a young American journalist named Neal had just been expelled from Uganda.

The conflict between the two men was clear, but the play gained dramatic energy when two Africa prostitutes stepped out of the darkness and entered the stage light. In Kampala, I had lived in a hotel called the Tourist Lodge -- a cheap hotel close to the train station and taxi park. The Tourist Lodge was home base for a multi-national group of prostitutes who hung out on the third floor balcony. I spoke to these women often and admired their wit, strength and bravery. No matter how many beers were served, the women remained sober and skillfully manipulated their drunken customers.

My agent sent the play out to a variety of theaters, receiving a positive reaction from John "Joey" Tillinger, the associate artistic director of the Long Wharf Theatre. Oddly enough, I had already seen Joey naked. He had played one of the athletes in the Long Wharf production of *The Changing Room* that I had seen when I was a Yale undergraduate.

An aspect of Joey's background proved to be crucial to the formation of the play. He had been born in Tabriz, Iran, then schooled in London, Joey understood every detail of the expatriate life style. He had an intimate knowledge of why Dove and Neal lived in a country that was not their birthplace.

Readings and workshop performances allow theaters to "try out" new plays. But Joey wanted to premiere *Rebel Armies Deep Into Chad* and he used our two-week workshop as an opportunity for me to rewrite the play - under extreme pressure. After attending rehearsals during the daytime, I began rewriting around four o'clock in the afternoon, not stopping until past midnight. In general, Joey wanted me to dramatize all of my painful memories about the genocidal civil war in Uganda - the massacres and killing fields, my fear and exhaustion.

During the workshop and the first two weeks of rehearsals for the premiere, I rewrote dialogue and cut various scenes. Dove, Neal and Mary stayed the same throughout the rewrites, but the character of Christina was transformed. This change was influenced by Gail Grate, the actress who played Christina. When a playwright knows that a particular actor can perform emotionally difficult scenes, it liberates the writer's imagination. Watching Gail arrive at the theater and slowly make the transition into her character was an education about the power and skill that great actors can bring to a role.

***

REBEL ARMIES DEEP INTO CHAD was given its world premiere by the Long Wharf Theatre (Arvin Brown, Artistic Director) in New Haven, Connecticut on April 14, 1989. It was directed by John Tillinger. The set design was by John Lee Beatty. The cast was as follows:

Dove......Alan Scarfe

Neal......Joe Urla

Mary.....Pamela Tucker-White

Christina......Gail Grate

REBEL ARMIES DEEP INTO CHAD was published by Dramatists Play Service. Excerpts have appeared in *The Best Men's Stage Monologues.* It has been produced at a wide range of American theaters including The Old Globe Theatre in San Diego, the Roundhouse Theatre in Washington, D.C. and American Stage in St. Petersburg, Florida,

REBEL ARMIES DEEP INTO CHAD

A Play

by

Mark Lee

ACT I

A cottage in the Karen District of Northern Nairobi: an area that was once Isak Dinesen's coffee plantation. The cottage is surrounded by a forest and is a mile from the main road. It is being rented by Charles Richardson-Dove: an Englishman who is the East African Bureau Chief for Reuters News Service.

We see a cross section of the building that reveals the surrounding porch and the large central room. An open doorway covered with a curtain leads to the bathroom. A door on the right leads to the only bedroom.

An old couch, a rattan easy chair, and a coffee table are in the center of the room. An end table with a dial telephone is to the right of the couch while a low wooden stool is on the left.

A sink, food table, a portable radio, and refrigerator are near the front door. A writing table with a typewriter is near the entrance to the bedroom. The house has no running water. Metal jerry cans and boxes of Tusker beer are stacked against the wall.

It's about eight o'clock in the evening. We hear the sound of cicadas as Dove steps out of the darkness.

                    DOVE
     This way. This way.

He stops and looks back at Neal Bateman: a young American journalist.

                    DOVE
     Hurry up, Neal. You should have
     waited until we got inside. I'd
     put it back in if I were you. The
     mosquitoes are going to use it
     for a landing strip.

Dove walks towards the front door. Neal emerges from the darkness and almost trips stepping onto the porch.

                    DOVE
     Watch your step.

They reach the front door and Dove fumbles with his keys.

                DOVE
     Here we go. Now, where's the
     bloody key?

He slams open the door and steps into the dark house.

                DOVE
     Shoot me, you bastards! This
     is your best chance! Fire!

Neal immediately steps out of the doorway.

                DOVE
     I said fire!

Dove looks out the doorway and sees Neal.

                DOVE
     A bit jumpy, aren't you?

                NEAL
     Jesus! What are you doing, Dove?

                DOVE
     It's the thieves in this country.
     They're all incompetent. They need
     some kind of educational program
     Bloody cultural exchange.

Dove switches on the light.

                DOVE
     I'm home, darling! What's for dinner?

                NEAL
     You're not married, are you?

                DOVE
     I don't think so.

He takes two bottles of beer out of the refrigerator and takes off the caps with an opener attached to the wall.

                DOVE
     I'm just trying to make things
     friendlier. Brighten up my shabby
     little pied-de-terre.

                NEAL
     It's not that bad.

                    DOVE
          Of course it is. Everything in
          this house was discarded by a
          departing diplomat or aid worker.
          This is a black hole, sucking all
          debris into its core.

Dove sees that Neal is about to sit on the couch.

                    DOVE
          Don't sit there! It's loaded!

                    NEAL
          The couch is loaded?

                    DOVE
          In a manner of speaking.

Dove places one of the beers on the refrigerator. He
hands the other bottle to Neal, pulls back the cushions
of the couch, and takes out a pump-action shotgun.

                    DOVE
          Sit down on my furniture the wrong
          way and you'll blow off your bum.

                    NEAL
          What's that for?

                    DOVE
          There was an attempted coup in
          Kenya a couple of years ago and
          unknown citizens stole ten
          thousand rifles from one of the
          armories. Ever since then, all the
          expatriates have been nervous.
          Clutching their Uzis...
                (gestures)
          Oiling them in public.

Dove takes the shotgun into the bedroom.

                    NEAL
          What else are you hiding here?
          A land mine? An atomic bomb?

                    DOVE
          That's all. I promise. Sit down
          and drink your beer.

Dove comes back out of the bedroom. He walks over to the desk and places a piece of paper in the typewriter.

> NEAL
> I still think we should have stayed in Nairobi. I could have checked into a hotel.

> DOVE
> A hotel? I wouldn't think of it. The cheap ones are full of drunken Africans and the expensive ones are full of drunken whites. Either way you can't get a good night's sleep.

> NEAL
> It can't be that bad.

> DOVE
> Besides, all your articles are here. Your clips. Remember?

> NEAL
> So, where are they?

> DOVE
> Start writing your story. Go ahead.

Neal types the article as Dove searches for the clips.

> NEAL
> You *do* have my clips. Right?

> DOVE
> Of course I do. Just start typing. Tap-tap-tap. Hurry up.

> NEAL
> I don't know why you want an article. None of this is news.

> DOVE
> I'll be the judge of that.

> DOVE
> There we go! That the American spirit!

Dove finds the clips on the side table.

> DOVE
> Ah-ha! Your clips. I knew they were here.

He finds a manila envelope and hands it to Neal.

                    DOVE
          I edited them, of course, and
          those anemic wankers in London
          chopped them up some more. But
          they *were* printed.

Neal checks the clips as Dove sits on the couch.

                    NEAL
          This is gold.

                    DOVE
          No. They're just little scraps
          of paper.

                    NEAL
          They're going to get me a job.

                    DOVE
          You already have a job, Neal...
          with Reuters.

                    NEAL
          A *real* job. Back in the States.
          A job where army ants don't eat
          the telephone wires.

                    DOVE
          There's nothing wrong with the
          telephones around here.

                    NEAL
          Tell you what. Let's go back to
          Nairobi. I'll finish this at the
          office.

                    DOVE
          Sorry. It's too late. There's a
          curfew these days. Roadblocks.
          General nastiness in the dark.
          Some nervous soldier might take a
          shot at the car. Relax, Neal.
          We'll have a pleasant evening
          together. In the morning, we'll
          drive back to the city, go to the
          bank, and get the money Reuters
          owes you.

                    NEAL
          How are you going to send this out?
          Is there a telex machine in the bedroom?

                    DOVE
          We'll use the phone. I do it all
          the time.

                    NEAL
          And you get through?

                    DOVE
          There's rarely a problem.

Dove starts to dial the overseas operator.

                    DOVE
          I call London just to get the
          weather report.
               (to the phone)
          Hello? HELLO THERE, MATTHEW! THIS IS
          RICHARDSON-DOVE! CAN YOU HEAR ME!
          DON'T SWITCH THE CIRCUIT! DON'T!
          DON'T...! What...why hello, Matthew.
          Yes, it worked this time. So, how are
          you? How's your family? You sound
          incredibly lucid tonight. Listen,
          could you place a priority call to the
          Reuters office in London? All right.
          Call me back.

Dove hangs up. Neal pulls his article out of the
typewriter and hands it to Dove.

                    NEAL
          Here it is.

                    DOVE
          Here's what? Your lead?

                    NEAL
          The article. The whole article.

                    DOVE
          I beg your pardon.

                    NEAL
          I told you it was going to be short.

                    DOVE (reading)
          Dateline, Nairobi."The last
          Western journalist to live in
          Uganda was expelled by the
          government today." That's it?

                    NEAL
          There's another paragraph.

Dove tosses the article onto the coffee table.

                DOVE
I know that Americans have short attention spans, but this is ridiculous.

                NEAL
Come on, Dove. Who do you think you're talking to? You just send this stuff out. I've been on the receiving end. When I worked for a newspaper in Buffalo, the teletypes were going twenty-four hours a day. We never used more than five percent of it.

                DOVE
I wouldn't expect a small newspaper to print every --

                NEAL
It was the same thing in New York when I was working on the magazine. There, it had to be a big story and preferably an American one. I remember my editor telling me that a Presidential hemorrhoid operation equals a mining explosion in Wales which equals a cholera epidemic in Naples --

                DOVE
Which equals thousands dead in Guinea-Bissau.

                NEAL
You got it. This is a small story. Nothing important. One inch above the underwear ads.

                DOVE
Then write it a different way. I promised Reuters that you'd do a feature. Something personal. Immediate. Sexy.

                NEAL
What do you mean, "sexy?"

                    DOVE
          How does it feel to be arrested
          and kicked out of a country?

                    NEAL
          I told you what happened. This little
          man from the Ministry of Information
          came to the hotel, took my press
          pass, and drove me to the airport.

                    DOVE
          And he didn't tell you why you
          were being expelled?

                    NEAL
          He said that the government was
          "disappointed" with me. I told
          him I was disappointed with the
          government.

                    DOVE
          There's got to be more of a
          reason. I'm trying to remember
          what you sent out recently.

Dove stands up and examines the clips Neal left on the
writing desk.

                    DOVE
          What...what do we have here?
          Coffee exports. Blown-up bridge.

                    NEAL
          No.

                    DOVE
          Speech by Uganda's President.

                    NEAL
          No.

                    DOVE
          Usual rubbish. Sounds all right.
                (holds up a clip)
          What about this? Your interview
          with those two guerrillas?

                    NEAL
          I doubt it.

                    DOVE
          It was picked up by quite a few
          papers. It certainly would have
          irritated them.

                    NEAL
          Everything irritated them. If they
          hadn't been trying for a World Bank
          loan, I wouldn't have lasted a week.

                    DOVE
          Regardless of the reason, I need a
          good article. I'm having problems
          with Reuters these days.

                    NEAL
          What's wrong? Aren't your stories
          "sexy" enough?

Neal sits on the stool.

                    DOVE
          It's a bit more serious than that.
          Two months ago I met this woman
          walking down the road...from the
          Dinka tribe in the Sudan.

                    NEAL
          They're the tall ones, right?

                    DOVE
          Exactly. She was well over six
          feet tall. Six foot four, I
          should think. Anyway, I brought
          her back here, made her take a
          bath, then we went outside on the
          grass and engaged in various
          physical activities.

                    NEAL
          This is a good story. Very sexy.

                    DOVE
          Afterwards, we just lay there in the
          sunshine among the butterflies and
          bougainvillea. And then this six-
          foot naked woman with a crocodile
          tattooed on her back took out a
          little wooden flute and started
          playing it beautifully and...and I
          never did drive into town to see
          General Mbale arrive at the airport.

                    NEAL
          Wasn't he assassinated by his
          bodyguards?

                    DOVE
          Yes, he was. Inconsiderate fucking
          bastard. And everybody was there...
          BBC, Associated Press...everybody
          but *me*. And when Reuters called I
          sort of panicked and told a silly
          lie about stomach problems and
          things haven't been the same since.

Dove sits on the couch.

                    DOVE
          They've been questioning my
          accounts, spiking my stories,
          and this little twit named
          Simon is constantly asking me:
                    (Oxbridge accent)
          "You think you're up to this,
          Dove? Ever thought about moving
          back to Britain?" I don't want to
          move back to Britain! What am I
          going to do there?

He stands and paces the room.

                    DOVE
          Live in some shabby little flat and
          work for a suburban newspaper?
          Snivel and sniff and stand in a
          damp queue?

                    NEAL
          Relax, Dove. You're not going
          to end up in a queue.

                    DOVE
          It would help me immeasurably
          if you wrote an article. It
          shouldn't be that difficult.

                    NEAL
          I'd like to help you, but I
          can't change the facts.

                    DOVE
          I know that. Better than you.
          But we can pick which facts we
          want to mention, use a bigger
          lens, show more of the world...

Dove sits down at the writing table and places a sheet
of paper into the typewriter.

DOVE
It's easy. I'll help you. Tell me what it was like living in Uganda. Describe it to me.

NEAL
Cockroaches.

DOVE
Would you care to elaborate on that?

NEAL
The cockroaches in Kampala were as big as your thumb. At night, they'd crawl up the walls, scurry across the ceiling, and then fall on my pillow.

DOVE
So, you learned to sleep with your mouth closed.

NEAL
It was just life, Dove. The whole country was crawling with life. I used to walk through the market-place and see witches. Street butchers. Charcoal sellers stained with soot. Soldiers...ten and twelve-years-old...swaggering about with these huge rifles while the German ambassador's white Mercedes pushed through the crowd.

DOVE
And you were in the middle of it.

NEAL
I could go anywhere I wanted. Walk into any hut. You could see babies being born. Men being buried. Children singing Anglican hymns in Swahili. And there I was...on my own... without a half-dozen editors looking over my shoulder.

DOVE
Just one doddering reprobate in Nairobi.

Neal stands and approaches Dove.

NEAL
All the news was "life and death." The whole damn county was life and death. I didn't have to cover meetings of the zoning board. Check the facts on press releases.

DOVE
Exactly.

Neal wanders around the room.

NEAL
So, I liked Uganda in general. It was the people in particular that started to wear me down. Back in the States, people wanted "good press." A favorable article. All right, I can deal with that. In Kampala, if you were white and a journalist, it was more like... "save my life, please." People started to come to my room at night...desperate, frightened... telling me that their village had been destroyed, their families had been killed. As if I could do anything about it.

DOVE (writing)
This is good, Neal. Very good. Now, if you could relate it to what happened today.

NEAL
Forget about what happened today. Forget about your damn article. I've got my clips. I'm going home.

DOVE
Back to your old job? Sitting at a little desk while someone...

The phone starts ringing.

DOVE
London's calling for your story. Do you think you can finish it tonight?

NEAL
I'll write the facts, Dove. Two paragraphs. That's all. I'm not going to hype it up for you...or London.

                    DOVE
          What are you talking about?
          Don't you understand that --

He picks up the phone and instantly becomes polite.

                    DOVE
          Hello?...Simon, how wonderful to
          hear your voice. How's the weather
          in London? Drizzling? Well that's
          good for the complexion. Just a
          moment...
                    (hand over phone)
          Come on, Neal. Help me out.

Neal shakes his head.

                    DOVE
          Listen, Simon, about that stringer
          who got expelled from Uganda. Yes.
          Well, he's exhausted. Totally done
          in. He's been under a lot of
          pressure for the last few...

Dove rubs the phone handset on couch.

                    DOVE
          What...what's that? Bloody Africans
          can't maintain a decent phone system!
          Listen, I'll...I'll call you tomorrow
          morning, all right? There's no problem,
          Simon. Talk to you soon.

He hangs up.

                    DOVE
          Silly little prick.

                    NEAL
          Come on, Dove. Don't get angry.

                    DOVE
          Me? Angry? My heart overflows
          with affection.

                    NEAL
          You were the one who promised the
          big story to Reuters. I thought
          I'd come out here, get my clips,
          and take the first plane home
          tomorrow morning.

                    DOVE
          Why do you want to go home? Is some
          girl waiting for you? Heart-shaped
          locket and candle in the window?

                    NEAL
          Of course not.

                    DOVE
          You miss your mother. That's it.
          Plump little woman with graying hair.

                    NEAL
          My mother runs her own corporation.
          Everyone in my family has a resume...
          even the schnauzer.

                    DOVE
          Then why --

                    NEAL
          I'm tired to Africa. That's all.

                    DOVE
          You need to relax. Get rid of all
          the tension. Go...go to Club Med.

                    NEAL
          Did you ever see someone beaten to death?

                    DOVE
          What?

                    NEAL
          Someone beaten to death.

                    DOVE
          They don't do that at Club Med.

                    NEAL
          I'm not joking, Dove. It really happened.
          A couple of weeks ago, some soldiers
          caught a man outside my hotel room. It was
          night. He was out after curfew. They were
          from the Northern tribes...he was from the
          south...so they automatically assumed that
          he was a guerrilla.

                    DOVE
          And they beat him?

NEAL
You could hear him scream this wavering shriek like a frightened child. He was crying. Begging for his life. So, there I am, listening to this, and the hotel cook knocks on my door and says: "Save him! Save him! Go down there and tell them to stop." Meanwhile, the hotel manager comes in and he says: "Don't go. Stay here. They'll shoot you down on the street." And so I'm pacing back and forth and it's --
    (as cook)
"Save him!"
    (as manager)
"They'll kill you!"
    (as cook)
"Save him!"
    (as manager)
"They'll kill you!"
    (very angry)
So, finally, I said: "Get the fuck out of here! This is not my job! This is not my responsibility!" And then, they left. And the crying got weaker and weaker. And then, he was dead.

DOVE
I'm sorry. I'm sure that must have been...uncomfortable.

NEAL
"Uncomfortable." Right. I forget about British understatement. I guess the dead man was "indisposed."

DOVE
What word should I use? "Horror?" "Nightmare?" Would a bigger word make you feel better?

NEAL
I'm not asking for that.

DOVE
You're good journalist, Neal. But you've got to take one last step. One final progression. The world's bloody mess, but you can't let it bother you. You're the little man at the edge of the picture.

                    NEAL
          What are you talking about?
          What little man?

                    DOVE
          Take a look at any historical
          photograph...race riots in
          Detroit, Hitler addressing the
          Reichstag. People are screaming,
          fighting, throwing Molotov
          cocktails, but over there...in
          the corner of the picture...
          there's always some little man,
          cool and calm, watching the whole
          thing. He's just a bystander mind
          you. He's not a journalist. But
          he's showing us what we should
          be. We're in the middle of the
          madness, but we're not part of it.

                    NEAL
          I'm not sure if that's possible.
          Sometimes, things just happen
          even if you don't want them to.

                    DOVE
          And what happened to you?

                    NEAL
          Nothing.

                    DOVE
          Are you sure? Have you told me everything?

                    NEAL
          Listen, Dove, I like you...we've
          had some laughs over the phone. But
          if you're going to act this way,
          I'm walking back to the city.

                    DOVE
          It's a long way, Neal. It dark.
          You don't have any money.

                    NEAL
          I mean it. No more questions.
          I just want to go to sleep.

                    DOVE
          All right. If that's what you want.
          You've got the couch tonight. It's
          not that bad. Really.

Dove steps into the bathroom. He comes out with some sheets and tosses them to Neal.

> DOVE
> Now, let me see. What can I offer you. Here's a sheet. Another sheet ...No, this one's growing things.

> NEAL
> That's okay. One's enough.

> DOVE
> Here's a blanket. Pillow. There's no running water. Hasn't been for years.
>   (picks up jerry can)
> There's some over here in case you want to...

Mary Mungai and Christina Kagohyera approach the house in the darkness.

> MARY
> Hello, there! Dove! You bastard!

> NEAL
> Who's that?

> DOVE
> Nothing to worry about.

> MARY
> You dirty bastard!

> NEAL
> Somebody's out there.

> DOVE
> It's just the local whatever. They're always selling something.

> NEAL
> Isn't it a bit late?

Dove moves towards the door as Neal takes off his clothes.

> DOVE
> I'll handle it. You go to sleep.

> NEAL
> She didn't sound very happy.

Dove switches off the light. Wearing his underwear, Neal lies down on the couch.

                    DOVE
        Go to sleep, Neal. If that's
        what you want. Sweet dreams.

Dove leaves the cottage and steps out onto the porch.

                    DOVE
        Mary! Are you out there? Mary?

Mary and Christina come out of the darkness and step onto the porch. Mary is a Kenyan in her thirties. Christina is a Ugandan in her early twenties. Both women wear cheap print dresses and carry purses. Christina is carrying her shoes.

                    MARY
        Go to hell, Dove!

                    DOVE
        Mary...how pleasant to see you again.

                    MARY
        Why didn't you stop for us on
        the road? I shouted. I threw a
        rock at your car.

                    DOVE
        I needed more time. I wasn't ready
        for you, yet.

                    MARY
        Wasn't ready for what? What's
        going on?

Dove looks at Christina.

                    DOVE
        Is this the girl you told me
        about? What's her name?

Christina finishes putting on some lipstick.

                  CHRISTINA
        I'm Christina Kagohyera.

                    DOVE
        Ugandan?

                  CHRISTINA
        That's right.

                    DOVE
          One more refugee.

                    CHRISTINA
          Not at all. I came here on
          holidays and decided to stay.

                    DOVE
          Whatever for?

                    CHRISTINA
          I liked the weather.

                    MARY
          Christina...

                    DOVE
          Oh, she's a clever one. You've
          brought me a clever one, Mary.

                    MARY
          Christina...

                    DOVE
          Don't worry, Mary. You've already
          gotten the job. Now, come over here.
          I want to talk to you. Alone.

Dove leads Mary away as Christina sits on the edge of
the porch and puts on her shoes.

                    MARY
          What is it? What do you want?

                    DOVE
          We have a bit of a problem here. A
          special situation. There's a young man
          in there sleeping on my couch. This
          morning he was expelled from Uganda.

                    MARY
          What happened?

                    DOVE
          That's the problem. He won't really
          tell me what happened. Something's
          wrong about it. Something doesn't
          ring true. I've got to get all the
          facts before he leaves tomorrow
          morning. Don't want any nasty little
          surprises after he's gone.

                    MARY
          Give him some money.

                    DOVE
          I wish it was that easy.

                    MARY
          Shout at him. Tell him what to do.

                    DOVE
          If I push him any harder, he'll walk back
          to the city. But you can help me, Mary.
          You're my backup plan.

                    MARY
          Okay. 200 Kenya shillings. Apiece.

                    DOVE
          You don't have to kill him, Mary.
          Just get him drunk and get him
          talking. It'll be good for him.
          Really. In the long run.

                    MARY
          No problem. Just give us 200 shillings.

                    DOVE
          That's five times your normal price.

                    MARY
          I get your message and we walk here
          all the way from Nairobi... Past an
          army barracks and two police posts.

                    DOVE
          Look, I'm not some tourist with a
          fist full of traveler's cheques.
          I'll give you 60 shillings and my
          best wishes.

     Acting disgusted, Mary walks down the porch.

                    MARY
          We go.

                    CHRISTINA
          But we just got here.

                    MARY
          We go! Right now!

     The women start to leave.

                    DOVE
          One hundred shillings.

                    MARY
          One hundred and twenty.

                    DOVE
          If you wish.

Triumphant, Mary turns to Dove.

                    MARY
          Yes, I wish.

                    DOVE
          Payment will be made upon delivery.

                    MARY
          Noooo problem.
                    (turns to Christina)
          There is another man here. We
          get him drunk.

                    CHRISTINA
          Why?

                    MARY
          No questions. No problems.

She claps her hands and leads everyone into the house.

                    MARY
          Pah-pah, pah-pah, pah-pah, pah!

She slams open the door and switches on the lights.

                    MARY
          Hello there, handsome man! We're
          here! Aren't you happy? Aren't you
          glad to see us?

Neal sits up, sees the women, and realizes that they're prostitutes. He flops back down on the couch.

                    NEAL
          Oh, god.

                    MARY
          What do you mean..."oh, god?" We
          didn't bring him along.

                    NEAL
          Jesus.

                    MARY
          First, it's God. Now, it's Jesus.

CHRISTINA
He must be a very religious man.

DOVE
Come on, Neal. Wake up. I'd like to introduce you to some representatives of the National Tourist Board.

NEAL
Yes, I think I saw them on a poster somewhere.

DOVE
This nubile representative of the Kikuyu tribe is Mary Mungai and this is her friend, Christina. She's from Uganda...your favorite country.

NEAL
And you two just happened to be in the neighborhood, chasing butterflies.

MARY
What butterflies? Dove calls us. So, we walk here from the city.

DOVE
Wasn't that nice of them, Neal? They're going to explain the balance-of-payments problem.

MARY
And drink beer! I want some beer! Hurry up, Dove. You're a very bad house boy!

DOVE (African accent)
I'm sorry, muzungu. Right away, muzungu.

Acting like a house boy, Dove hurries over to the refrigerator. Dove takes out some beer as Neal pulls on his clothes.

MARY
What are you doing, Neal?

NEAL
Getting dressed.

Christina sits on the stool.

MARY
Why? There's no need for that.

CHRISTINA
You'll just have to take them off again.

NEAL
Why don't you ladies sit down and rest awhile. You both must have walked a long way.

Mary sits on the couch.

MARY
Okay. Now, you sit here.

She puts her hand on her face and laughs loudly.

NEAL
Just one minute. All right? I'll be back in a second. I want you to relax, concentrate on you navel, and repeat after me...ommmmm. Go ahead...ommmmm.

MARY
(very skeptical)
Ommmm.

NEAL
Great. Keep doing it. I'll be back in a second.

Neal walks past Christina.

NEAL
Ommmm.

CHRISTINA
Ommmm.

Neal approaches Dove as Mary gestures to Christina.

MARY
Very strange.

NEAL
You're really something, Dove. You should be a games director on a cruise.

DOVE
Bingo. Shuffleboard. Sex.
(offers Neal a bottle)
Here, take this.

NEAL
I don't want a beer.

DOVE
It's cold. You Americans are supposed to like it that way. You like cold beer, dental floss, efficient toilets...

He shoves the bottle into Neal's hand.

NEAL
Let me get this straight. These women walked here from Nairobi?

DOVE
Yes, they're quite athletic.

NEAL
This is very nice of you, Dove. I appreciate the gesture.

DOVE
You're most welcome.

NEAL
But I'd like it if you paid them both off and sent them back to the city. I'm not in the mood for this.

DOVE
One is rarely in the mood for anything. But that shouldn't stop us.

NEAL
I'm flying home tomorrow.

Dove crosses the room and serves the beer to the women.

DOVE
Oh, don't start talking about the glories of America. It's such a ridiculously boring country.

CHRISTINA
Have you been there? What's it like?

DOVE
Good teeth. Everyone over there has good teeth. It's disgusting.

MARY
Where's the food?

DOVE
There isn't any.

MARY
How can you drink without food?

DOVE
All right. All right. I'll dig
up something.

Dove stands up and walks over to the refrigerator. He takes
out a sausage and puts it on a plate with some crackers.

CHRISTINA
But you liked America? You were
happy there?

DOVE
They took me to a baseball game. God,
what a bore. It's worse than cricket
and you don't get cucumber sandwiches.

NEAL
Dove, listen to me. I like women.
I like sleeping with them.

DOVE
Good. I was beginning to worry.

NEAL
But I don't pay for it. It's not my style.

DOVE
You're not paying for it. Reuters
is. These two women are going to be
vouchered as "local informants."

NEAL
But...

DOVE
Relax, Neal. Don't think. It's part of
the Richardson-Dove Treatment.

NEAL
What treatment?

DOVE
It's a special method I've developed
for expelled journalists. Although
you've left the country, it's still
inside you. You've got to relax, get
it all out, then move on.

                    NEAL
          If we sleep with these women, we'll
          both need treatment.

                    DOVE
          Dear Boy, why do you think latex
          was invented?

He opens a small box on the table. It's full of condoms.

                    DOVE
          I've got gold ones, green ones,
          ones with textured sides...

He holds up one of the condoms.

                    DOVE
          This model glows in the dark.

Dove puts the condom in his pocket. He places a knife on the plate and takes it over to the coffee table.

                    DOVE
          Besides, they're checked every
          week by this doctor on Koinange
          Street. The famous Dr. Hassad.

                    MARY
          "Dr. Next."

                    DOVE
          What do you mean?

                    MARY
          He takes blood, puts his
          hand inside you, and --

                    MARY AND CHRISTINA
          Next!

Mary picks up the sausage.

                    MARY
          What is this?

                    DOVE
          A kosher sausage from Israel
          and relief crackers from CARE.

                    MARY
          Christina...food.

Christina moves over to the couch. The hungry women begin to eat as Dove shows Neal one of the crackers.

                    DOVE
          Just think, some little sixth
          form baton girl or whatever you
          call them in the States...

                    NEAL
          Cheerleaders.

                    DOVE
          ...giving up her lunch money so
          someone can flog this cracker on
          the black market.

He looks back and sees the women eating.

                    DOVE
          Gently. Gently, ladies. There's
          more if you wish.

                    CHRISTINA
          Where are you from, Neal? Are you
          American?

                    NEAL
          That's right.

                    MARY
          New York. Texas. Hol-ly-wood.

                    NEAL
          You got it.

                    CHRISTINA
          And you're a journalist, too?

                    DOVE
          Oh, let's not talk about journalism.
          We're just men and women huddling
          together in the night. Let's talk about
          truth and beauty, crackers and beer.

Dove crosses the room and sits back on the chair.

                    MARY
          Neal drinks like a leper at St. Matthews.

                    NEAL
          What?

                    DOVE
          The nuns at St. Matthews give the
          lepers a bottle of beer every
          Sunday. They drink it very slow.

                    DOVE
          I imagine if you're a leper it's
          the high point of the week. But
          we're not lepers. Are we?
                    (raises his bottle)
          To the ladies!

                    MARY
               (joking)
          Pip! Pip!

Dove and the two women drink. Neal remains by the table.

                    DOVE
          Come on, Neal.

Mary stands up and walks over to Neal. She grabs the bottle
and forces him to drink.

                    MARY
          More, Neal! More! Come on!

Neal sputters as beer spills on his shirt. Mary wipes Neal
with a towel. Dove sits next to Christina on the couch.

                    DOVE
          There you go! That's what made
          America great! Now, Christina...stop
          eating and say something clever.

                    CHRISTINA
          I don't know anything clever.

                    DOVE
          I'm sure you do. Give it a try.

                    CHRISTINA
          What do you want to talk about?
          Thomas Aquinas? Picasso?

                    DOVE
          Not that clever. Good Lord, where
          did you find this one, Mary?

                    MARY
          She's okay. No problem.

                    CHRISTINA
          I'll be glad to talk about
          anything you want.

                    DOVE
          Tell us about sex. What's the biggest
          male appendage you've ever seen? The
          longest? The shortest?

                    CHRISTINA
          The night isn't over.

                    DOVE
          Oh, what a cruel woman. So very cruel.

                    MARY
          Christina. What are you --

                    DOVE
          No, don't stop her. I like a little
          resistance. We're entering a different
          realm, now. A world of happiness and light.

                    NEAL
          It looks the same to me.

                    DOVE
          You're stuck, Neal. You're lagging
          behind. An extra twenty shillings
          to anyone who can make him smile.

                    MARY
          Truly?

                    DOVE
          You know me, Mary. I always pay...
          eventually.

                    MARY
          This is extra.

                    DOVE
          Of course.

                    MARY
          Noooo problem.

Mary stands beside Neal.
                    MARY
          Touch me, handsome man.

                    NEAL
          Can't we just play bridge?

                    MARY
          What bridge? Forget about bridges!

She slaps Neal's hand on her thigh and rotates her pelvis.

>   MARY
>   Touch me. High. Very high. Oh,
>   yes. Very good. Touch me high.
>   Very high and --

She suddenly whoops and Neal smiles. Mary walks over to Dove and holds out her hand.

>   MARY
>   Twenty shillings.

>   DOVE
>   It's not that easy.

>   MARY
>   He smiles. Twenty shillings.

>   DOVE
>   I want a long-range smile. A satiated
>   grin resulting from exquisite psycho-
>   sexual manipulation.

>   MARY
>   A white man with white words.

>   CHRISTINA
>   You better give her those shillings,
>   Dove. Mary always gets her money.

>   MARY
>   This one knows me.

>   NEAL
>   Dove, could you...

>   DOVE
>   Another beer? Coming right up!

Dove hurries over to the refrigerator and pulls out another beer.

>   NEAL
>   I don't need another beer. I'm
>   not done with this one.

Dove shoves another beer into Neal's hand.

>   DOVE
>   Have another. African germs have
>   already taken over the old bottle.
>   They're breeding. Festering. Making
>   battle plans of your bowels.

Dove stands behind the couch as Mary leans against the writing table.

                    NEAL
          That's just one more reason to go home.

                    DOVE
          "Go home?" Why would anybody
          want to go home?

                    NEAL
          I like it there. It's taken me a
          while to realize that.

                    CHRISTINA
          I think I would also like
          America. Is it pretty?

                    NEAL
          America starts the moment you get on
          the flight at the Nairobi airport. The
          seats are soft and comfortable. The
          air is cool and filtered. God, I never
          thought I'd feel nostalgic about those
          little packets of processed cheese.

                    DOVE
          You've got the disease.

                    CHRISTINA
          What's this?

                    MARY
          What disease?

                    DOVE
          No. No. Nothing like that. Neal's
          got "the expatriate disease." It's
          an uncontrollable tendency to
          idealize life in the motherland.

                    NEAL
          I remember what it's like.

                    DOVE
          Really? When you finally return, I
          think you'll be surprised how much
          of the "Third World" has oozed across your
          pristine borders. Life in the West is
          getting frayed at the edges these days.
          People are living in the streets. Things are
          starting to break down. Just like Africa.

                    NEAL
          Are you saying that it's all the same?

Dove approaches Neal.

                    DOVE
          No, Africa's better...for us. We
          can be something here. Something
          important. We can write about wars
          and famine and rampaging elephants.
          Back home, it's dog shows and garden
          clubs. Thousands of elderly women
          chasing you around the community
          center clutching their nasturtiums.
          You know that, Neal. That's why you
          came over here in the first place.

                    MARY
          Is that it, Dove? Are you done talking?

                    DOVE
          I'm talking for a reason, Mary.

Dove puts his arm around Neal.

                    DOVE
          We're not in the States...yet.
          We're in Africa. We should act
          accordingly.
               (to Mary)
          Neal's got to live in the Present
          Tense and answer this essential
          question...
               (to Neal)
          "Which one do you want?"

                    NEAL
          I want to go home without some
          exotic social disease.

                    DOVE
          Then stay away from relief workers,
          missionaries, and ambassadors' wives.

                    NEAL
          I'll try to remember that.

                    DOVE
          Now, Mary is a basic, dependable
          commodity...like a sack of millet
          or a can of lard. I've never met
          this Christina girl before, but
          she's an obvious refugee.

NEAL
So, it's either lard or refugees?

DOVE
Exactly. And for that reason, I think I'll take Christina. All this is designed to relax you. There's no reason to hear anymore horrid little tales about Uganda.

NEAL
Of course. I forgot. I'm getting "The Richardson-Dove Treatment."

DOVE
The deluxe version. No charge.

DOVE
All right, ladies. Time to get going! Madame Christina...if you would retire to my boudoir.

Christina walks into the bedroom.

DOVE
Dearest Mary, why don't you take off your knickers and discuss existentialist ethics with this young man.

MARY
What about the extra shillings?

DOVE
You'll get it if everything works out. Remember what I told you?

MARY
I remember.

DOVE
Have a pleasant evening, Neal. Help yourself to everything. Sorry that you have to use the couch, but you're more flexible than I am.

Dove enters his bedroom and closes the door. Neal stands near the refrigerator as Mary watches him.

MARY
Okay. O-kay.

> She takes off her shoes and walks over to Neal.

> MARY
> Do you know "pole-pole"? Do you know this word?

> NEAL
> It's Swahili, isn't it?

> MARY
> It means "easy-easy." Go gentle. Go slow.

Mary takes Neal's beer off the top of the refrigerator. She stands behind him, pushing her chest against his back, and slips the bottle into his hand.

> MARY
> So, you'll drink some beer and then some more beer and then...
>   (touches his groin)
> ...pole-pole.

> NEAL
> I'm sorry, but I'm just too tense. Tell you what...
>   (points to chair)
> You sit there. I'll sit there. And we'll both ommmmm.

> MARY
> No om. Forget om. Come here.

> NEAL
> What do you think about the depletion of the African forests? Some people think it might affect the ozone layer and --

> MARY
> You whites talk a lot. Don't you? You're like a little boy herding cows.

Mary unbuttons Neal's shirt.

> MARY
> Talk! Talk! Talk!
>   (bumps against him)
> Back! Back! Back!

> NEAL
> All right. Forget about the ozone.

MARY
And "pole-pole?"

NEAL
I'm tired, Mary. I don't want
to sleep with you. That's it.
No argument. Understand?

MARY
Yes, I understand. If you're
tired, you better sit down.

She grabs Neal's arm and pulls him over to the couch.

NEAL
I don't want to...

MARY
But you're tired. This is very
bad to be so tired.

She sits down beside him and strokes his leg.

MARY
Poor Neal. Poor little muzungu.
What's the problem? Are you scared
of me?

NEAL
Of course not.

MARY
Do you think I'm a leopard? Is
that it?

She stands up and moves around the room like a leopard.

MARY
Sleeping in the day...lazy in
a tree...then walking through
the tall grass. Soft. Soft.
        (standing on the stool)
She sees a zebra and --

Mary growls and jumps up on the couch.

MARY
Don't worry. I'm not hungry.

NEAL
No more leopards.

MARY
Okay. If that's what you want.

She sits down beside him and drinks some beer.

> MARY
> Listen to me, Neal. I know this world. I know how it is. Yesterday, you would drive by me in your car: "Watch out, black girl. Get out of my way." Tomorrow, you do the same thing. But we're in this house right now...together. We have beer. Food. And it's paid for.

> NEAL
> If Reuters only knew.

> MARY
> Who cares? Who cares about anything? Let's be happy. What do you want me to do?

> NEAL
> I want you to go back to Nairobi.

> MARY
> After I walked here...past two police posts? How can I go back with nothing?

> NEAL
> I'll pay you.

> MARY
> That would cost a lot of money.

Neal takes out his wallet.

> NEAL
> How much do you want? All I've got is Uganda shillings.

> MARY
> Uganda shillings? What can I do with Uganda shillings? You can't buy food with them. You can't buy anything. I wipe my ass with Uganda shillings!

> NEAL
> But I haven't been paid yet and...

Mary stands up and unzips the back of her dress.

> MARY
> No more talk. We do it. Take off your pants.

                    NEAL
          Dove!

Dove opens the bedroom door. He's unbuttoned his shirt.

                    DOVE
          I've read about premature ejaculations,
          but this is a new record.

Neal stands up and faces Dove.

                    NEAL
          I want the other one. Christina.

                    DOVE
          That wasn't the plan.

                    NEAL
          What plan?

                    DOVE
          The...arrangement.

                    NEAL
          All this is for my benefit. Right?
          Well, I want the other one.

                    DOVE
          As you wish.
                (turning to bedroom)
          Christina! Would you come out here!

Christina comes out of the bedroom.

                    DOVE
          If you don't mind, my dear.
          There's been a change of plans.
                (motions to bedroom)
          Mary, if you please.

Angry, Mary stalks into the bedroom.

                    MARY
          What do you want, Dove? Do I do
          this? Do I do that? There is too
          much scatter-scatter tonight.

                    DOVE
          I agree wholeheartedly. There's a
          depressing lack of decisiveness
          in the world today. We need women
          who can expose the key issue and
          deal with it firmly.

Dove walks into the bedroom. A Beat, then Mary shrieks with laughter. Christina walks over to the couch while Neal stands by the writing table.

CHRISTINA

Thank you.

NEAL

For what?

CHRISTINA

I dislike sleeping with older men. There's too big a difference between what you do with them and what you praise afterwards.

NEAL

What's wrong with lying?

CHRISTINA

The best lies are based on some truth.

NEAL

You've got a different way of looking at things.

CHRISTINA

Different? For a Nairobi prostitute?

NEAL

I guess that's what I mean.

CHRISTINA

There are a lot of women like me at the New Florida Bar. Women who worked for the government in Ethiopia. Women who taught school in Zaire. These days, we're all the same.

NEAL

What did you do?

CHRISTINA

I was a student at the university in Kampala. Three classes short of a college degree.

NEAL

How'd you end up here?

CHRISTINA

The usual reason. I hated trigonometry.

                    NEAL
          I don't quite believe that.

Christina walks over to the coffee table and picks up the
plate full of crackers.

                    CHRISTINA
          Cracker??

                    NEAL
          No.

Christina takes the plate over to the table.

                    CHRISTINA
          How about some beer?

                    NEAL
          No!

She stops and faces him.

                    CHRISTINA
          You don't have to shout at me.

                    NEAL
          Every time I turn around, some-
          body's trying to make me drink.

                    CHRISTINA
          You don't have to shout at me.

                    NEAL
          I'm sorry.

                    CHRISTINA
          A white man's apology. It's not
          the usual thing in Africa.

                    NEAL
          I've noticed that.

                    CHRISTINA
          So, why are you here anyway? They
          must pay you a lot of money.

Neal sits on the couch.

                    NEAL
          Journalists don't get paid a lot.
          Not by American standards. My
          family keeps asking me when I'm
          going to get a real job.

CHRISTINA
Then why does anyone do it?

NEAL
You get the right to ask questions to strangers and they answer. That's what has always amazed me about this job. People talk to you. They tell you things. You can find out what's going on inside their skulls.

Christina sits beside Neal.

CHRISTINA
That still doesn't explain why you're in Africa.

NEAL
I was trapped. Stuck at this news magazine in New York checking other people's --

He pulls away from her.

CHRISTINA
Don't you want me to touch you?

NEAL
It's been awhile.

CHRISTINA
We'll compromise. I'll just use one hand.

She unbuttons his shirt and touches his chest.

CHRISTINA
Go on. We're having a conversation, aren't we? You were working in New York...

NEAL
I was pushing paper around. That's all. Then I met this guy at a party and he told me about Dove. I called Dove up, he offered me a job, and I took the next plane to Africa.

CHRISTINA
So you had your own private country to write about. You must have been very happy.

                    NEAL
          It didn't work out the way I planned.
          When I was working on the magazine, I
          used to daydream about this huge
          headline: REBEL ARMIES DEEP INTO
          CHAD. I saw these tanks sweeping
          across the desert with an army of
          black soldiers.

Christina starts to unfasten Neal's belt.

                    NEAL
          Big things were happening and --
                    (reacts to Christina)
          Hey.

                    CHRISTINA
          All right. Don't worry. I won't
          use any hands at all.

She starts to kiss his chest.

                    CHRISTINA
          So, tell me...what was wrong
          with Uganda? No tanks?

                    NEAL
          Nothing dramatic. Just a lot of
          day-to-day killing. It wasn't
          "different." It wasn't "news."

Christina stops kissing Neal and sits back on the couch.

                    CHRISTINA
          The "news" is that the army is
          destroying the Baganda. My people.

                    NEAL
          I know that. I saw it every day.
          But you don't understand how it
          works. During the first few months,
          my biggest story was a feature on
          the Kampala golf course. How it
          felt to make a chip shot near an
          unexploded rocket grenade. If you
          think journalists are crazy, you
          should talk to some golfers.

Neal stands up and paces around the room.

                    CHRISTINA
          There's a war going in Uganda. A
          civil war.

NEAL
Right. And I went all over the countryside looking for it. A couple of weeks ago, I interviewed some rebels.

CHRISTINA
Is that why you were expelled?

NEAL
I don't know.

CHRISTINA
This article must have made the government angry.

NEAL
Swear to god, I don't know.

CHRISTINA
I...I think we should forget about journalism. Forget about all the things outside of this room.

NEAL
Is that possible?

CHRISTINA
We've done it already. You're the first white man I've met who isn't clapping his hands and shouting "Dance, black girl! Dance!"

NEAL
Don't you ever get tired of it? Wouldn't you rather just pick up your bag and go home?

Christina walks into the bathroom.

CHRISTINA
It's not so easy to go home. To get here, we had to walk past an army barracks and two police posts.

Christina comes out with a bowl of water, soap and towel.

CHRISTINA
There's a curfew at night. The police can beat you, take your money. Mary isn't scared of anything, but none of her friends would come along.

                    NEAL
          Are you brave, too?

Christina sits on the couch.

                    CHRISTINA
          "Much to gain. Little to lose."

                    NEAL
          Why did you leave Uganda anyway? I don't
          believe that it was trigonometry.

                    CHRISTINA
          I'm afraid that I'm just another small
          story, Neal. No "Rebel Armies In Chad."

                    NEAL
          Was it politics? The guerrillas?

Christina walks over to the food table.

                    CHRISTINA
          Did Dove give you an American sock?

                    NEAL
          What are you talking about? What socks?
               (looks at his socks)
          I got these at Macy's.

Christina takes a condom out of the sandalwood box.

                    CHRISTINA
          We call these things "American socks."
          You don't put them on your feet.

                    NEAL
          You women are very organized.

Christina soaps up the wash cloth.

                    CHRISTINA
          Not organized. Just careful.
          Please, take off your pants.

                    NEAL
          Why?

                    CHRISTINA
          So I can wash you. I don't want
          to get a disease.

                    NEAL
          There's no need. Really. I haven't
          slept with anyone in Africa.

CHRISTINA
Don't you like black women?

NEAL
It's not that at all. I think you're beautiful. I just didn't want to get involved with the people I was writing about. I saw what happened to some of the expatriates living in Kampala. You'd sleep with a woman, then she'd move in, then her whole family would move in. All of a sudden, you were part of the situation. You couldn't be objective.

CHRISTINA
I doesn't seem to bother Dove.

NEAL
As far as Dove is concerned, you're "just a African." I don't want to treat people that way.

CHRISTINA
So, come over here. We'll be two equals...together.

NEAL
All right.

CHRISTINA
Take off your pants.

NEAL
Goddamnit.

Irritated, he steps away from her.

NEAL
That was nice. We were getting somewhere. Then all of a sudden it's an industrial process.

CHRISTINA
In a way it is.

NEAL
Well, I don't like it.

CHRISTINA
I think I am the same as an American girl, but perhaps they're made differently.

                    NEAL
          It's the everything that goes before.
          That's what's different.

                    CHRISTINA
          Ahhhh. I see. The meeting and the greeting.

                    NEAL
          Exactly. Now, look...! know Dove's
          paid you and all this is standard
          practice, but it just doesn't work
          for me.

                    CHRISTINA
          I'm sorry. I apologize.

                    NEAL
          That's not necessary.

                    CHRISTINA
          So, tell me about these American
          girls. Where do you meet them for
          your evening together? In a bar?
          On the street?

                    NEAL
          You usually go to their homes.

                    CHRISTINA
          Good. You can come to my home.

She stands up, grabs his arm, and pulls him to the door.

                    NEAL
          Christina...

                    CHRISTINA
          Come on. It'll be fun.

She opens the door and pushes him out onto the porch.

                    CHRISTINA
          Now, don't be late.

She shuts the door and locks it. Neal knocks loudly as Christina smoothes down her dress.

                    CHRISTINA
           Who is it?

                    NEAL (outside door)
          Christina!

CHRISTINA
Oh, it is Neal. My American boy friend that I want to sleep with.

She opens the door and they smile at each other.

NEAL
All right. All right. You've made your point.

CHRISTINA
No, this is fun. I want to pretend I'm in America.

Neal walks inside and Christina embraces him.

CHRISTINA
So Neal, my dearest boyfriend, how was your day?

NEAL
I just got expelled from Uganda.

CHRISTINA
Oh, I'm so sorry.
    (breaks away)
So, tell me, where are we going tonight?

NEAL
Nowhere. There's a curfew.

CHRISTINA
Come on, Neal. I'm having fun. Where would we go on our outing? How would we travel? In a car? Did you own a car in America?

NEAL
I bought an old Triumph sports car when I first got out of college. My family thought I was crazy, but I managed to fix it up.

CHRISTINA
Oh, a sports car. I like this very much. What color?

NEAL
Metallic blue.

CHRISTINA
Very good. An excellent color.

She pulls him over to the couch and they both sit down.

CHRISTINA
So, we would get into your sports car and drive down these wide streets with no trash on them. No beggars.

NEAL
You haven't seen New York.

CHRISTINA
But no roadblocks? No soldiers with guns trying to take your money?

NEAL
No.

CHRISTINA
So we would drive in the car and then we'd go to a restaurant of gold and glass with soft music and flowers and men to carry the food.

Neal smiles and stands up.

NEAL
Good evening, madam. Table for two? This way.

Neal sits down on the stool and faces Christina.

CHRISTINA
Very good, I like this place. Now, what will we eat?

NEAL
Meat. Steak.

CHRISTINA
We have steak in Nairobi. Tell me something different. Something American.

NEAL
Hot dogs.

CHRISTINA
You eat dogs?

NEAL
It's a kind of sausage.

CHRISTINA
No more sausages. Something that sounds pretty.

                    NEAL
          Vichyssoise.

                    CHRISTINA
          Very good! What else?

                    NEAL
          Honey-glazed ham.

Christina smiles and begins to say each word slowly.

                    CHRISTINA
          With mushrooms.

                    NEAL
          Scallions.

                    CHRISTINA
          Truffles.

                    NEAL
          Smoked salmon.

                    CHRISTINA
          And to drink?

                    NEAL
          Beaujolais.

                    CHRISTINA
          And after eating all these wonderful
          things, we'd hold hands and look at
          each other and talk...What do you
          talk about with your American girl
          friends?

                    NEAL
          Their careers.

                    CHRISTINA
          We're not going to talk about
          my career.

                    NEAL
          Why not? I'm curious. Who do you
          sleep with most of the time?
          Africans? Swedish tourists?

Trying to keep the fantasy, she pulls him up the stool.

                    CHRISTINA
          The music has started. Stand
          up. It's time to dance while
          men with violins play and play.

They begin to dance.

                    CHRISTINA
          And then we would drive down the
          street in your blue Triumph sports
          car, moving quickly, passing shops,
          countless shops, with thousands of
          things in the windows. And there
          would be lights everywhere, red and
          green, blue and golden, flashing,
          flashing as we pass.

Christina moves closer to Neal, embracing him. Neal
resists for a few seconds, then holds her tightly.

                    CHRISTINA
          We can move over to the couch. Neal?

Neal pulls away from her and crosses the room.

                    CHRISTINA
          Are you all right?

                    NEAL
          I'm okay.

                    CHRISTINA
          You don't seem "okay."

                    NEAL
          I've been under a lot of pressure.

                    CHRISTINA
          I understand.

                    NEAL
          Do you? I spent my whole time in
          Uganda knowing that I was going to
          fuck up. I just wasn't sure how it
          was going to happen.

                    CHRISTINA
          You've got to be careful.

                    NEAL
          That's not enough. You could talk to
          someone in the marketplace...just a
          casual conversation...and they'd be
          picked up and executed that evening.
          And you'd never know why. You'd
          never know anything.

CHRISTINA
You're back in Kenya, Neal. You can relax.

NEAL
Some soldiers came to my hotel room this morning. I thought they were going to kill me.

CHRISTINA
Did they hurt you?

NEAL
They wanted to scare me and they succeeded. I was "officially scared."

CHRISTINA
They're experts at that.

NEAL
Yeah, well...you're right about one thing. It's over. Done.

Neal walks over to Christina and starts to kiss her.

NEAL
We don't need to talk about it. We don't need to talk at all. We're hermits. We've taken a vow of silence.

CHRISTINA
You're not acting like a hermit.

NEAL
It's a very sexy order with...

He touches her breasts and stops.

NEAL
What...what's this?

CHRISTINA
Neal, there's something I have to explain to you.

She steps away from him.

NEAL
Christ, they're padded. You must be the only woman in Africa with a padded bra.

CHRISTINA
Usually, the men I'm with are so drunk I don't have to explain anything.

NEAL
Explain what?

CHRISTINA
Nothing's wrong. We're going to have a good time this evening. It's just that my breasts are...bad.

NEAL
What do you mean "bad?"

CHRISTINA
I don't have a left breast and my right breast is scarred.

NEAL
Did you have cancer? An operation?

CHRISTINA
It's nothing. All my other "working parts" are in order.

She embraces him, but he pulls away.

NEAL
So what happened?

CHRISTINA
I'm sorry, but it's not news.

NEAL
What happened? Tell me.

CHRISTINA
About a year ago, I was picked up by soldiers in Uganda. I was slashed and left for dead. You must have heard about similar things when you were there.

NEAL
Why did they do it? Did they pick you up at a roadblock or at the University?

CHRISTINA
You enjoy asking questions. That's why you're a journalist. But it doesn't mean other people have to answer.

                    NEAL
          I just want to know where they --

The bedroom door opens and Dove walks out.

                    DOVE
          Sorry to interrupt, but I didn't
          hear any moans and groans.

                    NEAL
          What's wrong?

                    DOVE
          Nothing at all. One of the joys of
          growing older is that your bladder
          acquires a personality of its' own.

Dove picks up a jerry can and enters the bathroom. Neal sits on the couch.

                    NEAL
          Come here.

                    CHRISTINA
          Are we back on our date in America?

                    NEAL
          Forget about America. Come here.

Christina sits beside Neal and he holds her in his arms.

                    NEAL
          I'm sorry.

                    CHRISTINA
          You mean you're not going to ask
          for a discount?

                    NEAL
          Don't joke about this. Don't be
          like Dove. I'm really sorry.

He touches Christina's breast and she kisses his hand.

                    DOVE (from bathroom)
          What's that?

                    NEAL
          We're talking about the balance
          of payments problem!

                    DOVE
          Good for you. Now, listen, I just used
          up one of my gallons. Does anyone else
          have something they want to flush?

                    NEAL
          Go ahead, Dove. Flush away. Enjoy life.

                    DOVE
          No, I'll wait a bit. Don't want
          to waste any water.

Dove comes out of the bathroom and stares at them.

                    DOVE
          So, how are my two little lovebirds?

                    NEAL
          Just fine.

                    DOVE
          Really.
               (turns to bedroom)
          Mary!

                    MARY (from bedroom)
          Dove! Get me beer!

                    DOVE
          Mary, come out here.

                    MARY (from bedroom)
          Just one little beer!

                    DOVE
          I want to see you! Right now!

Mary comes out wrapped in Dove's bedspread, a British flag.

                    MARY
               (European accent)
          Good evening. How are you?

                    NEAL
          You're looking very patriotic, Mary.

Mary walks over to the refrigerator and takes out a beer.

                    DOVE
          Isn't she? That's my bedspread.
          I took it off the coffin of one
          of the old ex-paits.

                    MARY
          So, what do you want?

                    DOVE
          I'd like Neal to come outside with me.

                    NEAL
          Why?

                    DOVE
          I want to tell you something.
          Some-thing off the record. Come
          on. Let's take a look at the moon.

Neal hesitates, then walks out of the cottage. Dove turns
to Mary.

                    DOVE
          Mary, talk to Christina.

                    MARY
          Why? What's the problem?

                    DOVE
          I want passion. Spilled beer.
          Naked bodies. These two are
          acting like they're married.

Dove leaves the cottage. He stands outside the front door
and lights a cigarette as Mary stares at Christina.

                    MARY
          What's wrong, Christina?

                    CHRISTINA
          Nothing's wrong.

                    MARY
          Don't you know how to guide him?

                    CHRISTINA
          I'm not guiding anyone. It's not
          that way.

                    MARY
          What way is it? You're supposed to
          get him drunk...relaxed. Dove wants
          to know what he did in Uganda.

                    CHRISTINA
          Why should we care what Dove wants?

                    MARY
          He's paying.

                    CHRISTINA
          I'll do what I always do. That's all.

Mary walks back to the bedroom.

MARY
I brought you here, Christina. Our names are together. Don't forget that.

CHRISTINA
I won't.

MARY
Think about the money. If you don't do your job, we don't get paid.

Mary returns to the bedroom. Sound of cicadas as Dove walks down the porch to Neal and looks up at the sky.

DOVE
There's the moon. Should be full in a few days.

NEAL
So what?

DOVE
It's a fact, Neal. There's a certain purity in a good clean fact. It's like an egg still warm from the hen.

NEAL
Is that all you wanted to tell me?

DOVE
I want you to relax. I don't know if Christina's doing the job.

NEAL
We're just talking. What's wrong with that?

DOVE
If you want to talk, talk to me. These women weren't hired for their conversational skills.

NEAL
Christina's an educated woman. She's not just a prostitute.

DOVE
Nobody's "just a prostitute" except for a few politicians I've known.

NEAL
So what am I supposed to do? Not talk to her at all? Just tell her to shut up and lie down?

                    DOVE
          You can joke, chat about little things.

                    NEAL
          But don't treat her like an equal?

                    DOVE
          You've got to be careful with the
          people around here. They're not just
          poor, they're desperate. If you give
          them the slightest bit of encouragement,
          their dreams will get out of hand.

                    NEAL
          I know that. You're not telling
          me anything new.

                    DOVE
          Have you looked at that girl? Have
          you really seen her? Her feet are
          dirty because she's walked here
          barefoot to save those cheap red
          shoes she bought on Moi Avenue. Have
          you examined her purse? I don't
          have to. I'm sure that she's got a
          plastic comb, about ten shillings
          bribe money, and some black beans
          to suck when she gets hungry. Which
          is often. Right now, she's probably
          in there stealing some food.

                    NEAL
          You bastard. You think everybody's a
          fraud, don't you? Everyone's liar and
          a thief.

                    DOVE
          It takes some bravery to look at
          the world straight on. I don't
          know if you have it.

                    NEAL
          Have what? Bravery? Hey, you've been
          nice and safe in Nairobi while I've
          been shot at, threatened...

Christina walks over to the food table and puts some food in her purse.

                    DOVE
          Something happened to you in Uganda,
          but you don't have the courage to
          tell me about it. Come on, Neal. Spit
          it out. You'll discover that it's
          just another story...like everything
          else in this bloody world.

                    NEAL
          Nothing happened.

Dove walks away from Neal. Inside the cottage, Christina returns to the couch.

                    DOVE
          You're never going to be a
          journalist, Neal. You want to turn
          away from things. Cover it all up.

Dove enters the house. He nods to Christina.

                    DOVE
          Did Mary talk to you?

                    CHRISTINA
          Yes.

                    DOVE
          Don't forget. I'm the one
          who's paying tonight.

Dove walks into the bedroom as Neal enters the cottage.

                    CHRISTINA
          Hello...Hello, there. Did you see
          the moon?

                    NEAL
          Yeah, I saw it.

                    CHRISTINA
          Is that why you're so angry?

                    NEAL
          I'm not angry.

                    CHRISTINA
          All right. If you say so. While you
          were gone, I decided to change my
          identity. From now on, I'm a virgin
          from Hollywood with a red sports
          car. What do you think?

                    NEAL
          Dove says I don't want to face up
          to things.

                    CHRISTINA
          Really? Is that so? Why don't you
          come closer so you can face up to me.

Neal walks over to end table and picks up Christina's purse.

                    CHRISTINA
          What are you doing?

                    NEAL
          I'm just looking at your purse.

                    CHRISTINA
          Put it back.

                    NEAL
          Why? What's the problem?

                    CHRISTINA
          There's no problem if you give
          it back to me.

                    NEAL
          Dove said that you had a plastic comb.

                    CHRISTINA
          Do you want to borrow it?

                    NEAL
          Is there any money?

                    CHRISTINA
          Very, very little.

Neal circles the room as Christina follows after him.

                    NEAL
          Any food?

                    CHRISTINA
          Don't open it, Neal.

                    NEAL
          Did you steal some food?

                    CHRISTINA
          Don't!

Neal opens the purse and takes out one of the crackers.

                    CHRISTINA
          I'm hungry, Neal. These days, I'm
          always hungry.

                    NEAL
          Why didn't you just ask me? I would
          have given you anything you wanted.
          The whole damn refrigerator.

Neal gives her the purse.

                    CHRISTINA
          When I first came to Kenya, I spent
          a few weeks in a refugee camp.
          People were starving there...
          desperate for food...but when we got
          our daily ration each person took
          his little tin bowl and went off to
          eat alone. We were ashamed to see
          the hunger in each other's eyes.

                    NEAL
          I'm sorry, Christina. I just
          wanted things to be honest
          between us. For six months, I've
          been surrounded by lies.

                    CHRISTINA
          All right. It's over. Forget
          it happened.
                    (puts purse on table)
          So, are we still on our date in
          America? We've just had our dinner,
          gone back to your apartment and --

                    NEAL
          We're not in America.

                    CHRISTINA
          I know that. I know where we are. But
          what's wrong with making this room, a
          restaurant, and these crackers...a
          feast? I do it all the time.

                    NEAL
          It's just a fantasy, Christina. It
          isn't true.

                    CHRISTINA
          The truth is that we were happy
          until you went outside and
          talked to Dove.

                    NEAL
          He thinks I'm not brave enough to
          see what's going on.

Christina approaches Neal.

                    CHRISTINA
          Who cares what he thinks? I like you,
          Neal. Let's be happy tonight.

Christina pulls Neal back to the couch and embraces him.

                    CHRISTINA
          Now, where were we sitting before
          he came in? I think we were right
          ...right here. Now, I remember.
          You were kissing my neck. Or was
          it my left ear?

                    NEAL
          We were talking about the soldiers.

                    CHRISTINA
          Forget about them, too.

                    NEAL
          Tell me about being slashed. The
          whole story.

                    CHRISTINA
          I've already explained it to you,
          Neal. I'm not tanks and planes and
          "rebel armies." My life is not news.

                    NEAL
          What's the big secret. Were you
          working for the guerrillas?

                    CHRISTINA
          Not really.

                    NEAL
          Were you making speeches? Passing
          out leaflets against the government?

                    CHRISTINA
          Everyone from my tribe was
          against the government. You
          could get in trouble for making
          a joke or writing a letter.

                    NEAL
          So, what did you do?

CHRISTINA
Neal...

NEAL
Did you write a letter? Is that it?

CHRISTINA
Why do you whites get to ask the questions? What gives you the privilege?

NEAL
You were with the guerrillas, weren't you?

CHRISTINA
No.

NEAL
Then who was it? Who were you working for?

CHRISTINA
No one. It was just an accident. A foolish thing.

NEAL
Go on, Christina. Tell me.

CHRISTINA
And will that satisfy you? Is that all you really want?

NEAL
Tell me and then it's over. Done.

Christina hesitates, then faces him.

CHRISTINA
There was this organization at the university..."The Makerere Student Union." It was nothing important, just a debating society. But I was stupid enough to try to be the secretary even though another girl wanted the post. She told her soldier friends that I was a rebel so I was arrested, slashed, and left for dead.

NEAL
Where'd they arrest you?

CHRISTINA
That's it, Neal. It's done. It's in the past. I just want to forget about the whole thing.

NEAL
You think that's possible?

CHRISTINA
Of course it is.

Neal stands up and moves towards the writing desk.

NEAL
I wish I could believe that. I really do. I'd like to forget about everything that happened to me and walk away. But I can't, Christina. Neither one of us can. Dove's right. We've got to spit it all out before we can get on with your lives.

CHRISTINA
Well, I don't want to talk about the past. Let's just take off our clothes and make love.

NEAL
That's not going to change anything.

Christina walks over to Neal and takes off his shirt.

CHRISTINA
Maybe. It's possible. Perhaps we could discover a solution for all the pain in the world.

NEAL
I don't think so...

Christina stands up and takes off her shoes and dress. She's wearing a bra and underwear.

CHRISTINA
I'm serious. I think it's a wonderful idea. Maybe your American President should go to the U.N. and say: "Sex will solve your problems! Everyone go home!"

NEAL
Christina...

CHRISTINA
Please, Neal.

NEAL
Just one more question.

CHRISTINA
No.

NEAL
Where were you arrested? On the street?

CHRISTINA
No.

CHRISTINA
Come over here, Neal. We'll be more comfortable.
        (forces a smile)
This takes two people...or so I've been told.

NEAL
One question. That's all.

CHRISTINA
No!

NEAL
Was it at the university? In one of the classrooms?

CHRISTINA
Please, Neal.

NEAL
Tell me.

CHRISTINA
I can't...

NEAL
Tell me!

CHRISTINA
Neal, don't do this.

NEAL
I want to know. I need to know.

                    CHRISTINA
          It was night...near the student
          huts below the cricket fields. We
          heard gunshots. Girls screaming.
          And I ran outside and they found me.

                    NEAL
          Soldiers?

                    CHRISTINA
          Yes.

                    NEAL
          How many of them?

                    CHRISTINA
          First two men, then three, and then another
          with a car.

                    NEAL
          Where did they take you?

                    CHRISTINA
          I don't remember.

                    NEAL
          To a prison? To the barracks?

                    CHRISTINA
          To...the graveyard behind Rubaga
          Cathedral. And they kept laughing.
          All of them laughing. "Teach us,"
          they said. "You are our little
          schoolgirl. Teach us. Teach us."
          And they pushed me down and held my
          legs and raped me, filling my
          mouth with dirt. And I was nothing.
          I felt nothing. And the world
          passed through me as they took out
          their knives and cut. Cut. Wet.
          Blood. Burning. Burning.

She breaks down and cries. Stunned, Neal embraces her.

                    NEAL
          Oh, God...God...

Angry, she pulls away from him.

                    CHRISTINA
          Why did you want me to tell
          you this? Why? Did you want a
          little blood? Is that it? One
          last souvenir of Africa?

NEAL
I'm sorry. I'm sorry.

CHRISTINA
You whites! You come to Africa with your hard currency. We smile for you, sleep with you, satisfy your dreams. But you aren't content with that. You want our hearts, too.

NEAL
Soldiers came to my room this morning.

CHRISTINA
And they scared you? Poor Neal! You just had to show them your passport and get on the plane.

NEAL
They started kicking over the furniture. Tearing up my clothes.

Neal stands up.

CHRISTINA
A white man's clothes. What a terrible thing.

NEAL
One of them put a rifle here.
         (touches his neck)
Right here. Then they pulled me downstairs and threw me in a jeep and we drove up the northern road. And I kept thinking no. No. They're going to turn back. Turn around. But the rifle didn't go away and I didn't move until we came to a village. "Look at this," they said. "Look around you. I think you know the people here." And I got out of the jeep and they lead me down a hill and I saw this man... dead...his body all swollen up like a balloon. "Do you know these people?" they said. "Are they your friends?" And they kept pushing me forward and there were more and more bodies. A girl in a blue dress. A little boy. A woman still clutching a wooden spoon.

Neal looks at Christina.

NEAL
It was the same village where I'd
interviewed the guerrillas. Someone
must have told the army I was there.
So, they killed everyone.

CHRISTINA
Because you were there...

Neal approaches her.

NEAL
I don't really know what happened.
I wish I did. All I know is that
they're dead.

CHRISTINA
Why did Dove bring us here? Is he
that cruel? Doesn't he care what
happened?

Neal takes her hand.

NEAL
He doesn't know. And you can't tell
him. You can't tell anyone.

CHRISTINA
I won't.

Christina stands up and hurries back to the couch. She pulls on her dress and shoes.

NEAL
All Dove cares about is his job. If I
told him about this, he'd twist it
all around and blame it all on me.

CHRISTINA
Then why did you tell me?

NEAL
Because you understand! You know how
things can happen for no reason. I went
to a lot of villages looking for a
story, any kind of story, but this time
something went wrong. Maybe someone saw
me on the road. Maybe the guerrillas
betrayed their own people. Anything's
possible.

CHRISTINA
I suppose.

                    NEAL
          It was an accident. That's all. My
          luck ran out. I stayed too long.

Christina moves towards the door. Neal grabs her arm.

                    NEAL
          Where are you going?

                    CHRISTINA
          Back to the city.

                    NEAL
          There's a curfew. It's dangerous
          on the road.

                    CHRISTINA
          It's dangerous here. Some people are
          dead. Dove wants to question you. I
          don't want to be involved in this.

                    NEAL
          There's nothing to worry about,
          Christina. Something happened to
          both of us, but we survived.

                    CHRISTINA
          Let me go. I don't want to be here.

                    NEAL
          No more questions. I promise. I just
          don't want you to leave.

                    CHRISTINA
          This frightens me.

                    NEAL
          It'll be all right.

                    CHRISTINA
          Please, Neal. Let me go.

                    NEAL
          Come here.

                    CHRISTINA
          No.

                    NEAL
          Come here!

They struggle as she tries to get away. Christina drops
her purse and grabs the knife off the food table.

                    CHRISTINA
          Don't...Neal...Don't!

Dove opens the bedroom door carrying the shotgun.

                    DOVE
          Christina!
               (raises the gun)
          Put the knife down, Christina.

Christina hesitates.

                    DOVE
          Put it down! Now!

Christina drops the knife onto the floor.

                    CHRISTINA
          It was an accident. He was
          shouting at me and...

                    DOVE
          Place your hands on your head.

                    NEAL
          Dove...

                    DOVE
          Get down on your knees. Do it!

Christina kneels on the floor.

                    NEAL
          Dove, put the gun away. It's
          not necessary.

                    DOVE
          I'll be the judge of that.

                    NEAL
          We had an argument, that's
          all. You don't need the gun.

Mary comes out of the bedroom.

                    MARY
          What's the problem?

                    DOVE
          Get back in the room.

                    MARY
          Do not call the police.

                    DOVE
          I'm not calling anyone...yet.

                    MARY
          This is not my fault. She's not my
          friend.

                    DOVE
          Get back in the room!

                    MARY
          She's not my friend.

Mary returns to the bedroom as Dove turns to Neal.

                    DOVE
          What's going on? Did she try to
          steal something?

                    NEAL
          I told you, it was just an argument.

                    DOVE
          About what?

                    NEAL
          Nothing.

                    DOVE
          It must have been a rather energetic
          nothing.

                    NEAL
          Nothing important. It was just some
          general craziness. That's all.

Dove picks up the knife and tosses it into the sink.

                    DOVE
          Get up, Christina. Come on, get up.

                    CHRISTINA (mocking)
          Of course, sir. Anything else, sir?

                    DOVE
          Just do it.

                    CHRISTINA
          I am the black girl. He is the white.
          Everything must be my fault. Correct?

                    DOVE
          I'm going to find out whose fault
          this is. Until then, sit down and
          be quiet.

Dove places the shotgun by the wall. Christina sits down on the couch as Neal approaches her.

> DOVE
> Well...this has turned out to be quite an evening. Something for the scrapbook.

> NEAL
> Christina, don't...

> DOVE
> What are you talking about?

> NEAL
> Nothing.

> DOVE
> This is my house. An unpleasant incident has occurred here. I think I have the right to ask a few --

Wearing her dress, Mary opens the bedroom door. She hurries across the room.

> MARY
> I think I will go.

> DOVE
> I told you to stay in the room.

> MARY
> The night is over.

> DOVE
> If you want to get paid, you'll stay.

> MARY
> Why? What am I supposed to do?

> DOVE
> You can sleep, drink, count the cracks on the ceiling. I don't care.

> MARY
> This is extra. Remember that.

Mary returns to the bedroom. Dove picks up Christina's purse.

> DOVE
> Why were you arguing with Christina?

NEAL
She...she wanted to leave.

DOVE
Why?

Dove opens the purse and finds the stolen food.

NEAL
This has nothing to do with you.

DOVE
Why, Christina? Tell me what happened.

NEAL
She doesn't have to answer your questions.

DOVE
Come on. Tell me what Neal said. You don't want to get into trouble. Do you?

CHRISTINA
I..I was slashed in Uganda. Neal wanted to hear about it and I didn't want to tell him. I tried to run away.

DOVE
(to Neal)
And you stopped her?

NEAL
I tried to.

DOVE
Because you wanted to hear about this incident?

NEAL
That's right.

DOVE
Whatever for?

NEAL
I thought it could be a story. Some kind of article. Maybe "sexy ."

DOVE
When did this happen, Christina?

                    CHRISTINA
          More than a year ago.

                    DOVE
          Sounds like current news.

                    NEAL
          I'm tired. Dove. Everybody's
          tired. We've all been drinking.

                    DOVE
          No, it's more than that. Over the years,
          I've met dozens of journalists who've
          just been expelled. I know how they
          drink, what they say...the rhythm of the
          evening. They don't act like you, Neal.

                    NEAL
          None of this would have happened
          if you had taken me to a hotel.
          Instead, you had to drive me out
          here, bring in these women.

                    DOVE
          Don't be ridiculous.

                    DOVE
          You were already acting
          strangely when I met you at the
          airport. You reminded me of a
          gazelle caught on the road at
          night...ears up, legs quivering,
          eyes staring at the headlights.

                    NEAL
          You're forgetting where I've been
          for the last six months. I was
          alone...under fire...while you were
          sitting at your telex machine.

                    DOVE
          Neal, you're not there anymore.
          You're back in Kenya. It's time to
          move forward.

                    NEAL
          Right. And that's what I want
          to do. Move forward. Get out of
          here and go home.

                    DOVE
          If you'd just tell me all the facts.

                    NEAL
          Why should I tell you anything?
          You'd never believe it.

Neal turns to Christina.

                    NEAL
          Journalists are supposed to be
          suspicious. It's the nature of the
          job. But Dove refuses to believe
          that the sun comes up in the morning.

                    DOVE
               (lighting a cigarette)
          Haven't you heard? It's done
          with mirrors.

                    NEAL
          When I showed up in Nairobi, he
          called my old editors...read my
          clips. That would be enough for
          anyone, but no...not Dove.

                    CHRISTINA
          Please, Neal. I don't want to
          be part of this.

                    NEAL
          Three weeks after I arrived in Kampala,
          I traveled north of the city and found a
          dead man lying by the road. Someone had
          shot him and the whole village had run
          away. But the pigs were still there,
          they'd broken out of their pen, and they
          were eating his flesh.

                    DOVE
          Neal...

                    NEAL
          I saw it, Christina. The whole
          thing. So, I went back to Kampala
          and sent out the article and two
          hours later Dove called to ask:
          "Did you really see that, Neal? Did
          it really happen? What kind of pigs
          were they? Can you describe them?"

                    DOVE
          I didn't know you then. I had to
          check your facts.

                    NEAL
          "What kind of pigs?" Can you
          describe the pigs? As if I'm going
          to make up the goddamn story!
                    (to Christina)
          But I answered him. I really did.
          I was so excited to be there.
          Proud. I thought I had finally
          reached the front line I'd been
          looking for all my life.

                    DOVE
          You did a good job, Neal. A
          damn good job --

                    NEAL
          Then why weren't you satisfied? You
          knew what was going on. You read all
          my articles. But you didn't bring me
          out. You let me stay too long.

                    DOVE
          What are you talking about? What
          do you mean..."stayed too long?"

Neal moves towards the door.

                    NEAL
          Go to hell, Dove.

                    DOVE
          It's already been arranged.

                    NEAL
          I'm out. I'm going home. I don't
          have to listen to you anymore.

                    DOVE
          I want to know...

                    NEAL
          That's it. I'm walking back to
          the city.
                    DOVE
          Neal!

Neal walks out of the cottage and disappears into the darkness. Christina stares at Dove.

                    CHRISTINA
          You whites are such calm, reasonable
          people.

                    DOVE
          Be quiet, Christina.

                    CHRISTINA
          We poor Africans should be honored
          to receive your insights.

Dove carries the shotgun into the bedroom.

                    MARY (inside bedroom)
          I want to go back to town.

                    DOVE
          Stay here until I get back.

                    MARY
          If the police come --

                    DOVE
          The policemen aren't going to
          come! Just go to sleep!

Dove comes back out and pulls on his shirt. He picks up the blanket and rearranges the chair.

                    DOVE
          Help yourself to the food, Christina.
          Have some more beer. I'll talk to you
          when I get back.

                    CHRISTINA
          Why?

                    DOVE
          I want to find out what's troubling
          Neal. If I can't find him, you'll
          have to provide some answers.

                    CHRISTINA
          He didn't tell me anything.

                    DOVE
          We'll see about that.

                    CHRISTINA
          I don't have to stay here. I can
          just forget about the money.

                    DOVE
          You're a whore and refugee, Christina.
          I'm sure that your papers are false.
                              (more)

> DOVE
> It would be easy for me to contact the District Police Captain and wave some money in his face. They'd track you down in a day.

> CHRISTINA
> And arrest me?

> DOVE
> That's possible.

> CHRISTINA
> And send me back to Uganda?

> DOVE
> That's also possible.

> CHRISTINA
> The soldiers would kill me if I went back there.

Dove walks to the front door.

> DOVE
> It's your decision, Christina.

> CHRISTINA
> But you'd cause it to happen.

> DOVE
> It's your decision.5

Dove leaves the cottage. A Beat, then Christina stands up and walks quickly to the door. She touches the door, hesitates, then steps back --- alone, frightened, wondering what to do.

BLACKOUT

ACT II

Lights up on the same position at the end of Act I. Christina stands motionless as Mary comes out of the bedroom.

                  MARY
     Where's Dove? Where did he go?

                CHRISTINA
     He went to find Neal.

Mary walks over to the refrigerator and takes out a beer.

                  MARY
     So what happened? Did you want more money?

                CHRISTINA
     No.

                  MARY
     Did you steal his money?

                CHRISTINA
     It had nothing to do with money.

                  MARY
     Oh. Oh-Oh-Oh.
          (firmly)
     Everything has to do with money!

                CHRISTINA
     Maybe for you.

                  MARY
     For everyone! There are no whites and blacks...only dollars, pounds, and shillings. For-eign ex-change! Mjinga.
          (waits for a reaction)
     Mjinga!

                CHRISTINA
     I am not a fool.

MARY
Maaaaa-jinga.

Christina faces Mary.

CHRISTINA
You don't know what happened. You weren't here in the room.

MARY
I know you had a knife in your hand.

CHRISTINA
I didn't want to hurt him.

MARY
Ahhh, that makes it better.

She pretends to hold a knife.

MARY
Excuse me, sir. I don't want to hurt you.
    (stabs someone)
Oh, I'm very sorry, I don't want to cut you.
    (glances around room)
The police are here? No problem. I didn't want to kill him.

CHRISTINA
Even if the police had come, you wouldn't have been involved.

MARY
You think that? Truly? Then you are a fool!

CHRISTINA
Listen to me, Mary...

MARY
When we first meet on Kenyatta Avenue, I think..."Ahhh, a girl from Uganda. She knows about the world." Then I talk to you more and I think "Ahhh, a university girl. She knows how to handle the whites." I thought you could help me so I help you.

CHRISTINA
How lucky for me.

                    MARY
          Yes, very lucky. Some girls are
          dead, but you still eat.

                    CHRISTINA
          I should thank my teacher.

Mary sits down on the couch.

                    MARY
          Thank me for nothing. You never
          learn, Christina. You never
          open your eyes. You're still a
          little church girl in a white
          dress...first communion.

                    CHRISTINA
          What happened wasn't my fault.
          He shouted at me. He wouldn't
          let me leave.

                    MARY
          "He shouted at me. He wouldn't
          let me leave."

She spits on the floor.

                    MARY
          He is young. He is white. He is
          a man. All these things make it
          easy to guide him.

                    CHRISTINA
          You didn't "guide" him so well
          when you had a chance.

                    MARY
          I didn't try hard. I didn't care.
          Dove was paying and all this one
          had was Uganda shillings.

                    CHRISTINA
          He didn't want you. That's
          what happened.

Mary stands up and paces around the room.

                    MARY
          Ex-act-ly. It was your job. Not
          mine. So what did he want? A
          servant? A little mother? Did he
          want you to dance around the room?

CHRISTINA
It wasn't that way. He was hurt...drunk. I don't know.

MARY
A cow is as big as three men. But when I was a little girl I can guide them.
(pretends to herd)
Toka! Acha! Drink the water! Follow me! You beat them on the nose and tell them what to do.

CHRISTINA
Don't you ever get tired?

MARY
If I have no food. If I must walk into the city.

CHRISTINA
I mean, tired here...
(touches her forehead)
Tired of the manipulating and maneuvering?

MARY
Big words.

CHRISTINA
The push-push. Are you tired of that? Tired of being "Happy Mary, happy girl"? Tired of having to smile and think up tricks all the time? Sometimes, I wish they had killed me. Killed everything and everyone, then killed themselves. There'd be nothing but the forest and the river. The rain falling with no one to hear.

Mary shakes her head and sits back down on the couch.

MARY
If you want to die, go back to Kampala. Me...I have money. I will get more money. And then I will buy a little bar. A place for the men to drink. But I will have no husbands. No men at all. I will buy my children on the street. A son. Two sons. One daughter for the work. And I will make more money and buy land and die in my own shamba.
(more)

She raises her bottle and smiles.

                    MARY
          Drinking beer.

                    CHRISTINA
          What a wonderful life.

                    MARY
          A <u>life</u>! All the men can fight each
          other. The dogs can run in the
          street. But I will eat.

                    CHRISTINA
          You can do what you want, I'm
          going to London.

                    MARY
          Too cold.

                    CHRISTINA
          America.

                    MARY
          Too cold.

                    CHRISTINA
          You don't know that. They have warm
          places there. I've read about them.

                    MARY
          You will walk on cold streets. See
          cold white faces like ghosts. You
          will be a ghost, too.

Mary pretends to shiver as she imitates Christina.

                    MARY
          "Oh, I am sooo cold. I wished they had
          killed me. Killed everything and --

                    CHRISTINA
          Don't! You sound like you're on their side.

                    MARY
          I am on my side.

                    CHRISTINA
          Yes, I mustn't forget. You are
          Kenyan and I am just a refugee.

                    MARY
          So?

                    CHRISTINA
          Yes, of course. I'm forgetting
          what's even more important. You
          are Kikuyu and I am Bagandan.
          Different tribes.

                    MARY
          So? I came to Nairobi alone with no
          one to help me. I had to fight,
          steal, sleep in the streets...until
          slowly, slowly...I got money and
          clothes and --

Dove walks out of the darkness and steps onto the porch.

                    DOVE
          Neal! Are you out there? I'm
          getting mildly annoyed with you.

                    MARY
          Do you hear that?

                    DOVE
          Substantially annoyed.

                    MARY
          I think he's very angry.

                    DOVE
          Goddamnit!

Dove walks up the porch to the front door.

                    CHRISTINA
          Go back to the bedroom, Mary.
          I'll handle this.

Christina walks towards the front door.

                    MARY
          And make more trouble? I brought
          you here. Our names are together.
          You are a lucky girl, Christina. I
          will talk to Dove and smooth things
          down.

                    CHRISTINA
          You don't have to do anything. I've
          been with the tourists. I can...

                    MARY
          Dove is not a tourist. He is not
          African. He is his own tribe.

CHRISTINA
What difference does it make?
He knows I didn't do anything
wrong.

MARY
So? You think he cares? Let me
tell you, Christina...Dove can
joke and drink beer, but he's a
very dangerous man.
        (thumps her chest
         with her fist)
He's hard...hard right here, but
I know how to talk to him. For
me, it's easy. No problem.

Mary lies down on the couch.

CHRISTINA
If you're scared of the police,
then stay out of this. I will --

Dove enters the cottage.

DOVE
Well, Christina...guess you
decided to stay.

CHRISTINA
What happened? Did you find him?

DOVE
Not a trace. The fool must
have wandered off the road.

CHRISTINA
Maybe he got lost and...

Mary pops up from the couch.

MARY
Hel-lo, Dove.

DOVE
I told you to stay in the bedroom.

MARY
But I _missed_ you.

DOVE
Bloody Christ.

Mary stands up and approaches Dove.

                    MARY
          I am sorry for this, Dove. Very
          sorry. In two or three days, you
          will be happy and I will come
          back with some Kikuyu girls. No
          charge. No problem. And we will
          dance and dance.

She begins to move her pelvis back and forth.

                    MARY
          Pah-pah, pah-pah, pah-pah...

                    DOVE
          Sit down, Mary.

                    MARY
          Pah-pah, pah-pah...

                    DOVE
          Sit down!

Mary sits down on the couch.

                    DOVE
          No more talk. Do you understand?
          Not one word until I say so.

Dove enters the bathroom. A Beat, then Mary begins making a series of bird calls. After each call, she glances at the bathroom doorway.

                    MARY
               (quickly)
          Creak-creak-creak-creak-
          creak... A widow bird in the
          tall grass.

She makes a high-pitched whistle that fades at the end.

                    MARY
          A wild crane. He wants a woman.

                    DOVE (in bathroom)
          It's not going to work, Mary.

                    MARY
          Heeeeee, he-he-he.
               (looks for Dove)
          A little grey monkey. Very
          angry. He sees a black snake.

She throws one leg over the back of the couch as Dove comes out of the bathroom.

                    DOVE
          Believe me, I'm not in the mood for
          this. The three of us need to have a
          little chat before Neal returns.

                    CHRISTINA
          He's not going to return.

                    DOVE
          It's dark. There's a curfew. He
          doesn't have any place to go.

                    CHRISTINA
          He could get around the
          roadblocks and walk to the city.

                    DOVE
          And then what? Neal doesn't have
          any money. I'd find him tomorrow
          at his embassy or the telegraph
          office. He won't be able to hide.

                    CHRISTINA
          Mary was right. You are a dangerous man.

                    DOVE
          Me? Dangerous? I just have a great
          deal of curiosity, that's all. I
          like to hunt down facts, shoot
          them, and drag them back to camp.

Dove sits on the chair. Mary stands and approaches him.

                    MARY
          You do what you want, Dove. Just
          give us the money and we go. Right
          now.

                    DOVE
          No. No, I don't think so.

                    DOVE
          You women underestimate your influence
          on the evening's activities. If Neal and
          I had been here alone it would have been
          nothing but threats and bluster...two
          half-blind rhinos snorting at each other
          and pawing the ground. But with women
          around the world is changed. There's
          drinking and laughter. Male vanity.
          Perhaps a little truth.

                    CHRISTINA
          I've told you everything.

                    DOVE
          I'll be the judge of that.

                    MARY
          Forget about her. She's just a
          church girl.

                    DOVE
          Go back to the room, Mary. I want talk
          to Christina....alone.

                    MARY
               (pretends to be hurt)
          No.

                    DOVE
          I want you to --

                    MARY
          Don't worry. I'll help you, Dove.
          I'll be the police and ask the
          questions.

     Mary approaches Christina and pounds her fist on the stool.

                    MARY
          Hey, you! Church girl!

                    DOVE
          For godsake, Mary.

                    MARY
          What did Neal say?

                    CHRISTINA
          I've told Dove the whole story.

                    MARY
               (turning to Dove)
          You see?

                    CHRISTINA
          I was slashed by soldiers and Neal
          wanted to know about it.

                    DOVE
          What did you talk about earlier in
          the evening?

                    CHRISTINA
          Just little things. That's all.

                    DOVE
          For example.

                    CHRISTINA
          It wasn't important.

                    MARY
          That's right. It's not important.
          Why should you care about Neal?

Mary returns to the couch.

                    CHRISTINA
          This has nothing to do with Neal.
          It's me...from me. After I was
          slashed, I was in the hospital for
          more than two months. I lay in there
          and thought about everything
          ...what I was going to do.

                    DOVE
          And what did you decide?

                    CHRISTINA
          That I was going to live my
          life, but not hurt anyone. You
          can say what you want, Dove.
          Just don't involve me.

                    DOVE
          Sometimes, that's not possible.

                    CHRISTINA
          I'm going to try.

                    MARY
          What did I tell you, Dove? She's
          a church girl. That's all.

Dove stands and strolls around the room.

                    DOVE
          Morality is for tourists, Christina.
          Someone with a comfortable hotel room.
          Be like Mary. She'll survive.

                    CHRISTINA
          I don't want to be like Mary.
          I'm not going to hurt people
          and I won't help you.

                    DOVE
          Remember what I said about the
          police. It's very easy...

Mary stands and steps between Dove and Christina.

> MARY
> Stop it, Dove. This is a small problem. Very small. So, let's have some more beer and forget about everything.

> DOVE
> That's not possible. It would be a disaster if one of my competitors picked up a story that Neal wanted to hide. I'd lose my job in a second.

> MARY
> So what? You get another one.

Dove walks over to the writing desk.

> DOVE
> I don't think so. The other wire services want young blood these days...not this tired scrap of flesh. What could I do I was sacked? Go back to Britain and stand in queues for the rest of my life? Stay here and be a hotel clerk or a tour guide? One of those shabby, shuffling Englishmen that the little boys mock in the streets?

> CHRISTINA
> Now, I understand. You're frightened.

> DOVE
> "Concerned" is a better word. I think Neal made up a story...an interview with some rebels in Uganda.

> CHRISTINA
> Why would he do something like that?

> DOVE
> Because he's an ambitious young man. You should have seen him when he first arrived here from the States...sitting at the Thorn Tree Bar, popping water purification tablets in the gin and tonics. He kept telling me: "I can do it, Mr. Richardson-Dove. I can do it." For one drunken evening, I felt like I was still involved in something exciting, romantic, endlessly new.

CHRISTINA
So, you send him to Kampala. That
was a good thing to do.

Mary sits on the couch.

DOVE
Neal wanted to write a big story, but
all he got was a lot of day-to-day
killings. Maybe he became frustrated
and wrote his own interview.

CHRISTINA
Leave him alone, Dove. Who cares
if he made up something? Every
day there are thousands of lies
in the newspapers.

DOVE
Not from me.

MARY
Oh, you lie all the time!

DOVE
Everyone lies, Mary. It's as natural
as breathing. But when I see something I try to see it clearly. And
when I write something, I try to
write the truth.

MARY
What are you talking about? The
truth is I haven't been paid.

DOVE
If I want to get the facts about
something, I usually succeed.
Don't forget, both of you are
involved in this. And both of you
are going to help me.

MARY
I'm not "involved" in anything.

DOVE
It's not your decision.

MARY
You don't scare me. I know you. I've
seen you without your pants.

                    DOVE
          That hardly puts you in an unique
          category.

                    MARY
          I've watched you walk into the
          New Florida Bar a hundred times.
          I've seen you stand in the
          doorway alone...all alone...like
          a dog begging for food.

                    DOVE
          You're such a romantic, Mary.

                    MARY
          You don't have a country or a
          tribe. You don't have anything.

                    DOVE
          Just my natural charm and
          boyish good looks...

                    CHRISTINA
          Mary's right, Dove. You couldn't
          live in England so you had to
          come here. You're like one of
          those sick people they chase out
          of a village. They have to live
          in the bush. Die alone.

                    MARY
          Yes! That's him! That's how it is!

                    CHRISTINA
          You've always been alone. No
          family. No friends.

                    DOVE
          That's not true.

                    CHRISTINA
          All you have is your little
          facts. No one cares about you.

Dove turns and faces Christina.

                    DOVE
          That's not true. I once loved
          a woman very much like you.

                    MARY
          Liar! He's lying again!

CHRISTINA
Don't waste your time, Dove. No one believes you.

DOVE
We met while I was working in Ghana. She was a nurse, trained in London, with a peculiar obsession for vitamin A. We had tons of it. Boxes in the bedroom. She was going to give it to all the children in Africa. Try to keep them from going blind.

CHRISTINA
She was black?

DOVE
Dark black. Blacker than you. I scrubbed her neck. I braided her hair. We bought furniture together. We owned a dog.

MARY
So where is this woman? Did you bring her to Kenya?

DOVE
No.

CHRISTINA
Have any photographs?

DOVE
No. They were taken from me.

MARY
Oh, yes. They were stolen by monkeys.

CHRISTINA
I think you just invented this person, Dove. I don't think she ever existed.

DOVE
Of course she did! We lived together for a year, then...then I came home and found the dog hacked open and hanging on the door. She was gone. Our photographs were gone. Everything had disappeared.

CHRISTINA
Who did this? The police?

                    DOVE
          It could have been the police. It
          could have been the army. Everyone
          told me a different story. I heard
          that she had been taken to a
          barracks. I heard that she was
          being held at this little house
          outside of town where they beat
          people to death with hammers. She
          was alive. She had been killed. She
          was going to be released. She was
          dead. A few weeks later, I lost my
          press accreditation and had
          to leave the country. I never
          did find out what happened.

The two women look at each other, then they laugh loudly.

                    CHRISTINA
          Should we feel sorry for you?
          Is that it?

                    MARY
          You loved a woman and now
          she's dead! So what!

Furious, Dove walks over to the couch. He picks up the
phone and starts to dial.

                    DOVE
          I'm calling the police! We've
          had an attempted robbery here!
          An assault with a knife and...

Silence. The women are frightened. A Beat, then Dove
hangs up.

                    DOVE
          You see before you another victim of a
          classical education.

Dove drops the empty bottles into the trash. He picks up
the wash bowl and places it in the sink.

                    DOVE
          I should studied the Sciences or
          stayed away from college all
          together, but no...I had read
          Tacitus and his fellow historians. I
          admired them. I really did. Their
          elevated tone. Their calm voices
          describing scenes of human frailty.
                    (more)

DOVE (Cont'd)
They were always...above it all.
And that's the way I wanted to
be...above it all. For awhile, it
was all quite possible. I was well
on the road to becoming a Senior
Editor, one of those men who
interviews heads of state and
writes about the big picture for the
Sunday supplements. Then, they sent
me to Africa "for seasoning." Good
god. As if I was a piece of meat
that needed a little more salt.
So, I came here and stayed and stayed
and you destroyed me. Not you two
personally of course, but the whole
bloody continent. I didn't believe in
the big picture anymore. It was
lie. A total illusion.

CHRISTINA
You're making yourself sound very
noble, Dove.

DOVE
Not at all. I've fought this every
step of the way. Bit by bit, I've
given up parts of my future. And
it's going to get worse. Oh, I'm
sure of that. Somehow, this
stubbornness to know the facts, to
see things clearly...is going to
force me to give up the last
small scrap of my life. There'll
be nothing left of me but a few
empty bottles of beer.

CHRISTINA
Please, Dove. Do what Mary wants.
Give us the money and let us go.

DOVE
The money? Yes, you want the
money. Well, I can provide that.

Dove pulls out his wallet and walks over to the women.

DOVE
Here's forty shillings for you, Mary.
No, here's fifty. Make it sixty...

                    MARY
          This is extra.

                    DOVE
          Of course. I agree. Just take
          the money and have some more beer.

Mary snatches the money from Dove. He approaches Christina.

                    DOVE
          Now, Christina...we mustn't
          forget your effort.

                    CHRISTINA
          I don't want any money from
          you. It's dangerous to take
          things in this house.

                    DOVE
          Did you hear that, Mary? Did
          you hear what she just said?

                    MARY
          If she doesn't want it, give it
          to me.

Neal walks out of the darkness.

                    DOVE
          Not at all. That won't be fair.
               (offers the money)
          Come on, Christina. Take it.
          Just for being my friend.

                    CHRISTINA
          I'm not your friend!

Neal enters the cottage.

                    DOVE
          Good heavens. It's Neal. Our
          prodigal son.

                    NEAL
          Leave Christina alone.

                    DOVE
          Leave her alone? I'm offering her
          money!

                    NEAL
          It doesn't look like she wants any.

Dove puts the money back in his wallet.

                    DOVE
          As you wish, Christina. It's
          your loss. Not mine.

He takes out four bottles out of the refrigerator.

                    DOVE
          Well, our little family's back
          together again. How delightful!
          What about some refreshments,
          Neal? Another beer?

                    NEAL
          No.

                    DOVE
          Mary??

                    MARY
          I want the rest of my money.

                    DOVE
          Christina?

                    CHRISTINA
          Can't you see that we've had enough,
          Dove? No one wants to drink.

                    DOVE
          Why not? Here we are comfortable
          and happy...sitting on the veranda
          as the sun rises over the Green
          Hills of Africa. It's just like
          Hemingway, isn't it? The days of
          the Great White Hunter.
               (hands beer to women)
          We're going to talk about the
          news from home. The coffee crop.
          The servant problem.
               (hands beer to Neal)
          And...oh, yes...Neal's going to
          tell us about that clever little
          article he sent out last week. The
          interview with those guerrillas.

                    CHRISTINA
          You don't have to talk to him.

                    DOVE
          Stay out of this, Christina.

                    NEAL
          No, I don't mind. He doesn't scare
          me at all.

                    DOVE
          Really? I don't seem to frighten
          anyone tonight. Must be losing my
          touch.

Dove sits on the chair.

                    NEAL
          I hope you didn't let him intimidate
          you, Christina. I could have walked
          back to the city, but I knew he'd still
          be here...trying to push you into
          saying something that wasn't true.

                    DOVE
          We had a little chat. That's all.

                    NEAL
          I was out there, wandering
          around in the dark, until I
          figured out the whole situation.
          You want to know about the
          interview, don't you?

                    DOVE
          We can start with that.

                    NEAL
          All right. I'll tell you about
          it. I'll tell you everything.
          Then we can all go to sleep.

                    DOVE
          Good for you, Neal. That's the
          spirit. So, tell me...how did you
          meet those two guerrillas? Did they
          contact you in Kampala or did you
          organize everything yourself?

                    NEAL
          The whole thing was an accident. I
          bumped into them while I was looking
          for the head of an African priest.

                    DOVE
          A what?

                    NEAL
          Some people in the market told me
          that the soldiers had killed a
          priest, cut off his head, and
          forced it onto a pole.

DOVE
Is that true? Why didn't you write about it?

NEAL
I had to verify the story. Get the facts. Find some witnesses. It's not so easy in Africa.

DOVE
It's the nature of the job, Neal. People who decapitate priests rarely put out a press release.

NEAL
I borrowed a motorcycle and went up the country roads north of Kampala. I talked to people, lots of people, but nobody had seen anything. It was always "In the next village. Up the road." So, there I was...alone...risking my life for a rumor. A fantasy.

DOVE
"A headless priest." It's a good story. They would have printed that.

CHRISTINA
Did they kill his family, too?

MARY
Christina...

NEAL
I don't know if he had a family. I never found him...or his head. After two weeks of wandering around, I stopped at this village to ask for directions. I walked back to the motorcycle and all of a sudden two men in camouflage uniforms were pointing their rifles at my chest.

DOVE
The guerrillas?

NEAL
They talked to me for about a hour and I wrote it all down. It was real. It was news. I rode back to Kampala, sent it out on the telex, and...that's it.

                    DOVE
          The whole story?

                    NEAL
          Beginning, middle and end.
                (watching Dove)
          What's the matter, Dove? You
          look disappointed.

                    CHRISTINA
          He thinks you made it all up.

                    DOVE
          That's enough, Christina.
          You're crossing the line.

                    MARY
          Don't talk. Don't say anything.
          You'll get us into trouble.

                    CHRISTINA
          Dove's the one that's causing
          trouble. All he cares about is his
          job.

Mary stands up and walks over to the radio.

                    MARY
          Neal's right. Let us forget about
          all this. Okay? Let's be happy.
          Beer, Dove! More beer! Let's turn
          on the radio and dance and dance...

She switches on the shortwave radio and African music
blares out of the speaker. Mary begins to dance wildly.

                    DOVE
          Shut that damn thing off!

He hurries over to the table and switches off the radio.

                    MARY
          What are you doing, Mary?
          Who's side are you on?

                    MARY
          I'm on the side of no police.

                    NEAL
          Everyone relax. There's no reason
          to get angry. In a few hours, it'll
          be light and we can walk back to
          the city. By noontime, I'll be on a
          plane going back to the States. And
          that'll be the end of it.

                    DOVE
          Back to the comforts of home.

                    NEAL
          And what's wrong with that?
          I wasn't hurting anybody.

                    DOVE
          A safe world, a protected world, where
          people move from the house to the car
          to the office, then back again...
          avoiding unpleasant realities.

                    NEAL
          I'm not going to avoid anything,
          Dove. But I'm not going to keep
          looking for trouble.

                    DOVE
          Just close your eyes, Neal...
          tight, tighter...and join that
          vast nation of blind men tap-
          tapping their way down the
          street. How much longer can they
          lie to themselves and others?
          When will someone stop them and
          grab their coat and say: "now...
          now, you must see!"

                    NEAL
          Things are different these days, Dove.
          I think you've been away too long. The
          people in America and Europe don't
          want to hear about all the little
          horrors in the Third World. They have
          their own lives. Their own problems.

                    DOVE
          Then we should just forget about
          Africa. Ignore what's going on.

                    NEAL
          It's just going to get worse.
          Nothing we do will change anything.

                    DOVE
          So, in a way, all your articles
          were meaningless. There was no
          reason for anyone to read them.

                    NEAL
          Yeah. You could say that.

                              DOVE
                    Meaningless...and unnecessary.

                              NEAL
                    I guess.

                              DOVE
                    And it would be all right for one of
                    these meaningless and unnecessary
                    articles to be fiction?

                              NEAL
                    You're like a vulture, aren't
                    you? Always looking for something
                    rotten by the side of the road.

                              DOVE
                    Don't waste your time trying to
                    insult me. I'm a journalist.
                    Remember? I've been called everything
                    ...twice.

                              NEAL
                    I can believe that.

                              DOVE
                    Think about the next reporter who's
                    going to work in Uganda. If the
                    government knows your interview was
                    false, they're going to give him a
                    very bad time.

                              NEAL
                    The government knows it was true.

                              DOVE
                    How can you be so sure?

                              NEAL
                    They were angry about what happened.

                              DOVE
                    Who was angry?

                              NEAL
                    The soldiers that took me to the
                    airport!

                              DOVE
                    Neal, you said that some bureaucrat
                    took you to the airport. A "little man"
                    from the Ministry of Information.

                              NEAL
                    It was...soldiers, too.

                    DOVE
          What kind of soldiers? Special
          Branch? The Military Police?

Neal moves behind the couch. Dove approaches him.

                    NEAL
          I don't remember.

                    DOVE
          What kind of uniforms were they wearing?

                    NEAL
          I forget.

                    DOVE
          The whole thing happened this
          morning.

                    NEAL
          I was scared. I thought they
          were going to kill me.

                    DOVE
          What gave you that idea?

                    NEAL
          Go back to bed, Dove. I'm not
          answering anymore questions.

                    DOVE
          You don't have to answer any
          questions. Just tell me the truth.

                    NEAL
          The truth? What do you know about
          the truth? You're just a kind of
          factory manager, that's all. I
          went out there and harvested the
          story, then you squeezed it
          through your grinder and sent it
          off to London.

                    DOVE
          It's a job, Neal. I'll admit that.
          It's a job and I don't want to lose
          it. But there's another part of it,
          too...a certain kind of honesty...a
          way of looking at the world.

                    NEAL
          Come on, Dove. You don't believe in
          anything.

DOVE
I don't turn away. That's my morality.

NEAL
Well, that's just wonderful. You can stay here staring at every-thing while I go back home.

DOVE
You made up that article, didn't you?

NEAL
It all happened! Just the way I described it!

Dove walks over to the table and picks up Neal's clips.

DOVE
Is that so? Let's find this little work of art and take a look at it. Here we are...
    (reads the article)
"We will attack the capital in six months," said Michael Kirunda, a lieutenant in the Uganda People's Army. "We will attack and destroy the traitors there."
    (glances at Neal)
"Standing in the middle of Nakalambe, a small village north of Kampala, Lieutenant Kirunda described the goals of the largest guerrilla group currently fighting in --"

CHRISTINA
    (to Neal)
You gave the name of the village?

DOVE
What's that, Christina? You have a question?

DOVE
Yes, he named the village. So what? Have you been there?

CHRISTINA
That's how it happened, Neal. That's how it really happened. Just...like...that.

DOVE
What happened, Christina? What are you talking about?

CHRISTINA
If the village was in a safe area, an area held by the guerrillas, you could write about it. But not in a village north of Kampala. The soldiers read his article, then they went there and killed everyone. They took him there this morning. He told me about it.

DOVE
Good God.

NEAL
That's all wrong, Christina. None of those soldiers read anything. They don't subscribe to the London Times.

DOVE
They didn't have to. The article was picked up by the Nairobi papers.

Christina stands and approaches Neal.

CHRISTINA
And you blamed it on the villagers. Didn't you? You even blamed the guerrillas. You thought of blaming everyone, but yourself.

NEAL
I just assumed that, it seemed logical --

CHRISTINA
Logical for a white.

NEAL
I met the guerrillas there. That's a fact. I only reported a fact.

CHRISTINA
Your "fact" just massacred a village!

NEAL
It was Dove's responsibility. He should have crossed it out.

                    DOVE
You were the person who was there,
Neal. The only one who could make a
decision. I assumed you thought it
was safe...a guerrilla-held area.

                    NEAL
It was...fairly...secure. Look,
I was just following your little
moral code. Getting the facts.
Writing the truth.

                    DOVE
But you knew about the situation.

                    NEAL
I was trying to write an article. I
needed a place, a date, a name to quote.

                    CHRISTINA
And now you want to go home. How
easy for you.

                    NEAL
What am I supposed to do? Stay here?
Go back to Uganda? What's the point?

                    CHRISTINA
There's no point. Everyone's been
killed. So wave your passport and
run to the plane.

                    NEAL
It's finished! Don't you understand
that? Those people are dead. I can't
bring them back.

                    CHRISTINA
So forget about them.

                    NEAL
I didn't say that.

                    CHRISTINA
But that's what you want. Maybe
it's possible to forget about
everything...all of Africa. You
can remove it from your mind.

                    NEAL
Isn't that what you want to do? All
night long you've been talking
about going to England or America.
You want to forget, too.

                    CHRISTINA
          I'm not running from anything.
          Not like you.

                    NEAL
          Of course you are. You want to lose
          your past and get on with your
          life. Just like me.

                    CHRISTINA
          I didn't kill anyone.

                    NEAL
          I didn't either. Not...directly.

                    CHRISTINA
          Not directly! You whites move
          through Africa like a drunkard in
          an automobile. You make people
          turn away and smash up in their
          own accidents while you're still
          safe and speeding down the road.
          Each thing you do touches us and
          yet you keep saying: "No. No. I'm
          not responsible."
               (looks at Dove)
          Perhaps you didn't kill those
          people, but you were there...both
          of you...pointing each gun.

                    DOVE
          Nonsense! I'm not involved in this.

                    CHRISTINA
          Don't try to get out of this, Dove!

                    DOVE
          Africans have been slaughtering
          each other since Independence. It
          was Africans who slashed you.
          Wasn't it, Christina? Maybe they had
          the same color skin, but they...

Very angry, Mary steps forward.

                    MARY
          Dove!

                    DOVE
          Keep out of this, Mary.

                    MARY
          No.

                    DOVE
          This is none of your business.

                    MARY
          You know me, Dove. You know me.
          I want you to leave her alone.

Christina grabs her purse and walks to the front door.

                    CHRISTINA
          You don't need to defend me, Mary.
          I'm going back to the city.

                    DOVE
          I owe you some money.

                    CHRISTINA
          Forget about your money.

                    NEAL
          Christina...

She stops at the door.

                    CHRISTINA
          If there are ghosts in this world,
          I hope they come to you...both of
          you. Touching your hearts. Pushing
          into your dreams.

She walks out of the cottage and runs into the darkness.

                    DOVE
          Well, that ahhh...that wasn't
          very professional of her.

                    MARY
          Don't speak against Christina.

                    DOVE
          I'm not speaking against anyone.
          Christina's poor. Almost starving.
          She should have taken the money.

Dove takes out his wallet and walks over to Mary.

                    MARY
          Not from you.

                    DOVE
          You'll...you'll give it to her.
          Won't you, Mary? You don't forget
          about such crucial matters.

He counts the money onto her open palm.

                    DOVE
          Here we go. A hundred and twenty
          for you. A hundred and twenty for
          Christina. And...a little bit more.
                    (glances at Mary)
          All right, quite a bit more. Take
          it. It's yours.

Mary stares at the money as Dove tries to smile.

                    DOVE
          Is everything okay. No problem?

Mary drops some of the money onto the floor.

                    MARY
          This is too much. I'll take what
          is owed to me. Nothing more.

                    DOVE
          Don't be ridiculous.

                    MARY
          The night is over, Dove.

Mary slips the money into her bra. She picks up her purse from the top of the refrigerator and walks to the door.

                    DOVE
          Some of this money is for
          Christina. The poor girl needs
          every shilling she can get.

                    MARY
          Don't worry about Christina.

                    DOVE
          I want her to get paid.

                    MARY
          I'll take care of Christina.
          Good night.

Mary walks out of the cottage. Dove picks up the money.

                    DOVE
          Oh, to hell with it. You can't
          count on anything but the news.

He walks over to the phone and dials the operator.

                    NEAL
          What are you doing?

                    DOVE
          Placing a call to London. I want
          to send out this story as quickly
          as possible.

                    NEAL
               (sarcastic)
          Of course. Don't want to wait.

Neal turns away from Dove and crosses the room.

                    DOVE
          You better sit down.

                    NEAL
          No.

                    DOVE
          Go ahead, Neal. You must be
          exhausted. You had frightening
          experience this morning and now
          we've got to...
               (to phone)
          Hello, Matthew? Richardson-Dove
          here. Yes, I've want to make another
          call to Reuters in London. That's
          right. Push it through. Will you?
          That's a good man.

He hangs up and sits at the typewriter.

                    DOVE
          All right. Let's get all the facts
          in order. I'd like an exact
          description of those soldiers.
          Name and rank, if possible. I'll
          write the lead now and compose
          the rest over the phone.

                    DOVE
          Do you want to tell me the whole
          thing or shall I ask you questions?
          Neal?

Neal doesn't respond.

                    DOVE
          Why don't we just start from the
          beginning. Tell me...when did the
          soldiers arrive?

                    NEAL
          I didn't know this would happen.

					DOVE
		I understand that. It wasn't an
		intentional act.

					NEAL
		I made a mistake. A bad one.
		But writing this article won't
		change anything.

					DOVE
		We don't know that. It could
		have some kind of effect on the
		government.

					NEAL
		The army will deny everything.
		They'll keep on killing people.

					DOVE
		Of course they will. Thousands more
		will die unknown, unacknowledged.
		But not this village, Neal. Not
		the people you saw today.

					NEAL
		But it won't change the situation.

					DOVE
		That's not the issue here. You
		owe something to those people,
		Neal. Their memory.

					DOVE
		This thing happened to you. It's
		a fact. You can go back to the
		States, go anywhere you want, but
		you won't be able to forget it.

					NEAL
		I realize that. I just don't see
		why I have to tell the whole
		world what happened.

					DOVE
		It's part of facing up to it. If
		you don't write that article,
		you'll be a fraud. A liar. You
		wouldn't be able to get on with
		your life.

					NEAL
		Get on with what? I'm still going
		to have this memory in my brain.

                    DOVE
That's right. It's not going to go
away. But you won't have to lie to
yourself for the rest of your life.

                    NEAL
Do you believe that? Really? Tell
you what, Dove...I'll write the
article. I'll tell everybody the
whole story.

                    DOVE
Good for you, Neal. Very good.

                    NEAL
I'll write about it...if you put
yourself in the article.

                    DOVE
What are you talking about?

                    NEAL
I want you to tell everybody that
you had the article on your desk.
You were the one who knew all about
Africa. I was still learning. You
could have questioned any part of
the story...called me on the
phone...but you let it go through.

                    DOVE
It was your responsibility.

                    NEAL
No, Dove. Both of us were
responsible and you know it.

                    DOVE
Stop this. You're talking like a
madman.

                    NEAL
Then forget about the article.
I'm not going to back it up.

                    DOVE
I don't need you to write this.
Christina told me what happened.

                    NEAL
I'll say it was a lie. I'll call
up Reuters and tell them that you
made up the whole thing just to
keep your job. They won't sent it
out, Dove. You know they won't.

DOVE
Are you a coward? Is that it? Someone who won't admit his mistakes?

NEAL
I'll admit everything, but you've got to come along. This is going to be a long, dark road, Dove. I want a little company.

DOVE
You...you don't understand. I could lose my job.

NEAL
Why is your job any different from mine?

DOVE
You're a young man. You can work your way back up or do something else. This is it for me, Neal. I don't have anywhere else to go.

NEAL
So, the real question is...who's career is it going to hurt?

DOVE
You know what I'm saying!

NEAL
All night long, you've been telling me to write the truth...see the world clearly. Is that just talk, Dove? Is it just an excuse for all the crummy things we do?

DOVE
It's not a excuse. You know that. I just...! can't lose this job. I can't. There's not much of me left other than this phone and the telex machine. Without them I'd disappear like a wisp of smoke. Do you understand?

NEAL
Sure, I understand. It feels different when you're part of the story.

DOVE
I've never been part of anything.

                    NEAL
          Right. I remember. You're "the little
          man" at the edge of the picture.
          Always watching. Never caring at all.

Angry, Dove stands up and moves towards Neal.

                    DOVE
          And who am I supposed to care
          about? Every beggar on the street?
          Do you have any idea of what I've
          seen and walked away from in my
          life? Children...sick and starving
          with sunken eyes and rust-red hair
          coming off in patches from their
          skin. A woman shivering with
          malaria, dying for want of a grain
          of quinine. A man in Ethiopia
          about to be shot...his hands tied,
          his eyes pleading to me as if I
          could save him. And those are just
          the things I've seen. What about
          the daily dose of death and
          disaster that spews out of the
          telex? We have too much news
          today. Too much to really care.
          What can I do about the situation?
          What can anyone do but walk
          outside and howl at the moon?

                    NEAL
          But you were involved with this
          particular incident.

                    DOVE
          Not directly...

The word collapses in his mouth. He turns away.

                    DOVE
          I always knew there'd be a moment
          like this. A time when I'd have
          to choose. I've been waiting for
          it. Waiting for most of my life.
          But now that it's here, I must
          admit...I'm disappointed.

                    NEAL
          What do you mean?

                    DOVE
          I was hoping for something a bit
          more noble. Stylish. A firing
          squad on the edge of a forest.
                              (more)

                    DOVE (Cont'd)
          Men aiming their rifles while I
          flicked away the cigarette and
          said "No, I'm not going to..."
                    (gestures)
          Whatever.

                    NEAL
          Rebel Armies Deep Into Chad.

                    DOVE
          What?

                    NEAL
          My own little fantasy.

                    DOVE
          It's hard to feel noble when you're
          surrounded with secondhand furniture
          and mosquitoes squashed on the wall.

The phone starts to ring. It's London. For few seconds
neither man moves, and then Dove crosses the room.

                    NEAL
          What are you going to do? Dove?

Dove picks up the phone.

                    DOVE
          Hello, Simon. Richardson-Dove
          here. I've got a story for you.
          No, I'm...I'm home. I can't use
          the telex. You ready? Ready to go?
          Dateline, Nairobi. The...
                    (A Beat)
          The continent of Africa broke off
          from its foundation today and began
          to float north towards Europe and
          the United States. Birds screamed,
          the earth shuddered, as long vines
          trailed through the grey Atlantic
          water.
                    (firmly)
          No, I'm not drunk. I've got a
          story, but I'm not ready to send
          it out. Remember our stringer in
          Uganda? The one who sent out that
          piece about the guerrillas? Yes,
          well, he mentioned a village and
          I let it go slip through and the
          army went up there and destroyed
          the whole place. Yes, it...Yes,
          we're going to write about it!
                              (more)

                    DOVE (Cont'd)
          I know what it means...No, it's...
          Certainly not...It's my job, Simon.
          My decision...All right. Yes...Yes
          ...Call you in the morning.

Dove hangs up the phone.

                    NEAL
          What did he say?

                    DOVE
          He wanted to know if he was going to
          get blamed for anything.

                    NEAL
          That's all?

                    DOVE
          He said it was a good story.

                    NEAL
          Christ!

                    DOVE
          Everyone's dead or missing. All
          gone. All lost. And it's a good
          story.

Neal watches Dove.
                    NEAL
          Dove?...Dove?

Resolved, Dove looks up at Neal.

                    DOVE
          So, tell me...how do we begin?

                    BLACKOUT

PIRATES

When my son was in elementary school, he came home from the library clutching an illustrated history of pirates. I read the book and encountered the story of the pirate Anne Bonny, her lover "Calico Jack" Rackham and her fellow pirate, Mary Read. The main source of information about Anne, Jack and Mary comes from a 1724 book titled A *General History of the Robberies and Murders of the most notorious Pyrates* that was written by a pseudonymous author named Captain Charles Johnson. The captain's book is lurid mixture of facts embellished with stories that can't be verified.

As a playwright, I watched the rehearsals of my own plays and observed the way that actors shaped a role. It made me conscious of the artifice - the playfulness of theater. And once you're aware of performances on stage, you become more sensitive to the roles that all of us perform in real life. Although pirates did kill and enslave people, it was in their interest to exaggerate their own reputations so that they could board and loot boats without the danger of an actual battle. Looking and acting like a bloodthirsty pirate captain was often more performance than reality.

As I began writing scenes for a play about pirates, the idea of "doubling" roles on stage gave me the idea of a two-level plot - one set in a contemporary college and the other set in the 18th Century Caribbean. Doubling some of the roles dramatized the ironies inherent in our modern lives. We dream of waving a pirate sword, but have to attend committee meetings.

The other factor shaping the play was language. I studied several books of eighteenth century slang and created a private dictionary of expressions and swear words. The bold and colorful pirate language undercut the bland phrases that routinely are used in academic life.

Pirates premiered at the South Coast Rep with a theatrical pirate ship on stage. Five years later it was preformed a much small theater with set consisting of plywood cubes and a few ropes hanging from the ceiling.

In theater, less can be more. The most glorious pirate ships are the ones that appear in our imagination.

***

PIRATES was given its world premiere by the South Coast Repertory (David Emmes, Producing Artis Director) in Costa Mesa California on January 11, 1991. It was directed by Martin Benson. The scenic designer was Marjorie Bradley Kellogg. The cast was as follows:

Jack Rackham/Nathan Taylor......Robert Sicular

Anne Bonney......Katherine Cortez

Helen Raymond......Joan McMurtrey

Stuart Crawley/Isaac Fletcher/Porterfield......Richard Doyle

Michael Dobbs/Captain/Soldier/Parson......Larry Paulson

Cafeteria Worker/Rebecca Skolnik/Mary Read......Katherine Hiler

PIRATES won first prize in the American Express California Playwright's Competition.

The 1996 production of PIRATES, directed by Brad Hills at The Road Theatre in North Hollywood California, won six Los Angeles Drama-Logue Awards.

PIRATES

A Play

by

Mark Lee

Pirates is set in the Caribbean during the early 18th Century and at a contemporary American university.

Cast: three actors\three actresses. Four of the performers double roles.

Actress #1: Professor Helen Raymond

Actress #2: Anne Bonney

Actress #3: Rebecca Skolnik and Mary Read

Actor #1: "Calico" Jack Rackham and Professor Nathan Taylor

Actor #2: Professor Stewart Crawley, Isaac Fletcher, and Captain James Porterfield

Actor #3: Michael Dobbs, the captain on the seized ship, and the Parson.

PRODUCTION NOTES

This play should move effortlessly from our contemporary world to the 17th century world of the pirates.

The scenes should follow each other in rapid succession. These transitions can be aided by changes in light and the use of sound or music.

Pirates should be staged on a simple geometric set of various levels. Ropes and a sail can be at the upstage edge of the playing area. Furniture and props are carried on as needed.

ACT 1

Music. Sound of a crowd gambling. Lights up as Anne Bonney, an 18th century Irishwoman, enters carrying a bottle of rum. Anne wears a dress with long sleeves, petticoats, and a low-cut bodice.

The music fades. Rackham enters. "Calico" Jack Rackham is an 18th century Englishman who has gotten his nickname from his brightly colored clothes. Jack draws his cutlass and slashes the air.

          JACK
Yes! Yes! Yes!

          ANNE
I think it's safe to say that you nicked them.

          JACK
Not just "nicked" them, Anne. That's a niggling word. I killed them! I crushed them! I pushed my sword in their guts and pulled it up until I heard their ribs crack!

          ANNE
You won their money, Jack. It's the same thing.

Jack puts the cutlass back in his scabbard and pulls out a leather bag full of gold coins. Anne drinks some rum and places the bottle on the top of a barrel.

          JACK
I've had enough of the Bahamas. I'm going to take these gold fellows, buy some slaves and start a sugar plantation in Jamaica. I'll just sit beneath a tree and watch them sweat.

          ANNE
You don't have enough gold for a plantation. Besides, you're going to be splitting the money two ways.

Jack puts the gold back into his waistcoat pocket.

                    JACK
    With who?

                    ANNE
    I stood beside you at the gaming
    table. I told you when to risk and
    when to decline.

                    JACK
    Any tosspot can say "wager this,
    wager that!" But it was my money on
    the table

                    ANNE
    And my dice.

                    JACK
    What?

Anne pulls one dice out of her sleeve and throws it on the floor.

                    ANNE
    Left sleeve...is a three.

She pulls another dice from her right sleeve.

                    ANNE
    Right sleeve...is a four.

She pulls a set of dice out of her bodice.

                    ANNE
    And the breasts...well, of course,
    that's a seven.

                    JACK
    Well, I'll be damned! False doctors
    for the even and odd. So, that's why
    you kept leaning over the table.

Jack kisses her and laughs.

                    JACK
    I owe you some gold for chousing
    those swabbers. But not half. Not
    close to half.

                    ANNE
    You wouldn't have won without me.

                    JACK
               (raising his fist)
          Shut it up, Anne. I'm warning you.
          Or I'll make you sing "Oh, be
          joyful" on the other side of your
          mouth.

                    ANNE
          What if I told the other men that
          you were a sharper?

Jack draws his cutlass and points it at her.

                    JACK
          And what if you died right now for
          being a cutpurse! Believe me, nobody
          would care. Some of the mad ones
          would buy your body just to watch
          the sharks eat a Englishwoman.

                    ANNE
          Irish...woman.

                    JACK
          They'd tie a rope around your neck,
          take you out in the bay and chomp!
          There goes your feet! Chomp! There
          goes your legs!

He's pointing the cutlass at her face. Anne lightly pushes it away and approaches him.

                    ANNE
          But that won't happen, Jack. We're
          going to be partners.

                    JACK
          Partners? With you? What do you
          think am? Some greenhead noddy
          boy? A county Harry?

                    ANNE
          Not at all. You're clever, Jack...in
          your way. Clever enough to be cautious.

Jack places his sword in its scabbard.

                    JACK
          I'm clever enough not to give my gold
          to someone I've only known for a
          fortnight. Let's stop this talk and
          play rantum scanrum.
                                             (MORE)

He grabs her from behind.

                    JACK
Unrig and pull out your dairies.

                    ANNE
Do you want to be rich? So plump in the pocket that you really could buy that plantation?

                    JACK
Of course I do. But I can't do that if I give my gold away.

She pulls away from him, holding the bag of gold. Jack realizes that she's picked his pocket.

                    ANNE
We're going to use that gold to get a boat and crew.

                    JACK
What crew? What are you babbling about?

Anne tosses him the gold and approaches him quickly.

                    ANNE
We're going to be pirates. Buccaneers. We're going to sail through the world and take what we want.

                    JACK
Have you gone mad, Anne? Or maybe you've been drinking that rum the blind man sells down by the harbor.

                    ANNE
You were a pirate before you came to Nassau.

                    JACK
That's right,And I learned that you don't just "sail through the world." Sometimes, the world shoots back. You've got to be careful.

                    ANNE
Yes, I know. Your crew voted you off the ship because you were a coward.

                    JACK
Who told you that? You better stop your clack right now!

ANNE
That's how you got your name...
"Calico" Jack Rackham. You were
famous for your clothes. Not your
bravery.

JACK
I said I was careful. That's all.

Jack sits on a bench and drinks some rum. Anne approaches him.

ANNE
There's twenty men to every woman
on this island. Why do you think I
picked you?

JACK
My gold. My wit. My little pego.
        (smiles at her)
We kept it up nicely last night.

Anne sits beside him.

ANNE
All the men on this island are like
bulls in a pasture...snorting and
sniffing and charging at everything
they see. You're a sly one, Jack.
You know there's more to the world
than what's floating on the
surface. There are things below the
water. Things you can't see.

JACK
I'll tell you what's below the water.
The bones of fools who tried to be
pirates. You can go out for a month and
see nothing but a few fisherman. Pretty
soon, the hull starts to leak and men
start sleeping with a pistol in each
hand. Look at someone cross-eyed and you
end up dancing with Old Mr. Grim.

Anne stands up. She takes a piece of paper out of the purse worn on her waist.

ANNE
Here's a list of the merchant ships
coming to Nassau in the next three
months. I even know what a few of them
are going to be carrying.

JACK
Let me see that.

Jack grabs the list and examines it.

JACK
Where did you get this?

ANNE
The governor of the island has a bed in his office. We've used it to discuss naval affairs.

JACK
I could do this. I could...

ANNE
We'll do it together.

JACK
Right. You stay here. Keep "talking" to the Governor.

ANNE
No, Jack. I'm going with you.

JACK
Don't be simple. No women are allowed on a pirate ship.

ANNE
I know the rule. That's why I'm going to be a man.

JACK
Really? Are you going to grow your own little stones and scepter?
    (clutches his groin)
You can't borrow mine.

ANNE
I already was a man for eight years.

JACK
Right. And I was the Queen of France.

ANNE
My father was lawyer in County Cork. My mother was his servant. He didn't want anyone to know that I was his bastard so he dressed me up as a boy and told everyone that he was training me to become a clerk.

JACK
And you were a boy?

ANNE
For several years. At first, I was too young to question the matter, but then I started to understand. I was playing a boy while others were pretending to be virtuous or brave. Everyone is disguised, Jack. But only a handful of us know it.

JACK
They must have been blind or simple. You've got two breasts as far as I can see.

She grabs the list away from him and slips it into her bodice.

ANNE
By the time I became a woman, we were on our way to the colonies. I lived in Charleston for a few years, then I ran away from my father and came to the islands.

JACK
Look, maybe you can fool the people in Cork, but you can't do that with the mob around here. They're all thieves and sharpers, whores and pirates...looking for the main chance.

ANNE
They'll close their eyes if we give them a reason.

JACK
And what's that?

Anne approaches him.

ANNE
They're going to be scared of you, Jack. You're going to be the kind of man that makes ships give up without a fight.

JACK
I'd like that. I'd like to be famous. But I don't want to be dead and famous.

He pulls away from Anne.

>   JACK
>   The only glory there is for the worms.

>   ANNE
>   I've already found a ship...a
>   brigantine. It's on the south end
>   of the island.

>   JACK
>   And what about a crew?

>   ANNE
>   You can get half your men out in the
>   tavern. Give them a few guineas and
>   they'll follow you down to hell.

>   JACK
>   You're right. They would sign on.
>   Simple bastards.
>   (moves away)
>   I must...I must think on all this.
>   Nothing should be done in haste,
>   but gripping a flea.

Anne approaches Jack.

>   ANNE
>   You're flush in the pocket, Jack.
>   You've got a ship and the men to
>   sail her. If you stay here any
>   longer, you'll die of the fever...
>   (pulls neck cloth)
>   Or the rope.

Jacks hesitates, then nods.

>   JACK
>   We'll do it!

>   ANNE
>   As partners?

>   JACK
>   Agreed. Partners in the Captain's
>   cabin. Partners when it's just us
>   two...alone. And you can't wear
>   your dresses on deck.

>   ANNE
>   I told you. I'm going to be a man.

JACK
But right now, you're a woman. So
lift up the petticoats and let's
see your commodity.

He tries to lift up her dress, but she slaps his hand away.

ANNE
No.

JACK
A new pirate signs the articles of
the ship. But you and I can do it a
different way.

ANNE
Take a look at me, Jack. This is
not what I want to do.

JACK
Who cares if you're smiling or
frowning or if you're half-asleep? A
man doesn't stare at the mantel-
piece when he's poking the fire
down below.

ANNE
You're not poking anything. Understand?

JACK
And why not?

ANNE
We're going to be stealing money
together. That's more intimate than
anything else we can do.

Helen Raymond, an Associate Professor of History, enters. Helen wears contemporary clothes and carries some library books. She watches as Jack removes his belt and cutlass.

JACK
No more jokes. Let's go. I know
you're a peppery wench.

ANNE
All right. If that's what you
want. One last time.

She moves away from him and reaches beneath her petticoats.

ANNE
How do you prefer to do it? Like a
monkey or a dog?

                    JACK
            A dog...of course.

He embraces her from behind. She pulls a knife from beneath her
dress and holds the edge against his neck.

                    ANNE
            Good. You can die like one.

                    JACK
            Don't...Anne...

                    ANNE
            Blood. Your blood. Warm and bright
            red. Flowing down the length of my
            blade. Touching my skin.

                    JACK
            You...you...aren't going to kill me.

                    ANNE
            Of course not. We're partners.

Anne lowers the knife, then walks away from Jack. She slips
the knife into the sheath strapped to her leg.

                    ANNE
            Hurry up, Jack. You better talk to
            the men before they get too drunk
            to listen. Go on.
                    (glances at him)
            Go on.

Jack gathers up his belt and sword.

                    JACK
            You're a mad one, aren't you?

                    ANNE
            I like the word...ambitious.

Jack starts to walk away, then stops.

                    JACK
            They're going to know my name?

                    ANNE
            Promise.

Jack exits. We hear music as Anne crosses the stage and picks up
the bottle of rum. Anne drinks the rum, then extends her hand
-- offering the bottle to Helen.

Suddenly, Anne turns and exits. The music fades as Nathan Taylor, an Associate Professor of History, enters. (This should the same actor who played Jack Rackham)

                NATHAN
I got your note, Helen. Helen?

Helen stops fantasizing and turns to face Nathan.

                HELEN
Oh...hello, Nathan.

                NATHAN
And the answer is "yes, yes, yes." I will escort you to the Basically Bach concert on Friday night.

                HELEN
My note didn't mention Bach at all.

                NATHAN
How about something more downscale? Beer and tequila at the Ugly Toad?

                HELEN
No Bach. No toads. I've got to grade 47 term papers on the French Revolution.

                NATHAN
Just toss them down a staircase. The ones that go the farthest get an "A."

                HELEN
I think I'll actually read them this time.

                NATHAN
It's my divorce, isn't it? That's why you don't want to go out with me. You think I don't understand women. Well, nobody understands women these days. But we're trying.

Helen moves away from Nathan.

                HELEN
I ran into Professor Goldman in the hallway this morning. He mentioned something about going to France for a conference.

NATHAN
Lucky bastard. He'll be eating *pate de fois gras* while we're gagging on meatloaf in the cafeteria.

HELEN
He was on the Search Committee with you and Stewart Crawley.

NATHAN
Our esteemed department chairman.
      (crosses himself)
Hallowed be thy name.

HELEN
I want to take Goldman's place.

NATHAN
Why? You don't have to. You've got tenure, Helen. As of what...three weeks ago?

HELEN
Three weeks. Two days.
      (checks watch)
Forty-seven and a half minutes.

NATHAN
They can't fire you unless you show up drunk and perform a striptease for the Freshman class. So relax and stop volunteering for everything.

HELEN
We're going to be hiring a new professor. I want to be part of the decision.

NATHAN
The whole thing's a waste of time. You should be working on your book about pirates.

Nathan inspects one of her library books.

NATHAN
This stuff is great. You've got peg legs. Parrots. Pieces of eight. It's really macho research.

HELEN
There were women pirates, too. A well-known one named Anne Bonney.

NATHAN
A historian writing about pirates is like a zoologist writing about large carnivores. It's the kind of thing that can get you on talk shows. God, I'd love to be on a talk show.

Helen takes the book away from Nathan.

HELEN
For six years, I've smiled serenely and kept my opinions to myself.

NATHAN
Then you got tenure...

HELEN
That's right. Now it's time to do something. Bring some people to this department who can inspire the students. Get them thinking.

NATHAN
That's always dangerous.

HELEN
Don't you want to be department chairman?

NATHAN
I never said that.

Helen approaches him.

HELEN
It might be possible if we brought in some new people. You'd get a secretary, more money, and grad students laughing at your jokes during faculty sherry hour.

NATHAN
I'd abolish sherry hour. Have a faculty vodka hour.

HELEN
Sounds good to me.

NATHAN
We've got to be careful. That's all. Remember...I'm "Amiable Nathan" and you're "Hard-working Helen." Stewart likes us that way.

                    HELEN
          He has to know how I feel about the
          situation.

                    NATHAN
          Don't say "feel." Stewart thinks
          that's a woman's word. If you like
          one of the job candidates, be
          methodical. Objective.

Lights fade on Nathan. The actor playing Nathan exits. Music as Anne enters wearing pants and a man's shirt.

Helen watches as Anne sits on a crate, removes her shirt, and starts to wrap a long strip of linen around her rib cage binding her breasts.

Anne pulls on her shirt and waistcoat. She puts on a man's hat, then bows to an imaginary woman.

                    ANNE
          My lady...
                    (deep voice)
          My lady...
                    (deeper)
          My lady...

Jack enters, carrying a cutlass in a scabbard.

                    JACK
          What's wrong with you, Anne? Have
          you gone simple?

Anne turns and bows to Jack.

                    ANNE
          Good day, Captain Rackham. I'm your
          new quartermaster.

                    JACK
          God save us.

                    ANNE
          How do you like my boots and breeches?

                    JACK
          Let me see you walk. Go on.

Anne walks across the stage.

                    JACK
          That's no good. No good at all.
          Strap on this cutlass.

He throws her the **sword**.

> JACK
> You've forgotten how it is to be a man.

Anne straps on the cutlass

> ANNE
> Don't worry. I'll remember.

> JACK
> Hurry it up.

> JACK
> Put it around this way. Like this.

Jack pushes the belt around so that the sword is hanging down between her legs. He steps away from her and walks like a woman.

> JACK
> A mort walks like she's squeezing butter between her legs. A man walks square-footed.

Anne tries to imitate him. Jack kicks her legs wider.

> JACK
> Square-footed.

He grabs the sword that's hanging between her legs.

> JACK
> Like he's got something hanging there.

> ANNE
> (pulling away)
> Some do and some don't.

She walks again. Jack shakes his head.

> JACK
> A mort moves her hands like a mouse nibbling at the cheese. A man moves his hands large...like he's swinging something.
> (demonstrates)
> You! Climb the foremast! Step lively!
> (turns to Anne)
> Now, you try. Easy now. Take your time.

Jack watches Anne. She hesitates, then draws her sword.

                    ANNE
          Climb the foremast, you bracket-faced
          gotch-gutted son of a whore!

Jack reacts, then exits. Spotlight on Anne as she moves forward. Still holding the sword, she runs through the basic fencing positions.

                    ANNE
          I remember when my father taught me how
          to use a sword. We went out just
          after sunrise to the woods below the
          river. It was the first time he ever
          smiled at me. First time he ever called
          me Anne instead of "Here, boy. Copy
          this, boy." We practiced all that
          summer. Lunge. Parry. Riposte. Our
          steel clanging together like a black-
          smith's shop while the morning dew
          flashed off the leaves. Then one
          September day, we were practicing and
          then we were fighting and then we were
          trying to kill each other. Lunging.
          Slashing away until I cut him on the
          chin. Blood. My father's blood. Red
          drops like jewels on the green grass.
          "That's enough," he told me. "You're
          learned your lesson."

Anne exits. Lights up on Nathan watching Helen.

                    NATHAN
          Hello? Earth to Helen! Come in, please!

                    HELEN
          I'm sorry. I've just been preoccupied
          late. I've stopped working on my
          book...working on anything.

                    NATHAN
          You need to expand your social life.
          That's all.

                    HELEN
          I need to get on the search
          committee. Is it possible?

                    NATHAN
          It would be good to have at least one
          woman on the committee...and you're
          the only one in the department.

                    HELEN
          I guess I qualify.

                    NATHAN
          Let me talk to Stewart. I think I
          can maneuver it.

                    HELEN
          I want to read all the *vitaes*
          you've received and the notes of
          your discussions.

                    NATHAN
          We've already done the drudge work. Last
          month, we winnowed it down to two
          candidates...a young man from Cornell
          and a woman from Columbia University.
          They're both going to deliver papers
          at the colloquium on Saturday.

                    HELEN
          Good. We'll listen to their
          speeches, ask a million questions,
          and make the right choice.

                    NATHAN
          Tactfully.

                    HELEN
          Decisively.

                    NATHAN
          We'll see.

The lights change. Music. Nathan exits. Anne enters carrying a
flintlock pistol and stares downstage at another ship.
Helen moves across the stage. She sits and watches Anne.

                    ANNE
          Dawn on the ocean. Mare's-tail clouds near
          the edge of the horizon as the sun burns up from
          the water. Waves falling. White scud slapping
          against the bow as our brig sails out of a
          cove and a man on the main yard shouts: "A
          ship! A ship! On the leeward side!"
                    (to the crew)
          Keep down. I want every man hidden. Their
          lookout sees us, but they don't know
          who we are. Load the cannon. Prime the
          cartridges. Set the tackle free.
                    (MORE)

                    ANNE
             (looks forward)
     It's a galleon. As plump and slow as a
     rich woman on a London street. Red-
     painted sails. Gold lilies on the
     stem post and the stern. Pitching
     and hogging as she rides over each wave.
             (to the crew)
     Close...Closer...Stay directly behind
     her, helmsman. The captain's on the
     thwart. He's waving at us...the
     fool. He wants to know where we're
     from.
             (to the crew)
     Ready? Everybody ready?
             (looks forward)
     Hello there! Yes!
             (draws a pistol)
     WE'RE FROM THE SEA!

Anne fires the pistol, then exits. Helen picks up a cafeteria tray and cross the stage. Professor Stewart Crawley, the Chairman of the History Department, and Michael Dobbs, a young graduate student, enter and approach her.

                    STEWART
     Helen! We've been looking for you!

                    HELEN
     Hello, Stewart.

                    STEWART
     This is Michael Dobbs. One of the job
     candidates.

                    MICHAEL
     Professor Raymond...

                    HELEN
     Hi.

                    STEWART
     God, what a morning. Woke at four o'clock,
     ran six miles, got home and corrected proofs
     for my book. Had breakfast. Yelled at the kids.
     Came here. Wrote half a grant proposal.
     Drove out to get Michael and now I've got to
     finish up my paper for the "19th Century
     Perspectives" conference in Las Vegas. So
     how about you, Helen? What's up? Have you
     picked those FEG-POC books?

Helen watches as Jack Rackham crosses the stage and exits.

STEWART
Helen?

HELEN
Yes?

STEWART
The FEG-POC books? Have you made your choice?

HELEN
Not yet. I've been busy.

Helen sits down and picks up a glass of milk from the tray.

MICHAEL
What's FEG-POC?

HELEN
Female. Ethnic. Gay. People of Color. The Dean wants us to pick some alternative books for the introductory Western Civilization course.

STEWART
The History of Art crowd thought up this plan and rammed it through the Academic Senate. As if we don't have enough things to worry about.

HELEN
I think it's a good idea, Stewart. It's about time we heard from some voices that aren't in the "canon" of history.

STEWART
Really? You didn't say that six months ago.

HELEN
I feel...that is...I have definite reasons...

STEWART
Good! You can tell me later! Right now, the schedule says you've got Michael for an hour, then send him to Nathan for an hour...then I get him back for lunch at Chez Jacques.

MICHAEL
We don't have to go someplace expensive.

STEWART
Of course we do. The school's paying. Wear a tie.

Stewart exits. Michael smiles nervously.

MICHAEL
He's really something.

HELEN
You mean Stewart? Yes, he is... something.

MICHAEL
He's got a lot of energy.

HELEN
You're the one with the energy, Michael. I read your vitae last night. You've already had two articles published. A fellowship. That's very impressive.

MICHAEL
Thank you.

HELEN
Now, you've got to spend an exhausting weekend being shuttled around the campus while all of us see how you fit into our various agendas.

MICHAEL
Stewart wanted to know if I could pitch.

HELEN
Excuse me?

MICHAEL
Pitch... for the department softball team.

HELEN
Yes. Of course. Softball is important. But I want to know about history. Why should we study it at all? What's our goal?

MICHAEL
We need to find out the truth about the past. What really happened.

HELEN
You think that's possible?

MICHAEL
You can do a lot with computers and the new techniques of analysis. When some historians at Harvard wanted to learn about slavery in America...they compared the mortality rates of slaves with the death rates of Northern industrial workers. Turns out that the slaves were healthier and lived longer.

HELEN
I'm sure they were very happy.

MICHAEL
I wasn't saying that.

HELEN
I know, Michael. I'm just wondering if there's any point to such a study. It seems to me that the "facts" about American slavery aren't as important as the myth that came out of it. A myth that still influences the racial attitudes in this country.

MICHAEL
We need to be objective, Professor Raymond. That's all we can do. Historians should be like scientists. Finding qualitative data. Analyzing it. Rejecting what can't be proved. When you get right down to it...history is just a series of facts.

HELEN
Perhaps history is a just a series of people being passionate about something.

MICHAEL
Passionate?

Blackout on Michael and Helen. Lights up. Jack sits upstage and holds a rag over one eye. Anne paces back and forth.

ANNE
It all went tick-rock. Just the way I planned. We stayed dead behind them so their cannon were useless. They had a scatter gun on the stern, but we fired our muskets and they had to crawl on the deck for cover. We got closer. A little closer. Then I sent a man up our bowsprit to hammer a wedge between their rudder and the stern. They couldn't steer. Couldn't do anything. Their sails started flapping like an old man's cheeks while their bow wallowed in the trough of each wave. I stood up, ran to the mast and started shouting: "Throw the grenades! Throw the smoke pots!" Nails and lead shot making them scream. Black sulfur clouds spewing into the air. Then we threw the grappling hooks and pulled ourselves up. Up. Smashing through the windows of the captain's cabin. Cutting and slashing. Firing our pistols. Everything helter-skelter until they threw down their swords and struck the yard!

JACK
So...it went well?

ANNE
Like god's bread melting on a virgin's tongue. How's your eye?

JACK
Bad. Very bad. I would have helped board the **ship,** but a half-blind captain's no good to anyone.

ANNE
Strange, isn't it? Their first shot strikes the bulwark and a splinter hits your eye.

JACK
Any gold on the ship?

ANNE
A handful of doubloons. That's all. But there's logwood. Sugar. Barrels of indigo. We'll sell it to the **smugglers** on Tortuga.

JACK
Good. Very good. All is fish that comes to the net.

He lowers the rag and starts to exit.

JACK
I better go up on deck and tell the men what to do.

ANNE
What about your eye?

JACK
It was ahhh...

ANNE
The left one, Jack.

JACK
It's much better.

Isaac Fletcher calls to them:

FLETCHER
Rackham! Are you hiding down here! Who the...

JACK
ANNE
It's Fletcher. Isaac Fletcher. That maggotty bag of guts. He was your idea for the crew.

Isaac Fletcher enters. (Fletcher should be the same actor that played Stewart Crawley)

FLETCHER
I'm surprised that you're not down in the hold. Mewling and puking like a little bantling.
    (to Jack)
I should have listened when they said you had milk in your belly.

JACK
I...I had a splinter In my eye. The left one.

FLETCHER
Did you now? That's a clever little splinter if it keeps you from harm.

ANNE
Get back to work, Fletcher.

FLETCHER
God's mercy! It's our quartermaster! We all wondered where you were... hiding down in the Captain's cabin. Then, the minute we see a ship, you're up on the bow giving orders like a Lord.

ANNE
You heard me.

FLETCHER
I'm not some hornless calf to lead about. I've sacked towns and taken ships, sworn my blood on a dozen pirate codes. I know the laws of the brotherhood.

ANNE
Got sand in your ears, Fletcher? Can't you hear me?

JACK
We'll talk on this tomorrow.

Fletcher points his finger at Anne.

FLETCHER
Cats. Brats. Witch and whore. You're a woman!

ANNE
I just took a ship. Go and count your share.

FLETCHER
That's what the rest of crew thinks. Greedy fools. You could be the devil himself as long as you find them things to steal.

ANNE
But you don't agree.

FLETCHER
I don't take orders from a bitch. Damn the crew. I want you off this ship at the first sight of land.

Anne turns away from Fletcher.

JACK
Anne...! mean, Andrew...! I mean...

ANNE
Are you sure I'm a woman?

FLETCHER
As sure as the nose on my face!

Anne draws her pistol and points it at Fletcher's head.

ANNE
Take a good look at me, Fletcher.

FLETCHER
I...don't...

ANNE
Take a very good look at my face.
My eyes. The little black hole at
the muzzle of this gun. Tell me
what you see, Fletcher? Answer me!

FLETCHER
You're...you're a man...sir.

ANNE
Good. You're beginning to see.

She motions with the gun and Fletcher exits. Anne turns to Jack.

ANNE
Now, get down on deck and tell the
crew to lower the sails. We're
bound for Jamaica!

Anne and Jack exit. A sail is lowered and it becomes a screen. We see a slide of a 17th century sailing ship. Lights up as Helen enters and begins to give a history lecture.

HELEN
Before we begin our examination of
the French Revolution, I'd like to
talk about one more aspect of the
early eighteenth century.

We see a slide of some pirates.

HELEN
Pirates...the people who attacked
colonial shipping in the New World.

A slide of a sailing ship.

                    HELEN
          Pirates called themselves "The
          Brethren" and considered themselves
          "artists" of the sea. They chose their
          leaders by majority vote and prohibited
          flogging...unlike the British navy.

A slide that shows a pirate code.

                    HELEN
          Each crew obeyed its own Pirate
          Code...a set of written laws called
          the "articles" of the ship. The
          articles contained basic rules of
          conduct as well as a sort of
          "workman's compensation" ...that
          required the payment of twenty gold
          pieces for the loss of an arm or leg.

A slide of pirates drinking.

                    HELEN
          Pirates saw themselves as belonging
          to an informal collective that was
          in complete opposition to authority.
          They even tried to organize their
          own country called Libertatia on
          the island of Madagascar.

A slide of pirates fighting.

                    HELEN
          These are some of the facts about
          pirates. And yet, it is the legend that
          fascinates us ...the vision of sailing
          your own ship through the world...
          unrestrained and free. We need to
          remember that there are two kinds of
          history: the facts of what happened and
          the myth that grows out of those facts.

We see a slide of Delacroix's Liberty Leading the People.

                    HELEN
          Both histories can be seen in this
          painting by Delacroix called
          "Liberty Leading the People."
          We see men with guns...the "facts" of
          the French revolution...marching
          through Paris with the idealized
          vision of freedom. It is the myth
          of the past that inspires us...
          guides us...leads us forward.

Sound. Helen moves upstage. She watches as Jack and Fletcher enter holding a British sea captain. They force the captain on his knees and pull him over a bench. Anne follows them and speaks to the crew of a seized ship:

                    ANNE
        When we "Brethren" seize a ship, we
        always search the Captain's cabin.
        Sometimes, we find gold. Sometimes, we
        find wine. This time we found a cat.

She displays a cat-o'-nine-tails: a whip made of nine knotted cords attached to a handle.

                    ANNE
        Looking at the backs of some of the
        men on this ship, I see that this cat
        has been a very active creature. It
        seems that your captain likes to flog
        someone before he drinks his morning tea.

She slaps the whip on the deck.

                    CAPTAIN
        Mercy! For godsake, mercy!

                    ANNE
        Your captain wants mercy...that
        holy virtue. But did he give you
        mercy when your wrists were tied to
        the capstan and the cat came howling
        through the air?

She slaps the whip again.

                    ANNE
        So, tell me...who wants to introduce
        this captain to his own cat? Who
        wants to take the clinkers off their
        wrists and join our congregation
        of the sea? It's a dangerous life
        ... I'll grant you that. But you
        won't be whipped for a handful of
        shillings. Join us. This is your
        only chance. Who wants to sign his
        mark upon the captain's back?

Blackout. The men exit, leaving Anne onstage. Lights up as Rebecca Skolnik steps out of the shadows. She approaches Helen -- who has just finished her lecture.

                    REBECCA
        Professor Raymond?

HELEN
The term papers are in a box outside my office.

REBECCA
Excuse me?

HELEN
A box. They're in alphabetical order.

REBECCA
I'm Rebecca Skolnik from Columbia University. I'm here for the colloquium and a job interview.

HELEN
I'm...I'm sorry.

REBECCA
Don't worry about it. I'm not exactly dressed like a Ph.D. I probably should have bought a suit for interviews, but I just couldn't do it. They always have these pinstripes and padded shoulders... And they keep trying to sell you these little ruffly blouses to wear with them. It's like telling the world..."hey, I may dress like a corporate banker, but the ruffly blouse means I've got a vagina."

HELEN
Yes, I suppose...

REBECCA
I might have fewer problems with all ruffles or all pinstripes, but the way it is now...fuck it.

HELEN
Ahhh...yes.

REBECCA
I liked your lecture. That stuff about pirates was interesting.

HELEN
Well, I hope the students thought so. Someone once wrote that history is "a love-song celebrating the triumph of life over death." (MORE)

HELEN
On this campus, history is...two tests and a term paper.

REBECCA
You have to keep talking about people. That's what makes it interesting.

HELEN
What kind of people?

REBECCA
Everybody! All of them shouting and laughing and fighting and preaching and having orgasms!

HELEN
Not...so...loud.

REBECCA
Dark caves on the island of Crete. A Minoan priestess standing at an altar with snakes twisted around her arms. A Celtic woman fighting with a bronze sword. A Roman weaver bent over her loom.

Sound of a flute. Anne moves upstage.

ANNE
A midwife. A bawd. A herb doctor.

REBECCA
A Queen with a hawk on her black leather glove.

ANNE
A little girl working as a chimney sweep...crawling through the soot towards a patch of sky.

REBECCA
A factory worker in a crinoline petticoat. A miner dragging her sack of coal. A woman with a golf club.

ANNE
A woman with an ivory fan.

REBECCA
A woman at Dachau with a shaved head and a striped uniform. A woman with a paintbrush. A woman with a gun.

Rebecca exits. Anne walks upstage and looks forward.

          ANNE
A woman at the wheel of a pirate ship watching the sails luff and snap and fill with the wind. White scud on the slate gray water. Sea birds keening *in* the sky. And we're sailing...I'm sailing...anywhere I please.

Anne remains upstage. Nathan enters carrying an athletic bag and a squash racquet.

          NATHAN
Helen! Wait up! Why don't you come to the gym with me? We can breathe heavily. Work up an attractive sweat.

          HELEN
With me, it's not attractive.

Nathan swings the racket.

          NATHAN
I've started playing squash. I thought ...if I played squash and wore tweed all the time...people might think I went to a better school.

          HELEN
Good luck. It's worth a try.

She starts to walk away.

          NATHAN
I had coffee with Stewart Crawley this afternoon. He was really annoyed. He said you challenged him in front of Michael Dobbs.

          HELEN
I only told him that I liked the idea of an alternative syllabus.

          NATHAN
Come on, Helen. If you really want to guide this department, you've got to be careful. Keep your opinions to yourself.

          HELEN
I'm not like you, Nathan.

NATHAN
What does that mean? Do you think I came out of the womb smiling and agreeing with everybody?

HELEN
I don't know. I'd have to ask your mother.

NATHAN
People don't want history these days...or historians. They can't deal with any idea that can't be shouted on a car phone.

HELEN
We can fight against that. If we make a choice...

NATHAN
Just play the game.
        (swings racket)
All right?

Nathan exits. Helen crosses the stage, then stops and watches Anne walk downstage. Isaac Fletcher enters.

ANNE
Take the helm, Fletcher. And keep her northwest. We'll anchor tonight at Magdalene Cove.

FLETCHER
There's coral reefs outside that cove. We might split the hull.

ANNE
Not if we send out the longboat and take soundings first.

FLETCHER
We didn't choose you quartermaster.

ANNE
What of it?

FLETCHER
We didn't choose Rackham either.

ANNE
It was our ship, Fletcher.

FLETCHER
But not your crew.

ANNE
Pipe the men up. Ask them how much gold is in their sea chests and who won it for them. They can show their hands.

FLETCHER
We didn't pick you. That's all I'm saying. You're not in the brotherhood.

Fletcher exits. Angry, Anne looks around for Jack.

ANNE
Jack? Jack Rackham?

Jack enters and bows to Anne.

JACK
Master Bonney...

ANNE
I want Fletcher off the ship when we reach land.

JACK
That's not wise, Anne. He's the one white bird in the mob of crows. The crew hates him. Take him away and they might hate you.

ANNE
I've taken twelve ships!

JACK
All the more reason not to change things. Fair and softly goes far in a day.

Jack starts to walk away.

ANNE
Where's the boy?

JACK
What boy?

ANNE
Matthew Read. The one who signed on after we seized the English ship.

JACK
You mean that little bantling? He's down in the hold. I think. Helping with the food.

Jack approaches Anne.

                     ANNE
Is the cook with him?

                     JACK
Why do you want to know?

                     ANNE
I want to talk to him alone.

Jack smiles and tries to embrace her.

                     JACK
If you're feeling ruttish, then you can do it with me. My dear nug. My little love...

Anne moves away from him.

                     ANNE
No.

                     JACK
You liked to be tupped when we were in Nassau. Four times that first night. I'm no different than I was, Anne. I can swear to that.

                     ANNE
Well I'm different. Everything's back ways now.

                     JACK
Aye. The world's turned around. Remember that last ship? The galleon? The captain lowered his flag without a fight! He'd heard of me. He knew my name.

                     ANNE
Isn't that what you wanted?

                     JACK
It's like we're walking on the top spar. The sea's flat. The sun's warm. There's nothing to worry about unless we stumble.

                     ANNE
That not going to happen.

                    JACK
          The crew knows that you're a woman,
          but Isaac Fletcher is the only one who
          croaks about it. The men will follow
          you, Anne. They'll take any ship you
          want as long as you...

                    ANNE
          Keep my breasts tied flat.

                    JACK
          Amen. That's what I'm saying. If you
          play rantum scantum with that scullery
          boy, It just might break the glass.

Anne and Jack exit as Helen and Rebecca enter. Rebecca
carries a blanket, two plastic cups and a bottle of wine.
Helen carries some sandwiches.

                    REBECCA
          So, tell me...did you ever seduce
          one of your students?

                    HELEN
          Of course not. That's very
          irresponsible.

                    REBECCA
          You did! Didn't you? I can tell.

Rebecca spreads the blanket and both women sit.

                    HELEN
          I knew we shouldn't have had this
          job interview in the park. It's too
          easy to get distracted from the agenda.

                    REBECCA
          Don't worry about the agenda. I'll
          give you all the facts, but that
          doesn't mean we can't have a
          conversation. I remember reading a
          poem about a march of mill workers
          in Lawrence, Massachusetts. One of
          the women carried a sign that read:
          "We need bread...
                    (raises the glass)
          And roses, too."

                    HELEN
          Yes. Yes, I guess you're right.

Helen drinks some wine and smiles.

REBECCA
So, how did you meet this handsome student? Did you ask him to stay after class?

HELEN
He wasn't really my student. I was a teaching assistant in my fifth year of graduate school. He was a 19-year-old sophomore. Smart. Funny. Wild for knowledge. He reminded me of why I went to college in the first place.

REBECCA
Was he good in bed?

Startled, Helen opens a manila folder.

HELEN
Let's talk about your curriculum vitae. You're got a magna cum laude. Two articles. What did you do for Ernst Viltner?

REBECCA
I was a research assistant. Nothing important.

HELEN
It's very important. Ernst Viltner is considered to be God in bifocals around here. Is there any way you could get a recommendation?

REBECCA
What about this talk I'm supposed to be giving at the colloquium? Are you and the other two professors going to be evaluating that?

HELEN
Don't say anything controversial. Just be modest...with footnotes.

REBECCA
But then it wouldn't be my paper. My ideas.

HELEN
I don't want you to step on any toes. That's all. Play a role for few days and then you'll get what you want.

                    REBECCA
What I want is not to play a role at
all.

                    HELEN
That's what we all want, but it's
not always possible. Don't you
understand...

                    REBECCA
More wine? Have some more wine.
Did you always want to be a college
professor? Was that your plan?

                    HELEN
I'm supposed to be interviewing
you, Rebecca.

                    REBECCA
Come on, be a role model. Tell me
that you always wanted to teach.

                    HELEN
When I was younger, all I knew is
that I wanted to...stride.

                    REBECC
What?

                    HELEN
You know...stride. Like those
actresses in the 1940's films.
Katharine Hepburn. Barbara Stanwyck.
Rosalind Russell. They were always
striding into rooms. Being sure of
themselves. Taking charge.

                    REBECCA
Until Cary Grant showed up.

                    HELEN
Even then, they kept...striding.
And I tried to be that way as I
marched through graduate school and
my first job at this little college
in Pennsylvania. I wanted to do
everything then. Be everything.
I invited the students to my home,
started petitions about various
issues, wrote, challenged, stirred
up the waters until my contract
wasn't renewed at the end of the year.

REBECCA
What did you do?

HELEN
I managed to get a one-year contract at another university and then another job and then another. I became a nomad scholar. A member of the "part-time instructional staff." At my last job, there wasn't any health insurance. I got in a car accident and ended up in the emergency room with the other welfare patients, waiting my turn while I bled on the floor.

REBECCA
How did you get a job here?

HELEN
It was an academic miracle. A friend dropped out of a post-doc fellowship at Harvard and she was able to slip me into the position. I wrapped myself in the cloak of the Ivy League, got this job and held it. For six years, I've volunteered for everything. Wrote articles. Kept my opinions to myself.

REBECCA
That doesn't sound much better than being "a nomad."

HELEN
But it worked! Now, I've got tenure. I'm going have this baby, bring the child to faculty meetings, and change everything.

REBECCA
I guess it's worth it. But six years is a long time.

Helen stands and walks away from the blanket.

HELEN
I was teaching. Thinking. I started my book about pirates.

REBECCA
I'd like to read it.

The light fades. Rebecca exits. Spotlight on Helen.

                    HELEN
        I'm having some problems with the
        project. It's kind of a disaster.
        I read about this woman pirate...
        Anne Bonney...and then I started to
        fantasize about her. Think up
        little stories for inspiration.
        Now, I can't control it anymore.

Anne enters. She's carrying a lantern and smoking a pipe.

                    HELEN
        A year ago, I could picture her in
        my mind and manage the whole thing.
        I'd think...turn...walk away from
        the mast...and she would obey me.
            (Anne obeys her)
        Nowadays, this daydream has its
        own power. I'll see her doing
        something like...smoking a pipe.
        And I'll think: "No! Don't do that!
        I don't want you to smoke!" But
        she'll do it anyway.

Anne puffs a circle of smoke in Helen's direction.

                    HELEN
        It's as if I was a novelist who came
        downstairs one morning and discovered
        that her words had rearranged
        themselves upon the page. I can't control
        it. I can only watch what happens...

Helen exits. Sound of water sloshing against the side of the ship as Anne takes the lantern and walks downstage.

Matthew Read sits on a crate, peeling potatoes with his back to the audience.

                    ANNE
        Hello, Matthew. The cook said I'd
        find you here.

Matthew throws a peeled potato into a cooking pot. He pulls another potato out of a gunny sack and resumes peeling.

                    ANNE
        You look angry. Does it go against your
        grain to peel potatoes? Well, then
        don't peel them if it doesn't suit your
        humor. It's the cook's job anyway.

Matthew keeps peeling potatoes. Anne circles the boy.

ANNE
You're a gentleman, aren't you? I knew that when I first saw you walk across the deck. It's your manner. Your hands. The way you speak. So, tell me...why were you on that English ship? Were you pressed off the streets of London or was it something else? Were you a trimmer? A canticle who nicked the parish silver?

Matthew tosses a potato into the pot.

ANNE
There's nothing wrong with a gentleman pretending to be a sailor. But sometimes, the mask must be removed. I've...seen you in my sleep. Within my dreams. I was alone in my cabin when you entered and sat up upon my bed. And I took your hand and kissed your palm and traced the lines of your life with my lips and tongue.

Matthew raises his knife. Helen enters in the shadows.

ANNE
Yes. I see the dagger, Matthew. You don't have to cut me. Not yet. You think I'm some nazy cove who wants to box the Jesuit with you. But believe me...there are masks under masks in this world. My name is Anne Bonney. I'm a woman.

Matthew drops the knife, stands up and starts to laugh. He spins around, pulls off his cap and we see that "Matthew" is also a woman --- Mary Read. (This should be the same actress who plays Rebecca Skolnik)

MARY
So am I!

Anne and Mary exit. It's Saturday morning. Lights up on Helen as Nathan enters and offers her a plate full of doughnuts.

NATHAN
Doughnut?

HELEN
No, thank you.

NATHAN
You really should take one. They're an integral part of the colloquium. In fact, these doughnuts have been bought with a grant from the National Endowment for the Humanities.

HELEN
You mean they're humane doughnuts.

NATHAN
No, just free ones. Go on. Take one.

Helen takes one of the doughnuts.

NATHAN
Look, I know that we were going to pick somebody. That was the plan. But I think Stewart is leaning towards Michael Dobbs.

HELEN
So what? We've got two votes on the committee.

NATHAN
I don't want to make anybody angry. Understand? I'm a skater. Gliding through life. Watching out for holes in the ice.

Helen sees Rebecca walking across the stage.

HELEN
Good. You can take my doughnut.

She put the doughnut back on the plate and walks away.

HELEN
Hey, Rebecca...

Rebecca stops and Helen approaches her.

HELEN
We've got about a hour before the colloquium starts. Let's go to one of the empty classrooms and I'll take a look at your paper.

REBECCA
I'd rather not, Helen. You might want to change something and then we'd have an argument.

HELEN
I'll just make suggestions. That's all. You don't have to accept them.

REBECCA
It's not fair to the other candidate.

HELEN
None of it is fair. Don't you realize that? You've got to watch what you say.

REBECCA
I wrote a paper. I'm going to read it.

Rebecca exits. Helen starts to follow her, but Stewart enters. He carries a Styrofoam cup of coffee.

STEWART
Helen! There you are! I saw you in the park yesterday afternoon having a little feast with Dr. Skolnik.

HELEN
It was the scheduled meeting. I decided not to go to a restaurant. I thought I'd save the school some money.

STEWART
Great. No problem. It's just when I came back two hours later, you were still there with her. That's quite an interview.

HELEN
I'm a dedicated member of the search committee.

STEWART
What's this paper of hers going to be about? It's called: "The Lower Frequencies." Sounds like something from the engineering department.

HELEN
I really wouldn't know.

STEWART
You're kind of hostile these days, aren't you?

HELEN
Really? I haven't noticed.

STEWART
I don't expect everyone to like me.
But you're smart enough to realize
what I'm trying to do around here.

HELEN
And just what is that?

STEWART
When I first came to this university, the
history department was falling apart.
Only two people applied to our graduate
program one year... this guy from Taiwan
and a retired train conductor.

HELEN
Then you became chairman.

STEWART
That's right. I found some grants.
Started these conferences. Got rid
of the dead wood and hired some
people who could produce. People
like you.

HELEN
And just what are we producing?
Silly little papers that nobody
wants to read.

STEWART
I didn't make the rules, Helen.
Sometimes, I think this whole
academic system has gone crazy. But
that's the way it is. We don't
really have a choice.

Stewart and Helen exit. Anne and Mary enter.

MARY
My father was a sailor who went off
to the Indies and never returned.
My mother starved for a year, then
she took me down to London to live
with my grandmother. She was a
crump-backed old woman with a face
like a shriveled apple and hands
curled up like a pair of claws. She
hated my mother, but she wanted
someone to keep the family name. A
girl wouldn't do of course, so my
mother dressed me up in breeches
and told everyone that I was a boy.

                    ANNE
          Did your grandmother believe her?

                    MARY
          Indeed. Every Sunday, she'd push her
          claws into a leather sack and pull
          out a crown in honor of my little
          pego. Thanks to god, she died
          before I had to grow a beard.

Anne and Mary sit down on barrels. Mary starts to pick the
lice out of Anne's hair.

                    ANNE
          So, you became Mary again. Mary Read.

                    MARY
          No point to that. My mother died
          and I decided that I didn't want to
          be a bawd or a wet nurse or a
          seamstress. Or a wife...that's a
          combination of the three. So, I put
          on my breeches again, took the
          King's shilling and went to
          Flanders to fight the French.

                    ANNE
          Then, you came back to England and
          became a woman again.

                    MARY
          I've always been a woman.

                    ANNE
          A woman...wearing a disguise.

                    MARY
          I'm not in disguise.

                    ANNE
          A woman...in a man's clothes.

They change places. Anne picks the lice out of Mary's hair.

                    MARY
          These aren't "a man's clothes."
          They're my clothes.

                    ANNE
          But you're pretending to be a man.

                    MARY
          I **suppose**. I don't puzzle my head
          about it.

                    ANNE
          We're women and we're pirates! It's a
          wonder! We're the only ones on the
          sea!

                    MARY
          Who knows? Perhaps half the men out
          there are really women in disguise.

                    ANNE
          Don't be simple.

                    MARY
          You've got drabs pretending to be
          ladies. Ladies dressed up as
          whores. I've seen men of god with
          their hands in a bawd's smocket.
          Men of property without two bits to
          rub together. You know the King?
          "The Great King George?" He's a
          droolin' ninny from what I've heard.
          The devil's a clanker and God's
          asleep. So, what's all the wonder
          about the two of us?

                    ANNE
          The fools don't know they're fools.
          We know who we are.

                    MARY
          Forget all that, Anne. Let's just
          be pirates.

Anne and Mary exit. Stewart enters and addresses the audience.

                    STEWART
          Good morning. I'm Stewart Crawley,
          chairman of the department, and I'd like
          to welcome you to this year's
          colloquium: "New Perspectives on
          History." After our morning speakers read
          their papers and answer questions, we'll
          adjourn for lunch at the student center.
          At one o'clock we'll reconvene in two
          groups for our panel discussions:
          "Japan In The Meiji Era" sponsored by the
          Sony Corporation and "Arabia and the
          Expansion of Islam" sponsored by Exxon.

He looks down at his prepared speech.

STEWART
We historians are an independent breed of scholar. Instead of being influenced by changing fads and fancies, we try to base our opinions on ideas that have been proposed and challenged within the ongoing academic dialogue. This morning we're going to hear the ideas of two young historians: Rebecca Skolnik and Michael Dobbs.

Stewart exits. Michael and Rebecca enter and stand upstage left and upstage right. Michael begins his lecture.

MICHAEL
Anyone studying historical documents begins to notice the recurrence of key words and phrases during a particular period of time.

A slide with the acronym WIFA appears on the sail behind him.

MICHAEL
This initial observation led me to develop what I call the "WIFA" system of Word Incidence Frequency Analysis...a tool that will help historians join the computer age.

Michael freezes as Rebecca speaks to the audience.

REBECCA
There is a church in Rome that shows three levels of faith. On the street level, there are stained-glass windows and wooden pews. But if you walk down some stairs you can find the remains of a Gnostic catacomb. Go deeper still and there is an altar to the sun. We historians need to make a similar journey as we go deeper and look beneath the surface of conventional history.

A slide shows text moving from a manuscript to a computer.

MICHAEL
Using WIFA, a documents are fed into a computer which tabulates the recurrence of each word. This enables us to discover a variety of historical data.

Michael freezes as Rebecca continues her lecture.

> REBECCA
> Many of the Neolithic and Bronze Age cultures in the Mediterranean area were guided by a hierarchy of women priests. Women were seen as the source of that magical power needed to sustain the life of an agricultural society. Eventually, the area was invaded by a variety of patriarchal cultures. These people were hunters and nomads. Cattle Kings and horse lords who worshiped the god of thunder.

We see another slide which shows a bar Graph indicating the use of the word "cod."

> MICHAEL
> For example, here we see the use of the word "cod" per thousand words in American colonial documents from 1520 to 1600 compared to documents from 1600 to 1680. Cod is mentioned more frequently in the later period ...indicating increased interest in this useful fish.

> REBECCA
> In my paper today, I will suggest that this earlier culture was not destroyed by the nomadic invaders. It has remained with us like radio waves broadcast on "a lower frequency." If we listen closely, we can hear their sound.

We see a slide of the acronym WIFA.

> MICHAEL
> Using WIFA, we will be able to present quantitative proof of historical changes. We historians will no longer be held captive in dimly-lit library carrels...clutching our pens as we thumb through moldy manuscripts. Switch on your computers because the study of history has finally entered the Digital Era!

Blackout. Michael exits. Lights up as Helen enters and approaches Rebecca.

                    HELEN
          Where have you been, Rebecca? I've
          been looking for you ever since
          they started the reception.

                    REBECCA
          I was out in the hallway with
          Professor Crawley. We were having
          a discussion.

                    HELEN
          How'd it go?

                    REBECCA
          Is there a plane out of here tonight?

                    HELEN
          Don't leave.

                    REBECCA
          Why not, Helen? Crawley and I
          couldn't agree about anything.
          What's the point of me staying?

                    HELEN
          Because you're not a coward. And
          maybe I'm not one either.

   Nathan approaches them carrying two plastic glasses.

                    NATHAN
          Hey, great paper, Skolnik. It was very...colorful.

   Rebecca touches Helen and exits. Nathan turns to Helen.

                    NATHAN
          What's wrong? Did I say something
          wrong?

                    HELEN
          Not really.

   He hands her one of the glasses.

                    NATHAN
          As a contemporary representative of
          the patriarchal hunting culture, I
          am fulfilling my function by
          hunting down a glass of punch and
          bringing it back to you.

   Helen takes the glass and sips some punch.

HELEN
This tastes terrible.

NATHAN
Oh, god. I've failed to sustain my heritage. I just know I'd never make it in the Neolithic Era.

HELEN
I liked Dr. Skolnik's paper.

NATHAN
So did I. But Stewart hated it. I walked past them in the hallway when they were arguing with each other. Stewart kept saying: "**What** are your sources? What are your sources?" I bet he asks that question before he has sex with his wife.

HELEN
I'm sure that Rebecca...Dr. Skolnik has done the necessary research.

NATHAN
Of course. But that's not the point. Stewart just doesn't believe that she's a "**real**" historian.

Helen and Nathan exit. Isaac Fletcher enters. He watches as Mary enters and crosses the stage.

FLETCHER
Been talking to the Quartermaster?

MARY
That's right.

FLETCHER
So what did "**Master**" Bonney have to say?

MARY
He said that...if we look to our work...we'll be rich in a year.

FLETCHER
And what's your work? Playing catch-fart for the Quartermaster?

MARY
I'm a gunner.

                    FLETCHER
          Right! And I'm the Pope of Rome. A
          little chit like you couldn't shoot
          a cannon in your dreams.

                    MARY
          Man the falls. Swab the barrel.
          Ram home the power bag. Add
          some wadding. Shot and more
          wadding. Prick the cartridge with
          your priming wire. Touch the powder
          with your linstock and...fire!

She starts to walk away.

                    FLETCHER
          It's simple to be a Gunner if no
          one's shooting back at you. I can't
          see you holding your ground when
          there's blood all over the decks.

                    MARY
          It depends whose blood it is.

                    FLETCHER
          What are you chowtering about? Speak
          up. You sound like a mouse in the cheese.

                    MARY
          The sight of your blood might be a
          pleasure.

                    FLETCHER
          Are you challenging me? To a duel?

                    MARY
          A "duel" is for a gentleman. I'll
          just be killing a reechy little
          bastard.

Mary and Fletcher exit. Nathan and Helen enter.

                    NATHAN
          It certainly was a contrast. You've
          Got to admit that. There's Skolnik
          talking about Deborah..."Judge of
          Israel"...while Dobbs drones on about
          logarithms. What is a logarithm
          anyway? It sounds like some sort of
          Catholic birth control.

Michael enters and approaches them.

MICHAEL
What's this about birth control?

NATHAN
Nothing. Really. I think I'll go see if there's anything stronger than punch.

Nathan exits. Michael turns to Helen.

MICHAEL
So, what did you think of my paper?

HELEN
It was concise. Well-organized.

MICHAEL
Do you have any questions regarding my methodology?

HELEN
Not at all. You're very intelligent, Michael. You've worked hard. I just wonder how your "facts" about the past are going to help us make choices about the future. How can they inspire us? Tell us what to do?

MICHAEL
That's not our responsibility.

HELEN
Then whose responsibility is it? Our school's philosophy department is lost in linguistic analysis. Our English department believes that words have no meaning. Our physicists are working on laser death-rays while our political scientists want jobs in the State Department.

MICHAEL
People have to come up with their own values.

HELEN
That's what we've been doing, Michael. I just don't think it's turned out very well.

Michael freezes. Helen watches Anne enter and cross the stage.

ANNE
Mary? Mary!

Mary enters upstage.

MARY
Behind you!

Anne raises her pistol as Mary grabs a rope and swings down to her.

MARY
Hello.

ANNE
You always surprise me.

MARY
Why the pistol? Are you going to shoot at the moon?

Anne slips the pistol into her belt.

ANNE
I have enemies in the crew. You're the only soul I can trust on this whole ship.

MARY
Well, I'm afraid that you're going to lose me. I plan to nick the dory and row to Jamaica.

ANNE
Why? What happened?

MARY
Isaac Fletcher...that parcel of guts and garbage...bullied me into a duel and the whole crew heard about it. I've got to fight him on Sunday or they'll start pecking at me like a flock of crows.

ANNE
Can't you face him?

MARY
No. I can shoot a pistol as well as any man. But we're supposed to fight with cutlasses and I've never been good with any kind of sword. I know...maybe we can duel with cannons at twenty paces.

ANNE
Don't jest about this, Mary. He can't kill me so he's trying to kill you.

MARY
Forget about Fletcher. Let's run away together. We'll wear dresses if you want or keep our breeches on. We'll have some adventures!

ANNE
This is my ship. I'm not giving it up to anyone.

MARY
Who cares about the ship? It's just a lot of wood and tar. Been down in the hold? It's all smutched and rotten and smelling like piss.

ANNE
I'm going to fight.

Anne and Mary exit. Lights up on Helen and Michael.

MICHAEL
Listen, maybe I shouldn't say this, but...

HELEN
Then don't say it, Michael. That's always the best policy.

MICHAEL
Professor Crawley told me something this afternoon. Something rather disturbing. He said that you might vote against me because I was a man.

HELEN
I find that statement very offensive.

MICHAEL
I'm sorry. I apologize. It's just that I've made the final round at four different universities and I've lost out to two women, an African-American man and a bi-sexual Chippewa Indian.

HELEN
We need to respond to past inequalities.

MICHAEL
I agree. But when does it become just another kind of discrimination?

HELEN
It means making things fair.

Anne enters upstage.

> MICHAEL
> Then be fair. That's what I want. If I'm truly the better candidate, then give me the job. I might not match your demographics, but I'll be a first-rate historian.

Michael exits. Helen watches as Fletcher enters and begins to coil some rope.

> ANNE
> So, Fletcher...! understand you're going to fight a duel this Sunday.

> FLETCHER
> That's right. With your own favorite.

> ANNE
> Answer a riddle. How can a dead man fight a duel?

> FLETCHER
> I won't be dead.

Anne approaches him.

> ANNE
> Yes, you will. Because you're going to fight a duel with me on Saturday.

> FLETCHER
> Are you challenging me?

> ANNE
> Unless you're a coward. With you, it's always a chance.

> FLETCHER
> Oh, I'll be there. Don't you worry.

> ANNE
> Good.

She starts to leave, then stops.

> ANNE
> Oh, Fletcher... one more thing. Divide up all your gold before the duel. I don't want any quarrels when you're feeding the sharks.

Anne and Fletcher exit. Nathan enters and approaches Helen.

NATHAN
Where did Skolnik go? I can't find her anywhere.

HELEN
She went back to her hotel. I think.

NATHAN
Some of her lecture was a little strident, but I liked all that "earth goddess beneath the concrete" stuff.

HELEN
Don't joke about this, Nathan. I'm not in the mood.

NATHAN
It's true! I'm not joking at all. I grew up next to this big barley field, but when I came home from college one summer they had dug it all up and built a "Pick 'N' Save" store full of Snoopy get-well cards, fuzzy toilet seat covers... that sort of thing. And I remembered walking through the field as a child, the wind blowing, the barley moving around me like a vast ocean and...oh, my god. I'm being sincere.
    (glances at Helen)
How disgusting. I feel like I'm standing here in my boxer shorts.

HELEN
I like it.

NATHAN
Well, I don't. People need their protective armor. Psychologically, I have knobby knees.

HELEN
Don't you get tired of hiding the way you feel? It's like having to wear a mask all the time.

NATHAN
Everything's hidden. There are secret messages all over the place, but most of us don't know it. See the border around the edge of these name tags?

He points to the name tag that everyone is wearing.

                    NATHAN
          When I handed them out this morning,
          I used a little system. Green is for
          a drone. Blue is for a competitor.
          Red is for someone who can help my
          career.

Helen looks down at her name tag.

                    HELEN
          That means I'm a drone.

                    NATHAN
          I only had three colors.

Stewart enters and approaches them.

                    STEWART
          Hail to thee, fellow thunder worshiper!
          How's your phallic symbol?

                    NATHAN
          I gave it a sabbatical.

                    STEWART
          Ahhh, yes. Such is the life of a
          Cattle King and Horse Lord.

Ahhh, yes.
                    HELEN
          I liked Skolnik's paper.

                    STEWART
          Come on, Helen. The whole thing is
          bogus scholarship and you know it.
          I read your dissertation when you
          were first hired here. It was a
          solid piece of work. You didn't go
          running all over the countryside
          with "Boudicca, Queen of the Celts."

                    HELEN
          It's a new theory. That's all.
          We'll have to study it.

                    STEWART
          No. That's where you're wrong. It's a
          very old-fashioned view of history.
          Throughout the 19th century, historians
          took a single idea and made some grand
          theory to explain the world.
                         (MORE)

                    STEWART
          Usually, it was based around the
          Europeans conquering the lesser
          cultures...a Darwinian progression
          until the white-skinned people were
          triumphant in the end. You don't
          like that, do you? It's offensive.
          But this is the same kind of crap.
          It just substitutes women for the
          "Aryan race."

                    HELEN
          She didn't make up any facts,
          Stewart. All of her ideas were
          based on solid research.

                    STEWART
          It was how she used the research.
          That's the issue. You can't explain
          the past with only one idea. What
          do you think, Nathan?

                    NATHAN
          Me? I think I need to freshen my drink.

He tries to move away, but Helen grabs his arm.

                    HELEN
          What's wrong with having alternative
          views in this department? Why does
          everyone have to agree?

                    STEWART
          We all have to agree about History.
          It's a discipline. A branch of
          knowledge. Not a new religion.

Helen turns away. Ignoring her, Stewart speaks to Nathan.

                    STEWART
          You know, Nathan...the computer stuff
          that Dobbs is doing could generate a
          lot of articles. I bet we could talk
          to IBM and get a some kind of grant.

Anne enters, wearing a sword.

                    ANNE
          To hell with these bastards! Put a
          dagger in their guts!

Startled, Helen drops her glass of punch.

NATHAN
Helen! What's wrong?

Anne moves toward Helen. Crawley leans down to pick up the plastic glass.

STEWART
What happened? Did you have a muscle spasm? Happens to me sometimes.

ANNE
Don't let them scare you. You've got to face up to them! Grab a sword and fight!

HELEN
(to the men)
Yes, I think it was some kind of involuntary...twinge.

NATHAN
You want to sit down?

HELEN
Perhaps I will just freshen up a bit.

She walks away from the men and they resume talking. Anne steps directly in front of Helen.

ANNE
Don't be a sniveling coward! I might die tomorrow because of my friend, Mary Read. Are you going to fight or are you going to run away?

Helen hesitates, then walks back to the men. Anne smiles and draws her sword.

ANNE
Keep your sword point up! Cut and parry! Remember, once you get your blade between their ribs...it goes in like butter.

Nathan smiles at Helen.

NATHAN
Feeling better?

HELEN
Yes. Much better.

NATHAN
Good.

STEWART
You know, the three of us are the search committee. We could make a decision right now about--

HELEN
No. We're not going to make a decision. Not until we figure out why we're historians in the first place. Is it just a career with a long vacation or is it a way to understand the past and influence the way we see the future?

STEWART
Don't tell me that you believe all that stuff about the lower frequencies of history.

HELEN
Not completely. But that isn't the issue here. At least Rebecca has a vision of the past...which is more than I can say for the three of us. Every year, we get another class of students who want to learn about the world...who want to understand things...and four years later they come out thinking that all knowledge is relative. Why can't we inspire our students? Excite them. Make them feel that history can change their lives. We need facts. They're the bread of our existence. But why not some roses, too! Don't you agree? You must agree!

The men look stunned. Anne pulls out her cutlass and thrusts it into the air.

ANNE
Yes!

Sound of a drum. Blackout.

ACT II

Lights up on Helen sitting upstage. It's the day after the colloquium. Helen watches Anne sharpen a knife on a whetstone. When Anne is finished, she slips the knife into a sheath strapped to her leg.

ANNE
Fletcher! Where are you, Fletcher!
You oozy little shanker of pus!

Mary and Fletcher enter from different sides. They both carry cutlasses.

FLETCHER
I've been waiting for you, Bonney.

ANNE
Is that so? What a brave little fish you are. So, tell me. What are the rules of our battle?

MARY
(offering the sword)
To hell with the rules. just kill the maggotty bastard.

ANNE
I want to know. What laws govern this duel? Can I choose the weapons?

FLETCHER
You challenged me. So, I picked the weapons. Hurry it up now. I'm going to serve you a little cold steel for dinner.

ANNE
But what are the weapons, Fletcher? Pistols? Can we use pistols?

MARY
What are you talking about, Anne? Stop this jabber.

FLETCHER
No pistols.

ANNE
How about muskets? Pikes? Cannons?

FLETCHER
Get a cutlass or I'll kill you
without one.

Fletcher cuts the air with his sword and steps forward.

ANNE
Boarding axes. What about boarding
axes? They'd spill a little claret
on the deck. Wouldn't they?

FLETCHER
There'll be blood enough in a minute
or so.

He moves towards Anne.

MARY
Anne! Take the sword!

Sound. Anne grabs a cutlass from Mary as Fletcher runs towards her. He drives her across the stage with a slashing attack that uses all his strength.

Fletcher swings his sword at Anne's head and she blocks the weapon. They stand close together while Fletcher pushes against Anne's hands.

FLETCHER
Have you seen your death, Bonney?
Is he whispering in your ear?

Anne slips away and they resume fighting. Once again, Fletcher slashes at Anne's face. She blocks him and he pushes her down onto the ground. Fletcher steps on Anne's sword arm and the weapon falls out of her hand.

FLETCHER
You're a flimsy piece of goods.
Aren't you? Just a weak...woman.

Fletcher raises his sword for the kill. Anne pushes him backwards with her foot. She pulls out her knife, runs forward, and stabs Fletcher in the stomach.

ANNE
What about knives, Fletcher? You
didn't speak of knives.

Fletcher falls to the ground and dies.

> ANNE
> So, I guess they're proper.

Anne and Mary approach Fletcher's body.

> MARY
> Let's toss him over the side. Feed the sharks.

The two women drag the body away. Helen enters her office.

> MARY
> He's a heavy sack of shit.

Lights up as Nathan enters with one hand behind his back.

> NATHAN
> There she is! The terror of the history department!

Surprised, Helen turns and faces him.

> HELEN
> What's this message you left on my answering machine? You said it was an emergency.

> HELEN
> Stewart Crawley wants to see us. You've got him on the run.

He hands her a rose.

> NATHAN
> You were magnificent at the party last night. You smashed him, crashed him, bashed him against the wall.

> HELEN
> I was...inspired.

> STEWART
> You inspired me. You know, I actually enjoyed history when I was growing up. I used to lie in my bed and read about the rise of Prussia.
> (leans toward her)
> Rigid lines of soldiers marching forward, bursting across the borders --

Stewart enters.

STEWART
What's this about Prussia?

NATHAN
It rose and fell...like all dynasties.

STEWART
Good. Just make sure that you get all the data before debating some issue. That includes our work on the search committee.

HELEN
And what "data" have we overlooked?

STEWART
A little matter of Rebecca Skolnik's work experience. I called up Ernst Viltner after the party last night and asked about her stint as a research assistant. He said she was with him for three days, then they started arguing about "patriarchal structures" and he fired her.

HELEN
Did you ask Dr. Skolnik about this?

STEWART
I don't need to. She lied, Helen. It's obvious. Nevertheless, it's a delicate situation. We don't want any problems coming out of this. Do we, Nathan?

NATHAN
Of course. No problems.

STEWART
You seem to be close to her, Helen. Tell her to go back to New York.

Stewart exits.

HELEN
We should talk to her, Stewart. Stewart!

Blackout. Lights up as Anne and Mary enter and cross the downstage area. Anne carries a bottle of rum.

ANNE
Jack said this rum was four years old. I don't believe him.

                    MARY
          Give me the bottle.

Mary drinks some rum and spits it out of her mouth. She starts
coughing. Anne pats her on the back.

                    MARY
          There's gunpowder in it. I swear.
          It tastes like gunpowder!

                    ANNE
          And smells like a dead man's fart.

Anne takes the bottle and drinks.

                    MARY
          Thank you, Anne Bonney.

                    ANNE
          For the rum?

                    MARY
          For being my friend.

Anne picks up the two swords left on the deck.

                    ANNE
          It's good to have friend, but you
          you should carry a sword.

                    MARY
          I'm a gunner.

                    ANNE
          No one's a gunner when the enemy
          boards your ship.

Anne hands one of the swords to Mary.

                    ANNE
          Come on! Defend yourself! Pretend
          I want to slice off your ears.

                    MARY
          Don't kill me, sir! I'm just a
          little bantling. A chitty-faced
          country girl.

Anne lunges and the two women begin to fence.

                    ANNE
          Don't hold your sword so hard.
               (strikes Mary's sword)
          That helps me knock your arm away.

Anne points her sword at Mary's face. Mary looks angry.

> ANNE
> Now, what are you going to do?

> MARY
> Defend myself!

The two women resume fighting aggressively.

> ANNE
> Don't just answer my attack.
> Know what your next move will be.

> MARY
> Should friends fight each other?

> ANNE
> Only if they don't get angry.

Mary steps sideways and cuts Anne's wrist with her cutlass. Wounded, Anne falls to her knees. Mary throws down her sword.

> MARY
> It was an accident! I swear!

> ANNE
> Yes. Just an accident. That's all.
> (forcing a smile)
> You've learned your lesson.

Anne and Mary exit. Lights up on Nathan and Helen.

> NATHAN
> You've got to do it. Track down
> Skolnik and tell her to go home.

> HELEN
> It's not fair.

> NATHAN
> What do you mean? She hyped up her
> resume and got caught. Everything's
> pretty clear.

> HELEN
> We don't really know what happened,
> Nathan. I think we should have the
> decency to talk to her.

> NATHAN
> To hell with decency. Getting involved
> with this might hurt your career.

                    HELEN
          Yes, of course. I wouldn't want to
          do that.

                    NATHAN
          Come on, Helen! I'm just being
          realistic. We lost this time.
          That's the way it goes. There will
          be other battles. Ones we can win.

                    HELEN
          I've postponed so much and I'm
          still doing it. Sometimes, I think
          my whole life is an exercise in
          deferred gratification.

                    NATHAN
          You've got to be careful these
          days. Believe me, it's cold out
          there in the real world.

                    HELEN
          I realize that.

                    NATHAN
          Years ago, I used to look forward to
          the winter snow. At night, I'd sit
          by the window with a book and my
          father would come in with some
          firewood and say: "Storm's coming.
          Time to hunker down." That's what
          it's like these days, Helen. That's
          what this era is all about. A
          storm's coming. It's time to lock
          the doors, close the curtains, and
          find some warm place to hide.

Nathan exits. Sound of drumming as Captain James Porterfield, a British naval officer, enters.

                    PORTERFIELD
          The Governor of Jamaica has issued
          this proclamation to all those living
          on the island!

He begins to read a proclamation.

                    PORTERFIELD
          Two years ago, His Majesty, King
          George, agreed to pardon any pirate
          who surrendered to the proper
          authorities.
                         (MORE)

PORTERFIELD
Although many men have taken advantage of this most generous offer, the notorious pirate, Calico Jack Rackham, has shown his contempt for the King's mercy. In response to this brigand's continued attack on British shipping, the Governor has authorized myself...Captain James Porterfield...to hunt down Rackham and his crew. Any pirates captured by my men will be brought back to Port Royal and executed at Gallows Point. Their bodies will then be covered with tar and hung in chains at the entrance of the harbor for a period of one year. The Governor hopes that such a display will encourage respect for His Majesty and the rule of law.

Porterfield exits. Michael Dobbs enters Helen's office.

MICHAEL
Professor Raymond...

HELEN
Hello, Michael. I thought you'd gone back to Cornell.

MICHAEL
Professor Crawley called me at the hotel this morning. He told me what happened and asked me to hang around for a few more days.

HELEN
Professor Crawley *is* a very efficient man.

MICHAEL
Look, I know you didn't want to hire me and I'm sorry that it worked out this way. I wanted to be chosen because of my own merits...not because somebody else made a mistake. If I'm going to be in this department, I'd like to be a colleague and a friend.

HELEN
I've been trying to figure out why I want to be an historian, Michael. I'm afraid that you got in the middle of it.

MICHAEL
(smiling)
Why don't you try my way? "The Scientific Approach."

HELEN
No. No. Don't you understand that the way you ask a question determines the kind of answer that you're going to get? You can't avoid moral choices just because you're wearing a white lab coat.

MICHAEL
I don't think I understand...

Rebecca enters the room carrying a vase full of silk roses.

REBECCA
Introducing the concept of color to a gray and dreary –
    (sees Michael)
Oh. You're here.

MICHAEL
I was just leaving.

REBECCA
You know, I feel like I've talked to everybody this weekend. But I haven't really talked to you.

Michael begins to exit.

MICHAEL
We never got the chance.

REBECCA
We're not all that different, Dobbs. We're both unemployed.

MICHAEL
Yes. Well, you're right about that.
    (to Helen)
Good to see you, Dr. Raymond. We'll talk later.

Dobbs exits.

REBECCA
I was going to make a joke about "cod-cepts" of reality. But I restrained myself admirably.

HELEN
Rebecca...

Rebecca places the vase on a table.

REBECCA
All this is for you. They're made out of silk so they'll last forever.

HELEN
Thank you. Everyone seems to be giving me flowers these days.

REBECCA
These flowers are not for decoration. They're kind of psychological first aid in disguise. For example, let's say that your car breaks down and it looks like you've got a yeast infection and some journal has just rejected one of your articles.

HELEN
Sounds like a typical morning.

REBECCA
Now, you could take a couple Valium, but instead...ha-ha!...You've got these roses that Rebecca Skolnik gave to you.

She approaches the vase.

REBECCA
You take three deep breaths. Very important. One. Two. Three. Then you approach the flowers and go AHHHH!

Rebecca throws the flowers into the air. She exhales and smiles.

REBECCA
Instantly, you feel better.

Rebecca picks up the flowers and places them back in the vase.

HELEN
I'll have to try that some time.

                    REBECCA
          Don't forget the breathing first.
          That's important.

                    HELEN
          Professor Crawley dropped by the
          office this morning. He said that
          your vitae was...misleading. That
          you never worked for Ernst Viltner.

                    REBECCA
          I worked with him for three days.
          And they were the longest three
          days in my life.

Helen moves away from Rebecca.

                    HELEN
          What else did you lie about?

                    REBECCA
          I didn't lie! My vitae said...
          "research assistant." It didn't
          state the exact length the year.

                    HELEN
          You seemed so confident. So sure of
          yourself.

                    REBECCA
          It's a way of dealing with the
          world. That's all. I've been honest
          with you.

                    HELEN
          Look, I'm trying to get you this
          job. But you've made it very
          difficult to --

                    REBECCA
          You weren't there, Helen! You weren't
          locked up in that smelly little
          office with the Great Ernst Viltner.
          On the first day...the first
          morning..I'm up on a ladder getting
          a book and suddenly he's behind me with
          his hands on my hips.
               (Viltner's voice)
          "Just steadying you, dear. Just
          making sure you don't fall." And
          he kept touching me all day.
          Patting me on the head like a
          goddamn cocker spaniel.
                              (MORE)

                    REBECCA
               (Viltner's voice)
     "You know, you're very pretty for
     an historian. Very pretty."

                    HELEN
     That's sexual harassment. You could have --

                    REBECCA
     I couldn't have done anything! To be
     accused of harassment at our
     school the professor would have to
     zip down his pants in the middle of
     the faculty lounge.

                    HELEN
     So, you quit.

                    REBECCA
     Yeah, I quit. On the third day, I
     was taking dictation and he leaned
     over and tried to kiss me. We got in
     a big argument about women and
     history, then I walked out.

                    HELEN
     It was a mistake to use his name as a
     reference. You should have known
     someone would call.

                    REBECCA
     Viltner smiled at me whenever we met in
     the hallways. He acted like he wanted to
     forget about it...that the whole thing
     hadn't happened. God, I was wrong.
               (turning away)
     I'm sorry, Helen. I better go.

                    HELEN
     There still might be a chance.

                    REBECCA
     Don't worry about it.

                    HELEN
     I'll talk to Stewart. Try to
     explain the situation.

                    REBECCA
     This isn't your problem. Look, I'm
     not even sure I want this job.

Helen faces Rebecca.

HELEN
I'll do what I can.

REBECCA
You don't have to.

HELEN
I'll do what I can.

Rebecca exits. Helen follows her. Jack and Anne enter.

JACK
It was a proclamation, Anne. From the Governor of Jamaica. And it was feathered with my name.

ANNE
You wanted to be famous, Jack. Now, you are.

JACK
Famous, but not stretched on the gallows. A live dog is better than a dead lion.

ANNE
Are we dogs then? Frightened of the moon?

JACK
I'm not saying that.

ANNE
Go to, Jack. You're all in a muck sweat. Shall we be hen-hearted...jump ship and let the ghosts take command?

JACK
I've grown large, Anne. Too large to hide in this world. God, I wish I'd stayed in England. Been Old Mr. Queernabs, scratching my chats.

ANNE
This Captain --

JACK
Porterfield. James Porterfield.

ANNE
He doesn't have to find us.

JACK
And he won't...if we stay quiet. We'll disguise ourselves as merchants. Burn up our names and hide in the smoke.

Jack exits. Anne smiles and follows him. Stewart and Helen enter together.

HELEN
If you get rid of all the smoke and look at things clearly, it's a simple case of sexual harassment.

STEWART
So what? That's not the point. The problem with her vitae just made me stop and reconsider. She wouldn't fit in around here.

HELEN
She'd be a better teacher. Better for the university.

STEWART
The university is a group of people working together. I'd rather not have a constant battle going in my department.

HELEN
So, we should all be the same? Is that what you're saying?

STEWART
Have you picked those three books yet? The Dean sent me a memo about it this week.

HELEN
Answer my question, Stewart.

STEWART
Have you picked the books? That's your job around here. Do your job.

HELEN
I am not going to be the token woman picking the token books for the goddamn token syllabus! I know what you're doing here. You're not fooling anyone.

STEWART
Oh, you understand me. It's nice to know that somebody understands me. I'm the person that finds money so that our faculty won't get laid off and our graduate students will have jobs. I'm the person that people go to when they have problems with the pension fund and the medical plan. I'm the one who organizes the blood drive and the Christmas party. But you understand that. Of course. You realized that I keep my lawn trimmed, pay my taxes, obey all traffic signs...do my little part to keep this chaotic world of ours from breaking down of neglect. How selfish of me. How evil. I certainly deserve your contempt.

Blackout. Stewart exits. Helen walks upstage. Music as Anne enters and stands stage right.

ANNE
When I knew they were hunting us...sniffing in each cove like dogs for a fox...the sea changed before my eyes. Each new mast emerging from the horizon seemed like a knife thrust out of the water.

Jack enters and stands stage center.

JACK
We were taking on water and dragging through the waves and Anne thought...I thought...that if this Porterfield bastard was going to be searching for us...we best scrape the hull and get things squared away. So we sailed into Magdalene Cove, hoved to, then broke out the cargo and piled it all up on the beach.
    (to crew)
"Step lively now! Step lively!"

ANNE
The anchor was fixed hard into the sand and its chain set on the port side. When the crew turned the capstan, the whole ship began to creak and crack like every rib was going to break.

PORTERFIELD
We came around the point. Sailing
with the wind. I spied the masts
first and then the ship itself.
    (to the crew)
"There they are! On the starboard
quarter! Man the guns and fire at
range!"

ANNE
Two sloops came cutting around the
point. Men on the ratlines.
Scrambling up the shrouds.
    (to the crew)
"All hands up! Get the muskets!"
    (looking around)
No guns on the ship! No guns at all!

Jack moves away.

JACK
It was time for this bird to hop
the twig.

PORTERFIELD
"Fire!"
    (to himself)
First shot wide. Spouting in the water.
    (to the crew)
"Up a little more. Slew her to the left!"
    (to himself)
The second round...a chain shot...
slashing through their rigging. Top
of their foremast chopped off and
hanging.
    (to the crew)
"Get the longboats ready.' Prepare
the boarding crews!"

ANNE
Shot cutting into the hull. Shrouds
falling on the deck. I hear a
splashing sound as the longboat
drops into the water. Look over
the side and there's Jack rowing for
the shore. He calls out to me...

Jack climbs a rope and waves his hat.

JACK
I don't want to be famous anymore!

Jack exits.

PORTERFIELD
Longboat leaving the ship and
heading for the shore.
    (to the crew)
"Second boat follow that man in and
hunt him down!"

ANNE
Mary and I firing the muskets,
trying to fight while the rest of
the crew hides down in the hold.
Flames. Black smoke. Grappling hooks
over side and then they're on the
deck. And we're fighting...still
fighting...with twenty against us.
Fighting alone.

Anne exits. Porterfield walks to a spotlight. The sound of the battle begins to blend into the sound of a phone ringing.

PORTERFIELD
We caught the man in the longboat
first. It was Jack Rackham. Then I
gave the order to cease firing
and the rest of my crew boarded the
ship. They were attacked by two
pirates. Just two. But they managed
to kill three of my men and wound
the bo's'n. Finally, they were
disarmed. Chained. And taken back
to my sloop. They were kicked and
beaten, of course. The usual thing.
Justly deserved. And that's when we
discovered they...they were women.

Porterfield exits. Anne and Mary enter the stage in darkness while we hear a phone answering machine.

HELEN
Hello, you have reached the office
of Professor Helen Raymond. My
office hours are between 9 and 11AM
on Tuesdays and Thursdays. Please
leave a message after the beep.

REBECCA
Hi. This is Rebecca. I've checked out
of the hotel and my plane's leaving
at four. I...I want to see you.

Lights up on Anne and Mary in a jail cell in Port Royal, Jamaica. Their wrists are shackled. Steel collars have been placed around their necks and attached to chains.

Anne eats some food out of a wooden bowl while Mary stares at the floor. Anne finds something in the bowl and smiles.

                  ANNE
     There's a maggot in my stew.

She holds it up on her finger.

                  ANNE
     And he's alive. In fact, he's doing a little jig. Maybe he's some kind of bog trotter maggot from Ireland.

                  MARY
     I don't want to hear your babble.

                  ANNE
     Oh, you're the techy one. Aren't you? I'm just talking. That's all. If we were on the boat, I'd say: "Look up. Look at the sky. It's as clean and clear as a blue china bowl," But we're in a prison at Port Royal. And there's no sky. So, we might as well talk about maggots.

                  MARY
     It's all over, Anne. Don't you know that? Look at us. We're chained up like dogs and they're going to hang us.

Anne extends her hand. The chains rattle around her.

                  ANNE
     Tip me your daddle.

                  MARY
     Can't.

                  ANNE
     Go to. Don't be a currish little chit. Let's see your hand.

Mary hesitates, then the two women reach towards each other. The steel chains pull on their necks as they move closer. Finally, their fingertips touch. Anne smiles.

                  ANNE
     There you go. As soft as a cade lamb.

The women hear the sound of someone unlocking a heavy door.

ANNE
Somebody's coming. Let me talk to them.

Captain Porterfield and the Parson enter.

MARY
It's just Captain Porterfield and that skinny-shanked Parson. The one who looks like death's head on a mop stick. He's bringing us the Weepy Jesus and asking if we're saved.

ANNE
We are going to be saved. No one's making me climb the ladder.

Anne pretends to pray. Holding handkerchiefs to their noses, the two men approach the prisoners.

PORTERFIELD
Good day. Have you two been enjoying the King's accommodations?

MARY
There's a maggot in Anne's stew. He looks like a British officer.

ANNE
Begging you pardon, Captain. But you've got a stout enough lock on the door. Do we have to wear these clinkers?

PORTERFIELD
The chains could be removed and better food provided. What do you think, Parson?

PARSON
Charity is one of the three theological virtues.

PORTERFIELD
We could give you some better clothes and maybe even some rum... if you confessed.

ANNE
There's nothing to confess, Captain. We're not pirates. We were forced onto that boat.

MARY
Anne!

PORTERFIELD
You haven't been condemned...yet. There might be a chance of a pardon A confession would make the trial go easier and give the Governor a proper declaration to send back to England.

MARY
You're not going to pardon us. That's a swinging great lie. A real clanker.

PORTERFIELD
(turning away)
Your turn, Parson.

The Parson steps forward.

PARSON
You should confess...for the good of your souls.

ANNE
Of course, Reverend Father, I agree. We just don't want our souls to leave our bodies too soon.

PARSON
We need only recall the passage in Isaiah: "For if thou art willing and obedient, thou shall eat the good of the land. But if thou refuse and rebel, thou shall perish by the sword."

MARY
That's a taradiddle.

PARSON
Are you doubting the word of scripture?

MARY
It's all moon and arse to me.

PARSON
Blasphemy!

MARY
Go lick your own ballocks, you bog house dog.

ANNE
Mary! Don't!

PARSON
I think they should hang, Captain. Their acts of brigandage are just another proof of the evil found in their sex.

PORTERFIELD
Agreed.

ANNE
Surely you don't think that all women are evil, Captain? What about your mother? Wasn't she a woman?

PORTERFIELD
My mother was...a mother.

MARY
She should have fed you to the sparrows.

PORTERFIELD
Enough of this!

He approaches Anne.

PORTERFIELD
Jack Rackham has confessed...told us everything.

MARY
That squeaking coward. It's no surprise.

PORTERFIELD
He said it was all your fault. Don't you want to tell your side of the story?

ANNE
Yes. Maybe I should.

MARY
Are you bird-witted, Anne? Have they turned you simple?

ANNE
If I could only talk to Jack alone. You see, Captain...One always doubts confessions when guards and parsons are about.

PORTERFIELD
Impossible.

Porterfield starts to leave, but the Parson stops him.

PARSON
Begging your pardon, Captain. But it's not a bad idea. "Where one goose leads, the rest will follow."

PORTERFIELD
Perhaps...

He gives some keys to the Parson who unlocks Anne's chains.

PORTERFIELD
Well, I guess it can't hurt.

ANNE
I'm sure that I'll be inspired by Jack's example.

PARSON
Indeed. The wise man is a candle in the darkness.

The steel collar is removed and Anne stands up.

ANNE
Thank you, Captain. It's easy to see that you're both gentleman.

PORTERFIELD
Follow me. Rackham's in a cell across the courtyard.

ANNE
One more favor, if you please. As you can see, my friend has not opened her heart to the mercy of God.

PARSON
She's a whore and a blasphemer. That's what she is.

ANNE
Perhaps if I could talk to her for a minute or so, I could convince her to see the light.

PORTERFIELD
One minute. That's all. And I'm not taking off her chains. Parson...

Porterfield exits. The Parson moves upstage while Anne hurries over to Mary.

MARY
You're going to peach to those bastards. I can't believe it.

ANNE
Stop it, Mary. We don't have much time. There's only one way out of this. One chance. We've got to plead our bellies.

MARY
What?

ANNE
It's against the law to hang us if we're heavy with child.

MARY
I'm not letting a man --

ANNE
We've got to do it or we're going to hang! I think I can get Jack's "help." While I'm gone, you can lie with the Parson.

MARY
Anne!

ANNE
He'll jump on you. I know he will. He stares at your diddeys every time he says his prayers.

MARY
I won't do it.

ANNE
There's no choice. With a baby in the pot, we've got nine months to plan an escape.

MARY
Fat tits and a swollen belly.

ANNE
It's better than hanging in chains at the entrance to the harbor. Worms in your guts and crows picking at your grinders.

MARY
That mewly little Parson won't come in
this room alone. He's scared of me.

ANNE
Don't worry. I'll get him to come
back.

Anne stands up and begins to walk away.

ANNE
Tell him that you want to touch his
Holy Salvation.

Blackout. Anne walks upstage to the Parson. Mary exits.
Helen enters. Lights up. Carrying a shopping bag, Nathan
enters and approaches Helen.

NATHAN
Helen! What are you doing here?

HELEN
Waiting for you.

NATHAN
If I'd known, I would have rushed
home from the Co-op. You're a good
deal more pleasant than surly
student employees.

HELEN
So what did you get? Books?

She tries to peer into the bag, but he closes it quickly.

NATHAN
I'm a college professor, Helen. I
don't have time to read.

HELEN
What about an adult magazine? You
could look at the pictures...

NATHAN
Something more shameful than that.

He reaches into the bag and pulls out a pair of hand weights.

NATHAN
Heavy hands!

HELEN
Excuse me...

NATHAN
That's what these things are called. Heavy hands. You carry them around when you're jogging.

HELEN
I didn't know that you jogged.

NATHAN
Actually, it's more of a controlled stagger.

He tosses the weights back into the shopping bag.

NATHAN
God, I never thought that I'd be the kind of man who worried about upper body strength. My father chopped wood every evening. I just chop up term papers.

HELEN
You don't even have a fireplace.

NATHAN
That's not the point. When I was growing up, I remember embracing my father and smelling pipe smoke, bourbon and the witch hazel he slapped on after shaving. I use an electric razor and drink Diet Coke.

HELEN
There's nothing wrong with that.

NATHAN
Sometimes, I wish I was one of those pirates you're writing about. Swashbuckling across the Caribbean. Making people walk the plank. These days, being a man is a muddled proposition unless you're a a lumberjack or something.

HELEN
Men know who they are. They're the ones with the power.

NATHAN
It's all a big fraud. We act like we're in control of the game, but the fact is...we've lost the rules.

HELEN
We can change things, Nathan. We can change anything we want. We could hire Rebecca Skolnik this afternoon.

NATHAN
Don't be ridiculous.

HELEN
We've got two votes. That's a majority. Stewart Crawley might growl a little, but he couldn't block our decision.

NATHAN
No, he couldn't. But next term, you wouldn't get a raise. I wouldn't get a sabbatical. And we'd both end up tutoring basketball players about the Thirty Years War.

HELEN
That might not happen. Not if we stood together.

NATHAN
Why are you pushing for this, Helen? Do you really loathe Michael Dobbs?

HELEN
Of course not. He's what my mother would call: "a nice young man."

NATHAN
He *is* more up-to-date than we are.

HELEN
Are you really interested in cod?

NATHAN
Not especially. Are you that interested in Rebecca Skolnik?

HELEN
She isn't the Issue here. I'm just tired of people telling me that we have no choice. What they're really saying *is* that we can't change ourselves.

NATHAN
Most changes take a long time. Believe me, I know. I'm an historian.

HELEN
Help me, Nathan. Because...
because we're friends.

NATHAN
Friends can get you into trouble.

HELEN
Risk something. Take a stand. Just
this once...be a pirate for a day.

Nathan hesitates, then smiles.

NATHAN
What the hell. Let's go down to the
Ugly Toad and drink some rum.

Helen and Nathan exit. Blackout. Lights up on Anne and the Parson standing upstage. The Parson helps remove her shackles.

PARSON
She's a blasphemer! A sinful woman!

ANNE
All of us are sinful. But all of us
can find salvation.

PARSON
Some won't.

ANNE
The loudest chick *in* the nest has the
most hunger. When we are both *in* the
cell at nig...our words fluttering
like birds *in* the darkness ...she has
told me her desire for contrition.

PARSON
I don't believe it.

Jack enters with some food and sits on a bench.

ANNE
It's the Captain's fault. When she
sees him, she remembers our fight
on the ship...the smoke, the fire,
the shot cutting through the
shrouds. If you talked to her alone,
I think you could touch her...soul.

PARSON
I suppose I should try.

ANNE
I hear her groaning at night. Thinking of your face. "My angel. My angel." That's her secret name for you.

PARSON
I *will* try.

The Parson exits. Lights up on Jack Rackham eating and drinking. Anne approaches him.

ANNE
Hello, Jack. Got a wolf in your stomach?

Startled, Jack spits out the wine. He turns and faces her.

JACK
How did you get in here?

ANNE
Through the door...like any common soul.

JACK
Keep away from me!

Anne picks up Jack's bread and eats it.

ANNE
Why the Friday face? Is this how you greet your old friends?

JACK
Jailer!

ANNE
No reason to shout for him. He's one who let me in here.

JACK
So you could stab me in my sleep?

ANNE
Oh, that's not going to happen. The people of Port Royal want to see you dancing in the air,

JACK
I'm not going to hang. The Parson said I'll be forgiven.

ANNE
Our Savior forgave the good thief, but nobody took him off his cross.

JACK
Get out of here! I don't want to hear your jabber!

ANNE
They just want to hang your name, Jack. "The Great Calico Jack Rackham." The only problem is... you're attached.

JACK
Then I'll change my name! Be Jack Nasty Face, the make-weight sailor.

ANNE
Good idea! I can be Annie Green Gown. The village virgin.
    (innocent voice)
"I beg your pardon, sir. A tumble on the grass?"

Anne embraces Jack. He smiles and touches her.

JACK
We'll go back to England.

ANNE
Ireland.

JACK
All right. Ireland. We'll sit in a village, drink old hock and scratch each other's arse.

He smiles for a second, then shakes his head sadly.

JACK
I don't want to ride to the gallows, Anne. It doesn't suit me. I've always been a bit of a false coin...my courage trimmed off at the edges.

ANNE
I can't save you, Jack. I wish I could.

ANNE
But I can give you some pleasure.

She kisses Jack, then begins to touch him.

JACK
Here? With the guard outside?

ANNE
Put a rag in your mouth, He won't hear you crow.

JACK
And what if he does?

He begins to kiss Anne and they both respond passionately, Suddenly, Jack pulls away from her.

JACK
Now, I understand! You got the clap and you want to give it to me.

ANNE
That's not true!

JACK
Of course it is. It's the whore's revenge. You're like a wasp who carries a sting in her tail!

ANNE
All right. Let's say I was clapped. What difference does it make? If you catch it and you're pardoned, you've got the rest of your life to sweat for the quacks. If you catch it and you hang, then the rope will be your doctor.

JACK
I suppose.

Anne approaches Jack and embraces him again.

ANNE
We're all going to die, Jack. This is one thing we do while we're waiting.

He hesitates, then kisses her aggressively. Laughing, they both exit, Lights up on Helen. She's rearranging the silk roses that Rebecca gave her.

HELEN
Fifteen women on a dead man's chest.
Yo! Ho! Ho! And a bottle of rum!
A drink for the devil and none...

Rebecca enters.

                    HELEN
Oh, you're here! I got your message
on the machine.

                    REBECCA
I just came to say goodbye. I'm on
the way to the airport. My flight
leaves in a hour.

                    HELEN
Well, get on the phone and cancel
your reservation. You're staying.

                    REBECCA
There's no reason --

                    HELEN
You're hired. You got the job. I
talked Nathan Into backing you.

                    REBECCA
I can't believe it.

                    HELEN
It's true. Crawley is going to have a
heart attack when we out-vote him.

                    REBECCA
Helen...

Helen sits down.

                    HELEN
Look, you don't have to thank me.
You're going to be good for the
students here.

                    REBECCA
I don't want the job.

                    HELEN
I beg your pardon?

                    REBECCA
I've changed my mind. I'm withdrawing
my application.

Helen stands and approaches Rebecca.

                    HELEN
It's...it's not a big salary of
course. And you would have to work
fairly hard.

REBECCA
I'm not scared of the work, Helen. I've just decided that I don't want to be here. Some friends of mine are starting a center for the study of women's history on the island of Crete. The whole thing's pretty disorganized right now. It just a house on the beach, a few hundred books and two typewriters, but I've been thinking about going there. Maybe you could come along. There's a stone patio that's sheltered from the sun by a trellis green with grape vines. A long wood table with a bottle of wine, a bowl of black olives and some bread still hot from the oven. And there are women. Women talking and laughing and trying to understand history. Our history.

HELEN
I bet everyone has their period at the same time.

REBECCA
Probably.

HELEN
That's not the real world, Rebecca. You're just postponing your life. I don't want you to make the same mistakes I did. Wasting years... walking around in a dream...until you wake up in some shabby little apartment with a cat box in the bathroom and a car with a bad clutch.

REBECCA
I'll take the chance.

HELEN
Look, I did a lot to get you this job!

REBECCA
I didn't ask you to do anything.

HELEN
I thought that --

                    REBECCA
          I don't want to live in an
          environment like this. There are too
          many compromises.

                    HELEN
          You compromise, you sacrifice, and
          then you get what you want.

                    REBECCA
          I don't want to be like you, Helen.
          Concealing my opinions for six
          years so that I can be a junior
          member of the Old Boys Club at this
          mediocre university. You can't give
          away little pieces of yourself and
          still remain whole.

                    HELEN
          How dare you judge my life.

                    REBECCA
          I'm not saying that I'm a perfect
          person...far from it. But I don't
          want to just "get by" with my life.
          The moment you start doing that,
          life goes right by you.

                    HELEN
          Don't you understand...

Nathan enters.

                    NATHAN
          Hello there, Skolnik. I assume
          Helen gave you the news. Hang
          around for another day. It won't
          take long to type up your contract.

                    REBECCA
          Goodbye, Helen.

Helen turns away from her.

                    NATHAN
          Now, you will have to take an
          office in the annex, but don't
          worry about it. We can probably get
          you out of there in two or three
          years.

Rebecca exits.

NATHAN
What's her problem? You didn't tell her about the rats crawling around the annex, did you? Maybe they're just mice that have been lifting weights or something.

HELEN
Nathan...

NATHAN
I left a note in Stewart's box. We'll drop by his office at ten o'clock tomorrow morning. I'll make the announcement or...no, you tell him. That's best. Be calm about it. Objective. Say something like: "Stewart, Nathan and I have considered all the data" and then Pow! Drop the bomb. He'll be surprised. A little angry. But we can handle that.

HELEN
Rebecca doesn't want to be here.

NATHAN
What?

HELEN
She's going back to New York.

NATHAN
Don't worry, Helen. We'll get another chance. Half the faculty is dead already. They just don't realize it. Things will change in a couple of years. It'll work out. Eventually.

HELEN
I'm tired of "eventually."

Blackout. Nathan exits. Lights up on Mary sitting on the floor with the steel collar around her neck. The Parson enters and approaches her warily.

PARSON
Your friend said that you needed spiritual instruction.

Mary stares down at the floor.

PARSON
Not that I alone can change a human soul. That's God's providence. But, like a careful seaman, I can trim another's sail so that the wind of holiness pushes you towards salvation.

He touches Mary and she moves slightly. The Parson stumbles backwards.

PARSON
Perhaps the time's not right. I'll come tomorrow.

MARY
No. Anne told you the truth. I need to be filled with the Holy Spirit.

PARSON
You've fallen far into the darkest pit, Mary Read. You'll need all God's mercy to climb back up to some small glimmering of light...

MARY
I never killed a man who wasn't trying to kill me.

PARSON
But you were a pirate. A thief. Remember Our Lord's commandment: "Thou shall not steal."

MARY
A privateer's just a pirate with a paper from the King. We didn't have the fucking paper. That's all.

PARSON
You wore breeches, Mary! You concealed your sex!
（approaching her）
Remember the Book of Deuteronomy 22-5. "The woman shall not wear that which pertaineth unto a man for that *is* an abomination unto the Lord!

MARY
I'm sorry! Please! I beg forgiveness!

The Parson kneels and embraces her.

PARSON
Mercy, my child. No tears. No tears.

MARY
I can't breathe. This foul vapor.

PARSON
Guard...

MARY
No. No. You can save me. Remove my head cloth. Please.

The Parson pulls off the rag covering Mary's hair.

PARSON
Yes...Well, I...Remember...Remember St. Paul's words in Corinthians. "But if a woman have long hair, it is a glory to her."

MARY
My dress. Remove my dress. It binds me. Can't...breathe...

The Parson pulls Mary toward him. Kneeling behind her, he fumbles with the laces of her dress.

PARSON
I'm not a true Parson, you know. The Governor wanted ministers in Jamaica so I was pressed off the streets of London because I was carrying a Bible and wearing black. They threw me in irons, put me on a ship and sent me here.

MARY
Better...Much better...Yes...Yes...

PARSON
I was a clerk. A church clerk. But I still can show you the way.

He pulls down the top of her dress. Mary is wearing a shift.

PARSON
You must learn obedience, my child.

He fumbles with his trouser buttons.

PARSON
Remember the Book of Genesis. Chapter Two. "And Adam said, this is now bone of my bones, and flesh of my flesh: she shall be called Woman...
  (lifts up dress)
because she was taken out of Man."

MARY
  (faintly)
No.

PARSON
Then there's Proverbs 31-19. "For the woman shall layeth her hands to the spindle, and her hands hold the distaff." If you could just hold my...

He grabs her arm, but Mary resists.

MARY
No.

PARSON
For *in* Colossians it *is* written:
  (strikes her)
"**Wives,** submit yourselves unto your husbands, as it is fit in the Lord."

Mary yanks the Parson forward and wraps a length of chain around his neck.

MARY
Remember the Book of Judith? Chapter 13? My mother liked to read that to me.

PARSON
It's...not...in the canon.

MARY
Then Judith took down Holophernes' sword and grasped his hair and struck at his neck and --

The Parson breaks free.

PARSON
Help! Guard!

The Parson **exits**. Blackout. Mary exits. Lights up on Helen, Nathan, **and** Stewart. Stewart is writing a **memo**.

                    STEWART
          Therefore, the search committee...
          let me write this down... agrees to a
          two-year contract for Michael Dobbs.
          At standard salary. Et cetera. Et
          cetera. That ought to be enough for the
          Dean. Don't you agree, Nathan?

                    NATHAN
          Sounds okay to me.

                    STEWART
          Good. I'll send it over this afternoon.

Stewart finishes writing. Nathan and Helen start to exit.

                    STEWART
          Stick around, Helen. I'd like to
          talk to you for a minute.

 Nathan glances at Helen, then exits.

                    STEWART
          Congratulations.

                    HELEN
          What are you talking about?

                    STEWART
          I was impressed with your little
          rebellion. You almost won.

                    HELEN
          Go to hell, Stewart.

                    STEWART
          I knew that you'd try something
          after you got tenure, but I didn't
          think you'd be so determined. You
          even got Nathan on your side.

                    HELEN
          I'm not giving up.

                    STEWART
          I admire what you did, Helen. It
          shows courage. Strength of character.
          You've got more balls than the rest
          of the department.

                    HELEN
          How lucky for me.

STEWART
We have a great deal in common. Don't you realize that? Nathan thinks that he's going to be department chairman. What a joke. You're the person who's going to take charge one of these days.

HELEN
And then I'll hire Rebecca Skolnik or someone just like her.

STEWART
No, you won't. You're the kind person who can play the game for six long years. Don't think I didn't notice you grinding your teeth at every faculty meeting.

HELEN
Now, I have tenure.

STEWART
You thought things were going to be different, didn't you? But it's not. The system always has new carrots to lure you on. Bigger salary. New title. Better job. Believe me, I know. When you reach the top of some ladder, there's always a new ladder to climb. Accept that fact. Accept the responsibility.

HELEN
And just what does that mean?

STEWART
You can start by picking those three books for the alternative syllabus.

HELEN
What's the point? We're not committed to teaching them.

STEWART
Of course not.

HELEN
We're not committed to teaching at all.

STEWART
The whole reward system isn't set up that way. I wish it was. I really mean that. I might enjoy giving out wisdom beneath a fig tree, but that's not the situation and --

HELEN
We don't have a choice.

STEWART
No. Not really.

HELEN
Well, I have a choice. I quit.

STEWART
Go home, have a drink and relax. Or...take a short vacation. I'll cover for you. It's no problem. We're going to be friends.

HELEN
My letter of resignation will be on your desk this afternoon.

Helen exits while Stewart follows after her.

STEWART
Helen, for godsake! You should think this over!

Blackout. Sound. Lights up on Mary lying on the floor. She looks sick and sweaty. Anne enters and approaches her.

ANNE
Mary, it's me. They told me you were sick.
    (touches her head)
God, you've got a fever.

MARY
How did you get here?

ANNE
The sergeant just let me in. He's guarding the door.

MARY
Did you spread your legs for him?

                    ANNE
          I didn't have to. I gave him a treasure
          map in trade.

                    MARY
          We don't have any treasure.

                    ANNE
          Remember that hole we dug on
          Tortuga Island? The place we went
          to move our bowels?

                    MARY
          You gave him a map...to our privy?

Mary starts laughing.

                    ANNE
          Well, why not? He's got to find
          something once he gets there. Now,
          stop laughing. Don't want to make
          you weak.

Mary touches Anne's stomach.

                    MARY
          You got a squaller in your belly?

                    ANNE
          That's what I told them at the
          trial. You were there.

                    MARY
          I didn't believe it.

                    ANNE
          It's true. Jack did his duty.

Anne searches the room.

                    ANNE
          Where's the water around here?
          Didn't those bastards give you any
          water?

She picks up a pewter mug and sniffs the contents.

                    ANNE
          Beer. Hard and stale. Drink some.
          It'll have to do.

She helps Mary drink some of the beer.

MARY
I want you to do something for me when I die.

ANNE
You're not going to die.

MARY
I don't want to be buried in a dress.

ANNE
You want to wear breeches? Mary...

MARY
No. Not men's clothes. I want to be naked. That's all. The same way I arrived in the world.

ANNE
The minister wouldn't like that. The Governor wouldn't either.

MARY
Tell everyone I had smallpox. They won't open the coffin.

ANNE
Right. That'll do it. But...you're not going to die. You'll break this fever.

MARY
Then they'll hang me.

ANNE
Maybe you could pretend to confess and...no. No, that's not right. At the trial, I just stood there with my hands on my belly crying: "Please, Captain...I've got a innocent soul here." While you stood up and shouted: "Go to hell, you greasy little bag of guts!"

MARY
He didn't like that.

ANNE
You were the pirate. I was still wearing a disguise.

Anne stands and drinks the rest of the beer. She puts down the cup and paces around the room.

                    ANNE
          God. I've got windmills in my head. The
          whole world's spinning. Maybe I shouldn't
          have bowed to their vanity. That first
          time...the first prize ship... I should
          have stood up on the quarter-deck and
          shouted: "I'm Anne Bonney! I'm the Captain!
          Raise your caps or walk the plank!" Do you
          think they would have followed me, Mary?

She turns and sees that Mary's eyes are closed. Worried, she
hurries over to her friend.

                    ANNE
          Mary?

Mary opens her eyes.

                    MARY
          I think about you, Anne. When I'm
          awake. When I'm dreaming. It's all
          the same these days.

                    ANNE
          And I think about you. Remember the
          times we took the night watch...you
          and sailing the ship on our own
          while all the men snored down in
          the hold.

Mary closes her eyes.

                    ANNE
          It was so quiet when the sun came
          up in the morning. All you could
          hear was creak of the rigging and
          the hush of the waves. We'd just
          stand there holding the wheel and
          watching the sunlight burn across
          the water. We were happy then.
          Weren't we, Mary?

Anne realizes that Mary is close to death.

                    ANNE
          We were happy.

Anne picks up Mary and carries her off-stage. Lights up on
Helen loading some books into a cardboard box. Nathan enters.

                    NATHAN
          I ran into Stewart at the Faculty
          Club. He said you were --

HELEN
Crazy?

NATHAN
"Seriously disturbed" was the term that he used.

HELEN
Yes, I suppose he would see it that way.

NATHAN
I know a very good psychiatrist who doesn't even look like a psychiatrist. He wears shorts and a T-shirt. The floor of his consulting room is covered with sand and you sit on this beach chair under a sun lamp. It's very relaxing and you get a good tan.

HELEN
I'm not crazy, Nathan. No, I'll take that back. I'm as crazy as a woman who wanted to be a pirate.

NATHAN
Is this some kind of mid-life crisis? Believe me, I understand. Right after my divorce, I had this desire to buy a red Porsche and date 18-year-old girls named "Cindy."

HELEN
No, that's not my problem. It was a bit more than that.

NATHAN
What are you going to do?

HELEN
Finish my book on pirates. I've done all the research. It's time to sit down and write.

Nathan smiles and approaches her.

NATHAN
I'll miss you, Helen. For six years, you've been putting up with my jokes.

HELEN
You've been a good friend, Nathan. More than a friend.

She kisses Nathan on the lips, then embraces him. Inspired, Nathan paces back and forth.

> NATHAN
> You know, maybe I should tell Stewart to go to hell and write my own book and lead the students to the barricades and...and maybe I won't.
>   (shakes his head)
> You're braver than me.

> HELEN
> Or more desperate.

Nathan exits. Helen turns and sees the silk flowers that Rebecca gave her. Helen stares at the flowers for a moment, then takes three quick breaths and tosses them into the air.

> HELEN
> AHHHH!

Helen smiles and looks forward. We hear music as she walks downstage

> HELEN
> Anne? Anne Bonney?

Anne enters.

> ANNE
> So now you're calling my name.

> HELEN
> I guess I am. Although you don't really exist. Do you? You're an historical figure. Something in my imagination.

> NNE
> And what of it? Any ship will do if it carries you in the right direction.

> HELEN
> So what happened to you? I couldn't find any mention of your name after Mary's death and Rackham's execution.

The two women approach each other.

> ANNE
> Yes. It's a great mystery.

> HELEN
> I have a few theories.

ANNE
Tell me. Please. I love to hear about my own legend.

HELEN
You had a child. A girl.

ANNE
You've got half a chance at that.

HELEN
You named her after yourself.

ANNE
Sounds right.

HELEN
You escaped from prison...I'm sure you figured out a way. You lived in the mountains for awhile, then you joined up with a few runaway slaves and some bondswomen who'd been beaten by their masters.

ANNE
And then?

Helen looks forward --- inspired by her own vision.

HELEN
You stole a boat and sailed west. And the men on the shore saw your ship grow smaller and smaller until it was absorbed into the sky and the curve of the world and the dark blue sea.

Blackout.

AN AMERICAN ROMANCE

One of the pleasures of writing for the theater is that the playwright can get an immediate response from an audience of strangers. I've written lines on a piece of scratch paper during the first act, given notes to actors during the intermission, and watched the results in act two. Sitting in the audience, a playwright must listen to people yawn, whisper and fidget. When the play is over, you hear compliments and criticisms as the audience grabs their coats and walk back up the aisle.

When *Rebel Armies Deep Into Chad* as running at the Long Wharf Theater, I knew that if I sat in the stage manager's booth at 8:52pm, I could hear the audience gasp and watch some of them cry when Christina described how it felt to be slashed and left for dead. *An American Romance* gave me another example of the power of theater. If I stood in the lobby of The Road Theater and glanced at my watch, I knew when I would hear laughter.

***

I spent several years researching a novel narrated by Nathaniel Hawthorne's only son. Julian Hawthorne worked as a journalist, then was convicted of stock fraud and ended up in Atlantic Federal Penitentiary. Julian's sardonic view of the Hawthorne family and their famous friends seemed promising material for a comedy.

Although I never finished the book, my research introduced me to one of the more amusing episodes of Nathaniel Hawthorne's life. When he was a young bachelor he lived at Brook Farm, a utopian community established in West Roxbury, Massachusetts. Although Brook Farm only existed for six years, it is a notable example of the American desire to transform social theory into reality.

After reading books about Brook Farm and the people who lived there, I realized that I had found a group of real-life literary figures that could become characters on the stage. I wrote biographies of each person and then began to create the world of the play.

George and Sophia Ripley were the founders of Brook Farm. After graduating from Harvard Divinity School, George Ripley started a Unitarian church on Purchase Street in Boston. For 14 years George tried to interest his parishioners in a spiritual awakening as well as awareness of the poverty around them. Brook Farm was a joint-stock company organized by Ripley; each member had to buy shares in the Association. Although Ripley begged Ralph Waldo Emerson to join the group, the most famous writer of the time rejected the idea.

Margaret Fuller was a famous intellectual living at Brook Farm. Educated at home by an obsessive father, she became a brilliant speaker who supported herself by a series of public "conversations" in which Boston women paid a fee to talk with her about philosophical topics. She was also edited *The Dial* magazine with Emerson who characterized her as "the greatest woman of modem times."

Fuller suffered from terrible headaches and dealt with the pain by using mesmerism: a method of inducing a hypnotic trance developed by Anton Mesmer, an Austrian physician. Mesmer believed in the existence of a power called "animal magnetism" that could be transmitted to and from all living things.

Charles King Newcomb was already known in literary Boston as a promising young poet when he came to Brook Farm. A graduate of Brown University, he had briefly studied for the Episcopalian ministry, and then scandalized his family by becoming a Catholic. Newcomb was strongly attracted to the brilliant, good-looking Nathaniel Hawthorne and, for a brief time, they were close friends.

Nathaniel Hawthorne didn't exactly fit into this crowd of idealists and reformers. After graduating from Bowdin College in 1825, he had retreated to the attic of his mother's house in Salem. There, he worked obsessively to create a new American literature. The resulting stories were published in a collection titled *Twice-Told Tales*. Although the book was not a financial success, it established Hawthorne as a leading American author. The young writer moved to Brook Farm with the hopes of building a home for his fiancée, Sophia Peabody.

I took this group of real-life individuals, and then added two fictional characters to my play. Kathleen Boyle and Michael James O'Connor are recent Irish immigrants. In the 1840's, New England was the textile and meat processing center for the nation where Irish immigrants found work in the factories and slaughterhouses.

The two emigrants are inspired by the American dream of success in their new country. In contrast, the intellectuals at Brook Farm have been influenced by transcendentalism: a literary and philosophical movement popular in the first half of the nineteenth century.

Transcendentalism suggested that a higher reality could be achieved through sense experience - not through human reason. The members of Brook Farm were also aware of the English Romantic poetry that celebrated passionate attachments and extolled the beauties of nature. In addition, the young Hawthorne had plans to write a literary "romance" - a novel set in an exotic or mysterious setting. Ten years after he left Brook Farm he published *The Blithedale Romance* - an acerbic portrait of life in a utopian community.

When I had finished writing the play, I contacted The Road Theatre - the North Hollywood theater company that had achieved success with *Pirates*. Taylor Gilbert, the company's artistic director, wanted to produce the play and was enthusiastic about John Lawler, my choice for director.

The staging of *An American Romance* was a series of pleasant surprises. In particular, we were lucky to cast the playwright and actor John Rafter Lee as Nathaniel Hawthorne. The play opened to rave reviews, won numerous awards and ran for more than a year.

An American Romance is about love - and the fact that someone has to milk the cow and clean out the barn. As time passes, I also see this play as my love letter to the theater.

> NATHANIEL
> I've been in Salem too long. Hiding upstairs in my little room. This country of ours is vast and unrestrained. There are unknown rivers and grasslands. A wilderness that has never been surveyed. All is possible here. All is possible. But only if we discover a New World in our hearts.

***

AN AMERICAN ROMANCE was given its world premiere by The Road Theatre Company (Taylor Gilbert, Artistic Director) in North Hollywood, California on July 11, 1997. It was directed by John Lawler. The set design was by Wes McBride. The cast was as follows:

Kathleen Boyle......Marci Hill

Michael James Connor......Rich Willis

Sophia Ripley......Taylor Gilbert

George Ripley......James K. Ward

Margaret Fuller......Ann Gillespie

Charles King Newcomb......David Holcomb

Nathaniel Hawthorne......John Rafter Lee

AN AMERICAN ROMANCE won Five Valley Theatre ADA awards (best production and best writing), two Drama-Logue Awards, two Back Stage West awards and The New England Theatre Conference's John Gassner Playwright Award.

AN AMERICAN ROMANCE

A Play

by

Mark Lee

The play takes place during the summer of 1841 in a tenement in South Boston and at Brook Farm in West Roxbury, Massachusetts.

CHARACTERS

Kathleen Boyle - an Irish immigrant in her 20s Michael

James Connor - an Irish immigrant in his 20s Sophia

Ripley - a woman in her 30s

George Ripley - a former Unitarian minister in his 40s

Margaret Fuller - the editor and writer in her 30s

Charles King Newcomb - a poet in his 20s

Nathaniel Hawthorne - the writer in his 30s

ACT I

The stage design should allow the natural world -- the blue sky and the green countryside -- to dominate the interior settings. An upstage series of archways can suggest a wall.

Furniture and props are carried on as needed.

Music. Darkness, then the stage is illuminated with a cold, gray light. It's 1841. We're in a tenement attic in the slums of South Boston.

We hear voices, then Michael James Connor enters -- dragging Kathleen Boyle.

Michael James is an Irish immigrant in his twenties who wears a cloth cap, a long coat, boots and work clothes. He carries a bundle of clothing.

Kathleen is a seamstress in her twenties. She wears a thread-bare dress and shawl.

                  KATHLEEN
Let go of me, Michael James!

                MICHAEL JAMES
Stop your howling or I'll give you a clout you won't forget!

                  KATHLEEN
Let go! Right now! What do you think you're doing?

                MICHAEL JAMES
We're going up to the attic.

He throws her onto the floor.

                  KATHLEEN
You can't...! won't...

                MICHAEL JAMES
Stop it! Right now!

                    KATHLEEN
          I'm not staying here!

Kathleen scrambles to her feet and tries to get away. Michael
James grabs her from behind.

                    MICHAEL JAMES
          We're just going to talk, Kathleen.
          That's all. Just a little talk...

                    KATHLEEN
          Let go of me!

                    MICHAEL JAMES
          Go ahead. Scream all morning if you
          want. Not a soul in Boston's going
          to hear you up here.

                    KATHLEEN
          You got no right, Michael James!

She elbows him in the groin, then pulls away.

                    MICHAEL JAMES
          I'm your husband.

                    KATHLEEN
          No you're not. We never went
          before the priest.

                    MICHAEL JAMES
          I bought that shawl you're
          wearing. That means something.

                    KATHLEEN
          Good. You can take it back.

She tosses the shawl at his face.

                    MICHAEL JAMES
          Stop it, Kathleen. No need for that.

                    KATHLEEN
          Drag me up here like some whore you
          found on the street...

                    MICHAEL JAMES
          A lad's got a right to ask his
          woman a few questions.

Michael James approaches Kathleen and shows her the bundle.

MICHAEL JAMES
What's this? That's all what I want
to know. This morning, I found it
stuffed in the wall behind the back
staircase.

KATHLEEN
My other dress. A few old stockings.

MICHAEL JAMES
Beggar me if you're not a liar. As
far as I can see, it's everything you own in the world.

KATHLEEN
I didn't want the other people in
the building to steal it. Steal
your toenails if they could.

MICHAEL JAMES
That's what I thought at first.
Then I found this.

He pulls out a piece of paper.

MICHAEL JAMES
Man with a shovel. Woman with a
rake. Looks like someone's looking
for harvesters.

KATHLEEN
You got that wrong.

MICHAEL JAMES
So what's it about?
         (offers her the paper)
Go on! You know I can't read.

Kathleen takes the paper and smoothes it out with her hand.

KATHLEEN
It's about a place called Brook Farm.
It's in the countryside, west of Boston.

MICHAEL JAMES
Brook has a "B." Doesn't it? I know
that letter well enough.

KATHLEEN
They're asking people to come and live...
         (reading)
"in a community of faith and hope
and goodwill."

MICHAEL JAMES
And what of it?

Kathleen folds the paper and puts it in her pocket.

KATHLEEN
Nothing. I liked the drawing. That's all.

MICHAEL JAMES
They're whoremongers. That's what they are.

KATHLEEN
You don't know that!

Kathleen sits on the floor.

MICHAEL JAMES
They send out these bills. Make sure they're found by a lass like you. Before you know it you're a dollar a tumble for the lads working on the railroad.

KATHLEEN
You're talking like a fool, Michael James.

MICHAEL JAMES
I know the world. Better than you. There's no kingdom of "faith and goodwill." Not on this earth.

KATHLEEN
It's a <u>community</u>.

MICHAEL JAMES
Community of whoremongers. I'm sure of it. Trust in their lies and you'll spend the rest of your life looking up at the ceiling.

He approaches her and places the shawl on her shoulder.

MICHAEL JAMES
Kathleen, please. Me love...

KATHLEEN
Ahhh. First you drag me up here like a dog. Then you talk about love.

MICHAEL JAMES
I know you're not happy. But I'm
working. Working for both of us. In a few
years, we'll have enough money to go west.
Ohio. Kentucky. Any place you fancy.

He embraces her from behind.

KATHLEEN
In a few years, we'll be dead.
They'll stuff us in a sack and
plant us in that weedy little patch
of ground near the harbor. Black
ink on a plank tombstone. Your name
fades away with the first rain.

MICHAEL JAMES
That's not going to happen. We'll
live long enough to have our own
children. Grandchildren.

KATHLEEN
I'm tired, Michael James. Don't you
know that? This pain in my skull
comes more and more often.

MICHAEL JAMES
It's eye strain. You've got to have
more light when you do your
seamstress work.

KATHLEEN
I've done my work standing in the
sunshine and the pain still comes to
me. It's this place. That's what does
it. There are vapors here. Poison
vapors that push through your skin.

MICHAEL JAMES
We've got no money. We'd just be
beggars on the road. We need enough
to buy a wagon, oxen, tools.

KATHLEEN
That'll take ten years.

MICHAEL JAMES
Maybe not. Yesterday, I got a new
job at the slaughterhouse. Mr.
Feely took me off the killing beds
and put me on the sausage machine.

Kathleen stands up.

                    KATHLEEN
          Still sounds like pigs to me.

Michael James stands and faces her.

                    MICHAEL JAMES
          It's more money. Ten cents more an
          hour. Ten cents closer to leaving
          this place.

Kathleen approaches Michael James and touches him.

                    KATHLEEN
          Be careful, Michael James. Half the
          men in this building don't have all
          their fingers.

                    MICHAEL JAMES
          Don't worry about me. I move quick
          enough when I want to.

He kisses her and steps away.

                    MICHAEL JAMES
          I better get going. Mr. Feely wants
          me to sharpen up the blades before
          the first bell.

He begins to exit.

                    MICHAEL JAMES
          Just stay away from those whore-
          mongers. You hear me? Don't talk to
          a man with polish on his shoes.

Michael James exits. We hear music, slowly building in volume, as Kathleen picks up her belongings.

Kathleen looks at the handbill for Brook Farm. The lights rise upstage and we see Sophia Ripley gazing at the horizon.

Fantasizing about Brook Farm, Kathleen smiles and looks downstage. A Beat, then she decides to run away. Carrying her belongings, Kathleen turns and quickly exits.

The music continues. Lights up on the entire stage. It's a summer morning in the fields of Brook Farm. Sophia Ripley looks out at the world with great pleasure.

Sophia is in her thirties. She's a neat, cheerful woman who wears the "ethical clothing" soon to be advocated by Amelia Bloomer. The costume consists of a blouse, short skirt, and matching knickerbockers.

George Ripley, Sophia's husband, enters carrying two rakes and two shovels.

George is a former Unitarian minister in his forties. He wears a distinctive style of Brook Farm clothing: a blue tunic, sack trousers and heavy work boots.

The music fades. We hear the sounds of a country morning (birds, wind, some distant cattle).

      SOPHIA
  It's so beautiful on this hill.
  You can see the dandelions on the
  lower pasture. The elm trees and
  the duck pond. The bright blue
  bowl of the sky. It makes me feel
  light on my feet, George. If you
  don't hold onto me, I'll float
  off into the clouds!

George places the tools on the ground. Amused, he turns to his wife.

      GEORGE
  What clouds, Sophia? What are
  you chattering about?

      SOPHIA
  There's a wonderful view from
  here, George. Come over and see.

George walks over to his wife and looks down the hill.

      GEORGE
  There's a hole in the fence.

      SOPHIA
  So?

George returns to the rakes.

      GEORGE
  So the cows will find it and get
  out and wander down to the
  parsnip patch and eat too much
  and get the bloat and die.

      SOPHIA
  You're always so optimistic about
  people, George. But when it comes to
  livestock, you're a complete Puritan.

George adjusts the tines of a rake with some pliers.

GEORGE
We've just got to be responsible, Sophia. Anticipate any problems. Brook Farm is like a child, taking its first steps in the world.

SOPHIA
Don't worry. Everything will be all right.

GEORGE
Emerson might see this place as 179 acres of pokeweed and puddingstone, but it's really just a beginning. Brook Farm must become a crucible for improving mankind.

SOPHIA
All right. I'm persuaded. Let's fix that fence and save the cows from destruction.

GEORGE
Not yet. We have a job to do right here. Margaret's coming to help us.

SOPHIA
What about Charles?

GEORGE
I sent him out to check the gopher traps.

SOPHIA
That will take awhile. If he finds some gophers, he'll read them his poetry.

GEORGE
Charles is a talented young man, but he has way of undermining things. I don't want him around when I talk to Margaret. We must persuade her to join Brook Farm.

Sophia approaches her husband.

SOPHIA
She doesn't have much money, George. She's worn the same three dresses for the last two years.

GEORGE
The money is not as important as
her public support. Margaret is a
writer, a teacher and the editor
of the *Dial*. She has an intelligence
unusual for a...

Margaret Fuller calls from a distance. Margaret is in her early thirties. She wears a light summer dress. Her hair is arranged in a smooth, simple style with a part in the middle.

MARGARET
Hello up there! Should I bring some
tools with me?

GEORGE
No, Margaret! It's not necessary!
I've got everything organized!

Sophia speaks quickly to her husband.

SOPHIA
George, listen to me. We don't feed
hay to the chickens.

GEORGE
What? What are you talking about?

SOPHIA
You're a wonderful man, George. But
you talk to everyone the same way.
Margaret is a gray hawk spiraling
alone up through the sky. Don't be
so practical when you talk to her.
Tell her...

Margaret enters briskly and walks toward them.

MARGARET
Hello. What's the conversation?

GEORGE
Nothing really. Sophia's babbling
about hawks and chickens.

Sophia laughs nervously.

SOPHIA
Have to guard the hen house...

MARGARET
So what's this morning's project,
George? Not more post holes, I hope.

(MORE)

MARGARET
There's nothing more uninspiring than a post hole. Let's build something grand at Brook Farm. A lighthouse flashing its fire through the night.

GEORGE
During these formative days, the light must come from our own words.

SOPHIA
It's cheaper, too.

MARGARET
Don't worry. I don't really want to build a lighthouse. But in the country, on a summer's day, everything seems possible.

SOPHIA
It sounds like you've enjoyed your two weeks here.

Sophia links arms with Margaret.

MARGARET
Indeed. I don't want to leave.

George approaches the two women.

GEORGE
Then don't leave. Become a member of Brook Farm and live here permanently.

MARGARET
I don't think...

GEORGE
Take the first step. That's the most difficult thing to do. When I was still preaching, I would look out at my congregation and see these frightened, desperate faces. I wanted to leap down from pulpit, grab them by the neck and shout: "Try! Dare! Dream! Change your life before it's too late!"

SOPHIA
Fortunately, he restrained himself.

GEORGE
All those people sitting around
Boston parlors chattering about
moral freedom. If you want to build
the City of God, then someone has
to lay the first brick!

MARGARET
You're more an optimist than I
am, George. I'm not sure if we're
ready to reconstruct society.

GEORGE
Then see this as an experiment...
a test to see if our country is
ready for true change.

MARGARET
I don't like joining things. It
reminds me of marriage.

Charles King Newcomb enters. The poet is in his twenties. He dresses like George, wearing the same kind of work boots and tunic.

CHARLES
I have an announcement to make!

SOPHIA
Hello, Charles!

CHARLES
I refuse to have anything to
do with the massacre of
innocent gophers!

Charles declaims a parody of Shylock's speech in "The Merchant of Venice." He approaches Sophia.

CHARLES
Hath not a gopher little brown
eyes? Hath not a gopher
organs, passions for his
little gopher friends?
    (approaches Margaret)
If you prick a gopher will he not
bleed? If you tickle a gopher
will he not laugh?
    (approaches George)
And if you wrong a gopher...
shall he not find his revenge?

Charles sits down.

                    GEORGE
          They dig up the pasture,
          Charles. The cows can step in
          the holes and break their legs.

                    CHARLES
          Then that's the cows' problem.
          Not the gophers'.

Sophia hurries forward -- eager to break up the argument.

                    SOPHIA
          Let's begin working. All right?
          We've been standing around for
          most of the morning and we
          haven't got anything done.

                    MARGARET
          It's post holes. Isn't it,
          George? I just know that it's
          post holes again.

                    GEORGE
          Don't worry, Margaret. All I
          want to do is move this pile
          over to the vegetable garden.

                    SOPHIA
          It's the dung hill. We kept the horse
          here before we moved the barn.

                    GEORGE
          This is not a dung hill. It's a
          gold mine...in a poetical sense.

George crosses the stage to a pile of horse manure.

                    CHARLES
          I wonder if the horse realized that he
          was creating such a vivid metaphor.

                    GEORGE
          This dung...when mixed with the
          soil over where Charles is
          sitting....will increase the
          natural vitality of the land.

                    MARGARET
          Yes. Of course. An excellent
          suggestion.

She picks up two shovels and gives one to Charles. Sophia
picks up a rake and goes to the garden area.

MARGARET
Come on, Charles. Let's finish this
and go milk the cows.

CHARLES
Those cows don't like me. I'm sure
of it. They remind me of my
relatives in Boston. Swallowing
gossip whole, then spitting it up
to chew it over again.

Margaret pushes her shovel into the dung pile and starts to
carry some over to the garden area.

GEORGE
Stop! Don't work. Not yet.

MARGARET
What's the problem?

GEORGE
Last week, during the nightly
discussion, we agreed that all
labor at Brook Farm should be
performed in a rational manner.

CHARLES
It's just a dung hill, George.
There's nothing rational about it.

GEORGE
The shoveling job requires more
upper torso strength. Therefore, it
should be done by the men. The
raking job is more of a nurturing
function. Thus, it should be done
by the women.

George exchanges his rake with Margaret's shovel. Margaret
reluctantly walks over to the garden.

CHARLES
Is there a third category?

SOPHIA
I've got a rake. Get your rake, Margaret.

MARGARET
Why can't men nurture as well?

GEORGE
In the wilds, the female animal
takes care of the young while the
male...goes forth to gather food.

CHARLES
Except for moose.

GEORGE
I beg your pardon?

CHARLES
Young male moose congregate like a virile brotherhood of Spartan warriors.

GEORGE
But the female moose takes care of the children.

SOPHIA
Margaret doesn't have any children, George.

GEORGE
What?

MARGARET
Does that mean I can shovel?

GEORGE
You can't discount the upper torso strength.

He lifts the shovel over his head.

GEORGE
That *is* an unassailable fact.

CHARLES
Take off your shirt, George. Give us an exhibition.

GEORGE
All I'm saying *is* that there *is* a natural order *in* the world which governs the rational use of labor which means...I shovel, you rake.

Margaret hesitates, then begins to rake.

GEORGE
Excellent. Good for you, Margaret. With each little step, we travel closer to our "Golden City."

George walks over to the dung pile.

                    GEORGE
          We'll build our own theatre. Our
          own library and school. Money will
          be abolished. Hunger and poverty
          will be outlawed forever.

Furious, Margaret faces George.

                    MARGARET
          I want to shovel!

                    CHARLES
          And I want to rake. Direct contact
          with this dung pile is a bit too
          intense for my nostrils.

Margaret and Charles quickly exchange tools. Charles starts
to rake with Sophia.

                    CHARLES
          Besides, I feel rather nurturing
          this morning. Perhaps this evening,
          I'll have more upper torso strength.

                    SOPHIA
          So...everyone's happy. We all get
          what we want.

                    GEORGE
          Agreed.

Margaret walks back and forth between the pile and the garden.

                    GEORGE
          In another sort of community, there
          would have been rules to govern
          this decision. Instead we have
          relied upon our natural sense of
          goodwill and cooperation.

                    CHARLES
          I wonder who the horse cooperated
          with to make this hill.

                    GEORGE
          We don't need rules and regulations if
          we listen to the natural impulse of
          our hearts. Once we realize that all
          our lives are bound together, what
          can possibly come between us?

Nathaniel Hawthorne approaches them. Although it's summer, he
wears black clothes and a long black cloak. Nathaniel carries a
carpetbag.

                    NATHANIEL
          Hello.

                    GEORGE
          Nathaniel! You were supposed
          to come next week!

                    NATHANIEL
          There was nothing holding me
          in Salem.

                    GEORGE
               (very pleased)
          Well...Well...Well...

     George puts down his shovel. He shakes Hawthorne's hand.

                    GEORGE
          You know my wife....and Margaret
          Fuller.
               (motions to Charles)
          This young man is Charles King
          Newcomb...a recent graduate of
          Brown.

Charles puts down his rake and approaches Nathaniel.

                    CHARLES
          A lifelong shame, I'm afraid.

                    GEORGE
          Charles is our farm's resident poet.
               (to Charles)
          This is Nathaniel Hawthorne. You
          must have read his Twice-Told Tales.

                    CHARLES
          Of course. Your stories are
          brilliant, Sir. They are the best our
          country has to offer the world.

                    NATHANIEL
          If that's true, then we must all
          try harder.

Margaret puts down her shovel.

                    MARGARET
          How long is your visit, Nathaniel?
          One week? A fortnight?

GEORGE
Mr. Hawthorne isn't a visitor, Margaret. He's bought two shares in the farm, at $500 apiece. Plus he's made an additional investment of another $500.

Sophia puts down her rake.

CHARLES
That's wonderful. You must have made piles of money from your book.

NATHANIEL
Not really. But George has convinced me of the worthiness of his idea.

GEORGE
It's not just an idea, Nathaniel. We have land here. And buildings and fields and apple trees.

CHARLES
And cocks and pigs and cows that don't like me at all.

NATHANIEL
It sounds very...vital.

GEORGE
But why just talk about it? Come with me and I'll show you everything.

Margaret takes Nathaniel's arm. George leads them down the hill.

GEORGE
We'll walk to the pasture first. Then the duck pond and the creamery and the...

The three exit. Charles wipes off his hands.

CHARLES
Well, that was a good day's work. Was there any pudding left over from last night's supper?

SOPHIA
I think so. A little.

CHARLES
I think I'll consume it in a rational manner.

Charles exits. Sophia picks up the tools and exits. Blackout. Music.

Later that day. Lights up on Sophia. Sitting on a chair, she churns butter in the barnyard. (Note: she uses a wooden, barrel-shaped butter churn in which the churning stick is pulled up and down)

Nathaniel enters and approaches her. He has taken off his black coat, but still wears black trousers, a white linen shirt, and a black cravat.

SOPHIA
Good afternoon, Nathaniel. I trust you found your room satisfactory.

NATHANIEL
It was...satisfactory. Where are the others?

SOPHIA
My husband is weeding the cornfield. Margaret is herding in the cows.

NATHANIEL
And Mr. Newcomb?

SOPHIA
Oh, he's wandering around searching for eggs. He really does have a genius for finding them...much better than the rest of us. He says he's able to empathize with the chickens.

NATHANIEL
You look tired, Sophia.

SOPHIA
I'm all right. We must have butter.

Nathaniel steps forward.

NATHANIEL
Allow me.

SOPHIA
No. You've just arrived this morning. There's no reason why you have to start work immediately.

NATHANIEL
Please. I insist.

Sophia stands up.

SOPHIA
Thank you. Thank you very much. It's almost time for me to start cooking supper.

NATHANIEL
Do you recall the first time we met? It was several years ago. At the home of Bronson Alcott.

SOPHIA
Yes. That seems likely. I used to go there quite often.

NATHANIEL
You played a violin piece...very beautifully. Perhaps I could hear you play again.

SOPHIA
I'm afraid my hands are rather cramped and callused these days. My violin playing would sound like the squallings of a hungry cat. Thank you for your help. I'll be in the kitchen.

She starts to walk away.

NATHANIEL
Are you happy here, Sophia?

SOPHIA
Yes. Very happy. We were poor in Boston and yet we had to keep up appearances. The ladies at the church would comment on my faded bonnet and the patch on my skirt.

NATHANIEL
And now you have money?

SOPHIA
Oh, no. Now we're completely destitute, but it doesn't seem to matter. These days, I only care about the cows and the chickens... the green world that surrounds us.

                    NATHANIEL
               (looking around)
          It is beautiful.

                    SOPHIA
          I do believe that the world is
          changed by our emotions. Love and
          hope and happiness are absorbed
          into the air. They give the atmosphere
          a certain power...like the way the
          wind feels just before a rainstorm.

                    NATHANIEL
          That is...very interesting.

Sophia looks down and shakes her head.

                    SOPHIA
          Oh. I'm such a silly goose. Aren't I?

                    NATHANIEL
          Not at all.

                    SOPHIA
          Must start supper or we won't eat
          tonight.

Sophia exits. Nathaniel moves the churning stick for a few seconds. He peers under the round wooden top of the churn -- expecting butter to instantly appear. Nothing.

Slightly annoyed, he resumes the work. Charles enters, carrying basket and whistling the "Ode to Joy."

                    CHARLES
          I see that George already has you working.

                    NATHANIEL
          Actually, I was encouraged to do
          this by Mrs. Ripley.

                    CHARLES
          Sophia gave you an order? That's
          not like her.

                    NATHANIEL
          She was churning the butter...
          looking exhausted...and I had an
          immediate desire to volunteer.

                    CHARLES
          Sophia can do that to people.
          Never underestimate the power of
          sympathetic guilt.

NATHANIEL
You sound as if you're immune.

CHARLES
Immune to guilt? Yes. I obey Sophia because her own passion inspires me. Brook Farm is a community. But it's also her creation.

NATHANIEL
Her creation could use a bit more furniture. My room has a corn husk bed and a blue enamel wash basin. Nothing more.

CHARLES
You're lucky! When I first arrived here, I coveted that same blue wash basin like King David lusting for Bathsheba.

NATHANIEL
I guess I should feel fortunate.

Nathaniel sits down and moves the churning stick.

CHARLES
So tell me, Nathaniel...what are you?

NATHANIEL
I beg your pardon?

CHARLES
Almost everyone here is something other than themselves. George is a Transcendentalist. Margaret is a bluestocking. I'm a converted Catholic. I have an incense burner and an altar to the Virgin Mary in my room. It makes Unitarians break out into hives.

NATHANIEL
I'm just a writer.

CHARLES
You can write in Salem. Why come here?

NATHANIEL
I have become engaged to Miss Sophia Peabody.

CHARLES
One of the three Peabody sisters, correct? The sick one.

NATHANIEL
I need a place to build a home. For most of my life, I've been living with my two sisters and my mother.

CHARLES
Oh, I'm an expert on living with mothers. For as long as I've known her, my mother has worn a formidable whale-bone corset. Embracing her, I sensed the presence of a vast and terrible leviathan.

NATHANIEL
I...I love my family.

CHARLES
So do I. The institution is designed to invoke our deepest affections... and loathings. Fortunately, I was able to escape to Brook Farm.

NATHANIEL
Well, I'm not escaping from anything. I need to build a place of my own. A home for Miss Peabody.

CHARLES
Why not travel west with an ax in one hand and a rifle in the other? Claim your 60 acres of land and commence to slaughter Indians.

NATHANIEL
The wilderness is...wilderness. I thought that Brook Farm would provide a pleasant setting with intellectual stimulation. I have hopes of writing a Romance.

CHARLES
A Romance? Ahhh, I see. A tale of amorous adventure.

NATHANIEL
No. You mistake my meaning. I would like to write a story of sensibility ...of fine and tender feelings... set in the American countryside.

CHARLES
It won't be a true pastoral. There
are no satyrs or nymphs in West
Roxbury. Although I've been looking

Nathaniel peers into the churn. Still nothing.

NATHANIEL
Perhaps this is the wrong kind of
milk for butter.

CHARLES
Has it thickened at all? Are there
little white lumps?

NATHANIEL
Not that I can see.

Nathaniel replaces the cover and moves the churning stick.

CHARLES
You're too tentative.

NATHANIEL
What do you mean?

CHARLES
You want butter, but some delicacy
of character moderates your efforts.

NATHANIEL
I've never done this before. We buy
our butter in Salem.

Charles grabs the churning stick and helps Nathaniel move it up
and down.

CHARLES
Think of milk, pure and sweet,
thrust back and forth within the
walls of the churn. Slowly, it
thickens and the stick in your hand
moves stiffly. You can feel it,
feel the transformation, as lumps
butter appear and merge and grow
harder and harder...

Margaret enters, carrying the stick she's used to drive cattle.

MARGARET
I didn't know this was a job for
two men.

Flustered, Nathaniel and Charles stop working.

CHARLES
Nathaniel needed some encouragement.

MARGARET
And Sophia needs some eggs. She called to me from the kitchen window.

Charles picks up the basket and starts to exit.

CHARLES
I hope she's making dumplings. I have the appetite of a young farm Hand, clutching his scythe, cutting a path through a golden ocean of grain.

Charles exits.

NATHANIEL
He's hungry?

MARGARET
I think that's what he was trying to say. Charles can't weed the parsnip patch without a few metaphors to help his labor.

NATHANIEL
He said he was a converted Catholic ...with an altar.

MARGARET
Charles is running toward religion while almost everyone else is running away from it. George used to be a minister. Then he decided that instead of talking about Paradise in the Hereafter, he'd try to create it in West Roxbury.

NATHANIEL
George didn't mention "Paradise" when we spoke in Boston. He said that Brook Farm would provide enough food and income so that everyone here could be self-reliant.

MARGARET
So you bought shares?

NATHANIEL
He said that was necessary if I was going to build my own house.

MARGARET
Yes. Of course. There's gossip in
Boston that you're engaged to Miss
Elizabeth Peabody.

NATHANIEL
You're misinformed. It is her sister,
Sophia.

MARGARET
Oh. The sick one.

NATHANIEL
She's getting better!

MARGARET
Has she tried mesmerism? I've
learned some of the techniques from
the practitioners in Boston. It's
good for headache, sleeplessness,
and spiritual fatigue.

NATHANIEL
On the advice of Bronson Alcott,
Miss Peabody is taking a series
of ice-water baths.

Margaret swings the switch through the air.

MARGARET
Ice-water baths! What idiocy. In
one form or another, they've had
ice water baths since the Puritans
landed in Plymouth.

She approaches Nathaniel.

MARGARET
We need to look out...and beyond.
There is an ether that surrounds
us. It's invisible, rarefied beyond
all comparison, yet able to affect
the human body like the movement of
the tides.

NATHANIEL
So...we're standing in it?

MARGARET
We're breathing it. The ether
penetrates our bodies. It is the
animate force. The wind that pushes
our sails.

NATHANIEL
And do ice-water baths...?

MARGARET
Forget ice-water baths! This energy in our bodies is called animal magnetism. Once you learn the techniques, you're able to concentrate your own magnetism and project it into the body of another. It invigorates. Animates. Heals.

NATHANIEL
You sound like a believer.

MARGARET
I've healed myself. And others. In fact, the only problem with animal magnetism is that it doesn't seem to work with animals.

NATHANIEL
You've experimented at Brook Farm?

MARGARET
I've tried to use it on my cow, Athena. It hasn't worked.

NATHANIEL
Not enough milk?

MARGARET
I thought that Athena would be happy at Brook Farm. She'd have fields of grass. A large barn. Bovine companionship.

NATHANIEL
What happened?

MARGARET
It turns out that there's a cow society in every herd. A hierarchy of leaders and followers.

NATHANIEL
And what was Athena's role?

MARGARET
They've rejected her entirely, kicking her and trying to gore her with their blunted horns. Right now, they're in the barn and she's out in the pasture.

NATHANIEL
So you're angry at the herd?

MARGARET
Heavens no. I'm angry at Athena for still wanting to join them. They don't like her, Nathaniel. It's obvious. And yet, she keeps attempting to graze with them. It's pathetic.

NATHANIEL
You should send her away.

MARGARET
No. I will not admit failure.

She approaches Nathaniel.

MARGARET
There's a black bull living in the pasture next to ours. He's young and vital. A suitable companion for Athena.

NATHANIEL
She and the bull would share the same pasture?

MARGARET
Yes. That's it. What do you think of the idea? They would increase each other's magnetism...like two mirrors reflecting the candlelight. Athena is a strong animal. Very strong. I'm sure the bull would prefer her over her sickly sisters.

NATHANIEL
I don't know much about animals.

MARGARET
Stay at Brook Farm and you'll learn. You'll learn a great many things...

Margaret exits. Nathaniel hesitates, then returns to the butter churn. He pushes the churning stick a few times, then pulls it out. Nothing.

Blackout. Music. Nathaniel exits.

Lights up on the parlor of the farmhouse that evening. The parlor has a writing table with a chair. Two other straight-backed chairs are in the middle of the room.

Nathaniel and Charles enter with Sophia. She now wears a long, flowing skirt that is a 19th-century attempt at a "Grecian" costume. The two men wear coats and cravats.

>NATHANIEL
>That was a delicious meal, Sophia. Especially the apple dumplings.

>SOPHIA
>Thank you, Nathaniel. You don't think they were overcooked?

Sophia and Charles sit on the center stage chairs.

>CHARLES
>Nonsense! If Shakespeare had eaten at Brook Farm, it would have changed his poetry:
>>(recites)
>Shall I compare thee to a summer's dumpling? Thou art more lovely and more temperate...

George enters from the farmyard and removes his coat. Sound of distant thunder.

>CHARLES
>How are the cows, George? I think it's awfully sweet the way you tuck them in at night.

>GEORGE
>There's a big thunderstorm coming from the east. It's starting to drizzle.

>CHARLES
>Does this mean we won't be able to work tomorrow? Pity.

>GEORGE
>Of course we'll be able to work. This is just a summer storm. We've got to take care of that dung pile.

>CHARLES
>>(to Nathaniel)
>George never forgets a task. Unfortunately.

>GEORGE
>All right. Let's get going. Where are the writing materials?

SOPHIA
I'm sorry, George. I'll get everything right away.

Sophia walks over to the table. She picks up a pen and a leather manuscript portfolio. George approaches Nathaniel.

GEORGE
Because you're new to Brook Farm, I should explain our nightly routine. Saturday night is our artistic evening. We recite poetry or play musical instruments.

Sophia sits at the table.

SOPHIA
Perhaps you could read us one of your stories, Nathaniel. That would be lovely.

GEORGE
Sunday night is for private contemplation while Monday through Friday nights we have philosophical discussions. I propose a topic, we debate it among ourselves and see how the conclusion relates to our life here at Brook Farm.

NATHANIEL
It all sounds very...interesting.

CHARLES
I sense a tepid enthusiasm.

NATHANIEL
I don't see how a declaration against slavery relates to the management of a cow barn.

GEORGE
We've already decided that, if presented with the opportunity, we'll hide runaway slaves in that barn.

NATHANIEL
But that's against the law.

GEORGE
Morality without action is meaningless. That's why I organized Brook Farm. Instead of talking about the future, we're going to create it.

                    NATHANIEL
          Ralph Waldo Emerson once said --

                    GEORGE
          Don't mention him!

                    CHARLES
          Now you've done it.

                    SOPHIA
          George, please calm down.

                    GEORGE
          Ralph Emerson always talks about the
          beauty of nature, but the man has the
          biggest coal bill in Concord! He's never
          had to plow a field or castrate a calf.

                    CHARLES
          Not before bedtime, George. Please.

Carrying a dish rag, Margaret enters the room. Charles stands
immediately. Margaret has also changed her clothes -- wearing a
long, flowing dress.

                    MARGARET
          Don't start arguing without me.
          It's very rude.

                    CHARLES
          George wants to interfere with the
          social life of our cattle.

She hands Nathaniel the dish rag.

                    MARGARET
          Here's a dish rag. Get familiar
          with it. You're washing the pots
          and pans tomorrow.

                    NATHANIEL
          Of course, I'll do my share of work.

Margaret sits on a center stage chair.

                    MARGARET
          It's not your share. It's your
          duty. These nightly discussions are
          important. But the true measure of
          any society is who washes the dishes.

Sophia picks up a pen and opens a bottle of ink. She places the
leather portfolio on her lap.

SOPHIA
Ready to go!

GEORGE
I haven't finished my point concerning --

SOPHIA
George, no more Emerson. Please. Not tonight.

Charles sits on the floor.

GEORGE
Very well. The topic I am proposing for this evening's discussion is: "What is the Purpose of America?"

MARGARET
Why should America have a purpose at all? You make it sound like one of the shovels.

George moves restlessly around the room.

GEORGE
Other countries in the Old World developed gradually over time. In contrast, the Puritans' arrival at Plymouth was a deliberate act. Each new generation in this country must decide why we are here and what we want for the future.

CHARLES
My mother would vote for better table manners.

GEORGE
I was trapped in Boston. Held prisoner by a religion that had lost all meaning. Because I was an American, I was able to break free and choose a new life. That is the purpose of our democracy...that our finest dreams may become real.

Finished with his statement, George sits next to Margaret. Sophia scribbles her notes.

SOPHIA
Good, George. Very, very good.

CHARLES
It was good. But limited.

                    GEORGE
          I'm sure you'll explain why.

Charles stands up and circles the room.

                    CHARLES
          Three thousand years ago, a mob
          of Mediterranean sea traders looted
          and burned a walled city. Those
          warriors are gone, dissolved into
          dust. We only remember them because a
          poet named Homer created the *Iliad*.

                    SOPHIA
               (cheerfully)
          I'm writing this down.

                    CHARLES
          A wealthy Italian woman still bewitches
          us because da Vinci painted her smile.
          Hundreds of years from now, the Kings of
          England will only be thought of as
          characters in Shakespeare's plays.

                    GEORGE
          What are you saying, Charles?

                    CHARLES
          That art is what is important in
          any society. Art is what survives.

                    GEORGE
          We are discussing the purpose of America.

                    CHARLES
          The purpose of America is to produce
          American art.

Charles sits back on the floor.

                    GEORGE
          What's your opinion, Nathaniel?
          You're a writer.

                    NATHANIEL
          I'm...still considering. What about
          Sophia?

                    SOPHIA
          Oh, no. Not me.

                    NATHANIEL
          Margaret?

Margaret stands up. She smiles, enjoying the discussion.

                    MARGARET
          I think that both arguments are
          total nonsense. How can we change
          our lives if our society will not
          permit this to happen? And how can
          we create a true American art if we
          allow a graceless aristocracy of
          wealth and power to rule our
          country? At least the princes of
          Europe had a better taste in
          mistresses and architecture.

                    SOPHIA
          "Mistresses and architecture."
          Oh, that's very good.

                    MARGARET
          America was founded on the proposition
          that "all men are created equal."
          That's what makes us different. That's
          what makes us unique. Equality should
          be our purpose and our creed.
                    (turns)
          Nathaniel...

                    NATHANIEL
          No. I'd rather not.

                    MARGARET
          You've bought two shares and
          they've given you the blue
          wash basin, so say something!

                    NATHANIEL
          I...I'm not a philosopher.

                    CHARLES
          Thank God.

                    NATHANIEL
          But my ancestor, William Hawthorne, was
          one of the first settlers of this new
          land...chief magistrate of the
          Massachusetts Bay colony. Judge
          Hawthorne, like most of the Puritans,
          could not tolerate the first few
          Quakers that came to America. They
          disrupted the church meetings, they
          refused to pay certain taxes, and
          claimed to be guided by an inner light.
          (MORE)

NATHANIEL
On one occasion, Judge Hawthorne ordered that a Quaker woman named Ann Coleman be stripped naked from the waist upward, bound to the tail of cart, and dragged though the main street of Salem at a brisk walk. A strong-armed constable followed her with a whip of knotted cords. And whenever he flourished his lash, you could see a frown wrinkling and twisting on his brow, and, at the same instant, a smile upon his lips. Down came the lash. And a bright stripe of blood appeared upon Ann Coleman's back. Ten such stripes were given in Salem, ten in Boston, and ten in Dedham, and then the woman was driven into the wilderness.

SOPHIA
Poor thing.

NATHANIEL
Of course, the purpose of America has been influenced by our desire for self-perfection and equality... and even for art. But sometimes, I think we regard this New World like a fresh painter's canvas...clean and untouched...ready to receive the scrawl of our intolerance.

GEORGE
I...don't...think...

SOPHIA
George...

GEORGE
We need to build, Nathaniel. We need to look forward. Away with history. We must forget the past. Ignore it. We must...

Drenched from the rain, Kathleen enters and collapses.

KATHLEEN
Help...me!

                    GEORGE
          Sophia! Start a fire and
          get some blankets!

Sophia runs out of the room.

                    MARGARET
          Who are you? Where did you come from?

                    KATHLEEN
          I am...

                    GEORGE
          Where is your home? Who is your family?

                    KATHLEEN
          Walked...from....Boston.

                    CHARLES
          My god, she's shivering.

Sophia enters, carrying two blankets.

                    SOPHIA
          Here we are! Blankets! Blankets!

She hands one of the blankets to her husband. George and Margaret wrap the blanket around Kathleen's shoulders.

                    GEORGE
          Give me some help, Margaret.
          There we go. Gently. Gently.

                    SOPHIA
          Who is she? One of those
          immigrants from Ireland?

                    CHARLES
          She's too pretty to be a servant.

                    GEORGE
               (to Margaret)
          All right, now let's get her up onto
          one of the chairs. One...Two...

                    KATHLEEN
          I'm sorry. I don't wish to...

Margaret and Charles help her sit on a chair. Nathaniel sits at the desk table.

GEORGE
There we go.
        (to Sophia)
Bring her some tea. There might be
some hot water left in the kettle.

SOPHIA
Yes. Of course. Right away.

Sophia leaves the room. George sits beside Kathleen.

GEORGE
Good evening, Madam. I'm George
Ripley.

KATHLEEN
Kathleen...Boyle.

GEORGE
Why were you walking about in this
dreadful storm? Are you looking
for your family? Friends? Samuel
Henderson has a large farm about a
mile from here. An old man named
Wilkes lives down the road.

KATHLEEN
Is this not Brook Farm? I asked
a drover at the crossroads. He
told me to walk this way.

CHARLES
She's looking for us! Oh, this
is a mystery!

GEORGE
This is Brook Farm, but why are you
here? I don't recall a prior acquaintance.

MARGARET
"A prior acquaintance?" For
heaven's sake, George! This isn't
the sculpture room at the Athenaeum.
        (touches Kathleen)
I'm Margaret Fuller. And I'm your
friend. Tell us why you've come here.

Kathleen begins to cry.

KATHLEEN
This is all wrong. Everything's
wrong. You think I'm a beggar.

NATHANIEL
She's a seamstress.

GEORGE
What are you talking about?

NATHANIEL
She wears no ring so I'll assume that she's not married. She lacks the appearance of schoolteacher or a --

CHARLES
"Woman of the town."

NATHANIEL
She's a seamstress. Or a similar profession.

KATHLEEN
I am a seamstress. Piecework, mostly, for Rutherford and Sons.

GEORGE
But why are you here?

KATHLEEN
A month ago, I was very unhappy. It was Sunday and yet the sky was as cold and gray as a piece of slate. I went down to the pump behind our building to get some water. I needed to finish 20 collars by Monday so that Rutherford and Sons would pay me 80 cents.

CHARLES
80 cents!

GEORGE
Yes. I'm sure that Rutherford and all his sons consider themselves good Christians.

KATHLEEN
I had to do the work. Had to...

She stands up and begins to move around the room.

KATHLEEN
But when I went outside, my feet seemed to have a different plan. I started walking through Boston, just walking, like a leaf blown wayward by the wind. After awhile, I became tired so I went into a church on Purchase Street and sat down.

                    GEORGE
The Unitarian church. My old pulpit.

                    KATHLEEN
No one was there. But the room
was so bare that I knew I couldn't
be accused of theft. There was
nothing much to steal.

                    CHARLES
There's the Protestant faith in a
nutshell, George. Nothing much to
steal.

                    KATHLEEN
I sat in the pew for awhile and
then I'm afraid I went to sleep.
When I woke up, it was almost
evening. The light seemed gold and
heavy, filling the room. I stood up
and started to leave and then I saw
a notice posted on the wall near
the door.

She takes the notice from her pocket. George stands up.

                    GEORGE
MY notice.Yes.

                    KATHLEEN
It said that the Reverend George
Ripley, his wife, and their friends
had purchased a property called
Brook Farm in West Roxbury. It said
that shares in the farm were
available or that people could
contribute their labor.

                    GEORGE
                (reciting)
"And that, in a community of faith
and hope and goodwill, we would
attempt to live by the example of
the Early Christian Church."

                    KATHLEEN
There was more. At the bottom of
the page, you said there were
Fields. Fruit trees. Ponds. A trout
stream. Livestock. Pleasant company
and surroundings.

MARGARET
Please sit down, Miss Boyle. Your clothes are wet and you still look rather pale.

Kathleen walks back to the chair and sits down.

KATHLEEN
I left the church and walked back home and each step I took seemed to repeat the words: "Pleasant company and surroundings. Pleasant company and surroundings." I laughed out loud. A man stared at me.

GEORGE
And so you came here?

KATHLEEN
Not immediately. I thought about it for days and days. It made me realize how ugly everything was where I live. The constant smell of cabbage. The cough of the old woman in the next room. Mud in the hallways. Mud smeared across the walls. And in the gutters outside.

GEORGE
We don't need to know what's in the gutters.

NATHANIEL
And so you came here.

KATHLEEN
Yes.

MARGARET
Did you tell your family?

KATHLEEN
My mother is dead. My father went out to Albany to get work on the new railroad, but then he disappeared. No one seems to know what happened to him.

GEORGE
And you have no protector?

KATHLEEN
What?

GEORGE
Someone who protects you because
you're a young woman.

KATHLEEN
I...I can protect me self. Please
don't think ill of me. Don't make
me go away.

NATHANIEL
Why didn't you write a letter
before you came?

KATHLEEN
I...thought...

MARGARET
Can't you see that she's tired,
Nathaniel?

KATHLEEN
I thought that you wouldn't let
me come if told you who I was.

GEORGE
Nonsense! We're open to anyone who's
sympathetic to our philosophy.

KATHLEEN
Yes, but...

CHARLES
What she's *saying* George is that
you put up the notice in the Cambridge
Unitarian Church. Somehow, such news
never gets posted in tenement buildings.

GEORGE
Well, she's here. And that's the
important thing.
    (looks up)
Sophia!
    (to Kathleen)
The woman getting your tea is my
wife, Sophia Ripley.
    (motions)
This is Nathaniel Hawthorne and
Charles King Newcomb.

CHARLES
You can call me Charlie.
    (to Margaret)
No one else gets that privilege.

Sophia enters with a tea pot and mug on a tray.

                    SOPHIA
          Here we are! Hot tea! It only took
          a minute!

Smiling at Kathleen, she puts the tray on the writing table and starts to pour the tea.

                    SOPHIA
          How are you, dear? You do look a
          little better.

                    GEORGE
          Her name is Kathleen Boyle. She's
          from Boston.

                    SOPHIA
          Oh, how wonderful! Do you know
          any of our friends, the Lowells?

                    GEORGE
          She's a seamstress.

                    SOPHIA
          Excellent. That's just what we need
          here. I'm all right in the kitchen,
          but I can barely thread a needle
          without stabbing one of my thumbs.
              (to Kathleen)
          Sugar?

                    KATHLEEN
          I...guess so.

Sophia adds sugar and hands the mug to Kathleen.

                    SOPHIA
          Mr. Hawthorne joined us today and
          now you've arrived. Oh, it's so
          exciting. I know we'll have lots
          of people here at Brook Farm,
          laughing and singing and...

                    CHARLES
          Shoveling gold.

                    SOPHIA
          That too, Charles. God will find all
          the wayfarers and the pilgrims and
          the prodigal sons and guide them to
          our door...even in the rain.

Holding the mug, Kathleen stands and approaches Sophia.

                    KATHLEEN
          You're so kind. All of you. The
          other farms I passed had dogs
          that smelled me and ran out to
          bark and snarl. I thought there
          might be dogs like that here.

                    CHARLES
          No. We just have Margaret's cow.

                    KATHLEEN
          I dreamed about this place. Every
          night. Before I went to sleep. I
          saw the trout stream and the pond
          and then I was walking up a path
          and I heard voices...your voices
          ...calling me.
               (moving quickly)
          I walked faster in the dream.
          Running. Jumping. Almost like
          a dance. I'm here now! Can't
          you hear me? I'm here!

She becomes dizzy, then faints and collapses onto the
floor. George runs over to her.

                    GEORGE
          Sophia! Help me!
               (panicking)
          SOPHIA!

The lights dim. Music. Sound of the thunder and rain.
Everyone exits except Kathleen and Sophia.

In shadowy light, Sophia helps Kathleen take off her
dress. Sophia places a long white nightgown over
Kathleen's shoulders. The two women exit.

Lights up on Nathaniel's bedroom. There's a bed, a
table and a chair. A blue wash basin is on the table.

Wearing a long nightshirt, Nathaniel gets ready for bed.
Nathaniel touches the corn husk mattress and tries to
smooth down the lumps. He sits on the bed, finds some
more lumps, and tries to pound them down with his fist.

He touches the mattress again. More lumps. Annoyed, he
stands on the bed and gets ready to jump on the mattress.
Margaret begins to enter the room.

                    MARGARET
          Hello? Nathaniel? May I come in?

NATHANIEL
I'm not presentable, Margaret. I'm wearing my--

Margaret enters, wearing a long white nightgown. Nathaniel immediately gets off the bed. Margaret is full of nervous energy. She moves restlessly around the room.

MARGARET
I thought you might want a report about our little seamstress. We just prepared a room for her and tucked her into bed.

NATHANIEL
Why did she collapse?

MARGARET
She was hungry. That's all. She hadn't eaten for two days. We gave her some bread and milk. Tomorrow morning, we'll bring out the wash tub and give her a good scrubbing. She has beautiful hair. Quite Beautiful. Did you notice?

Margaret sits on the bed.

NATHANIEL
Yes, I believe I did.

MARGARET
I feel close to Miss Boyle. I think we shall become good friends.

NATHANIEL
Miss Boyle needs a friend. She seems quite alone in this world.

MARGARET
Many women are in the same situation, Nathaniel.

NATHANIEL
Not in Salem.

Nathaniel sits on the other end of the bed.

MARGARET
In Salem. In Boston. It's all the same. A woman is alone whenever she rejects her fate and pursues her destiny. Perhaps this is why so many women remain silent.

NATHANIEL
I can't imagine you remaining silent, Margaret.

MARGARET
I speak of other women and a disappointment I had this Spring. As you might know, I've offered a series of Conversations for the women of Boston. They each pay $20 for 10 sessions. We meet on Saturdays at 11 o'clock.

NATHANIEL
I've heard about these meetings. You stand in front of the crowd and lead discussions about Love, Truth and Beauty

MARGARET
Yes. It's wonderful how all the women have joined in. This Spring, however, I decided to include men in the sessions.
        (very distressed)
All the women that had spoken so well before...sat mute while Emerson and his friends talked and talked and talked. Why can't we women speak? Why can't we tell men what we truly believe?

NATHANIEL
Women are angels, the better half of mankind. Perhaps, they guide the world in a more subtle fashion.

Furious, Margaret stands up and moves around the room.

MARGARET
Don't call me an angel! Angels have no sex, no free will and no desire. They sit on a cloud in a pure white gown and do God's needlework. Call me a scold or a bluestocking or a demon. But not an angel. An angel is a simpering idiot with wings!

Nathaniel stands and faces her.

NATHANIEL
I was merely giving a compliment to your sex. Men and women are different. That's obvious.

MARGARET
It's not a permanent division, Nathaniel. Male and female are perpetually passing into one another.

She reaches out and lightly touches Nathaniel's heart.

MARGARET
Fluid hardens to solid, solid rushes to fluid. There is no wholly masculine man, no purely feminine woman.

NATHANIEL
Someone must lead when dancing.

CHARLES
Nathaniel?

Wearing a nightshirt, Charles enters the room. He's surprised to find Margaret and Nathaniel together.

CHARLES
Oh...Margaret. Continuing the evening's discussion?

MARGARET
Yes. In a way.

Charles lounges on the bed.

CHARLES
Well, here we all are, wearing our nightshirts, debating the future of America. I think it's a wonderful idea! We forget that Socrates and Plato had their symposiums lying in white robes on couches while curly-haired slave boys brought them cups of wine.

NATHANIEL
Margaret wanted to tell me about the seamstress.

CHARLES
Yes. Of course. I went to her room and gave her a book of Keats.

MARGARET
Charles treats poetry as if it were a powerful medicine.

CHARLES
Not just poetry...but novels and paintings, too. Art can heal you and feed you and give you comfort on a dark night.

MARGARET
Nonsense. That girl needed dry clothes and supper. You can't fill an empty stomach with *Ode to a Grecian Urn*.

CHARLES
What do you think, Nathaniel?

NATHANIEL
I think...I'd like to go to sleep.

MARGARET
Point taken. We'll continue this in the morning. Good night, Nathaniel. Charles...

CHARLES
Pleasant dreams.

She exits. Nathaniel sits by the writing desk.

CHARLES
You're always watching, aren't you? One part of you is always distant, as cold as a marble statue.

NATHANIEL
I do not believe in public displays of emotion.

CHARLES
Then how can you write a Romance?

NATHANIEL
That's just a story. Fiction.

CHARLES
There's no such thing as fiction. All writing is confession. The only variation is the extent of one's disguise.

NATHANIEL
Nonsense.

CHARLES
You disguise yourself very well,
Nathaniel. Quiet. Discrete. Always
wearing black. Hiding yourself
like a cat in the dark.

NATHANIEL
And you seem to spend all your
time acting like a poor imitation
of an English fop.

CHARLES
Italian fop. Don't forget. I'm Catholic.

NATHANIEL
If you want to be an American
poet, then start acting like a
product of this nation.

CHARLES
So, tell me. How is an American
poet supposed to act?

NATHANIEL
He doesn't build an altar and
become a Catholic.

CHARLES
Should I get circumcised and
become a Jew?

NATHANIEL
He doesn't talk like that either!

CHARLES
How should I talk?

NATHANIEL
Calm. Direct. Proud of your country.

Charles stands up and faces Nathaniel.

CHARLES
All right. I'll change my manner.
Become more American.
    (a rural accent)
Tell you what, Mr. Hawthorne. I'm
not leaving this place 'til you
rassle me to the floor.

NATHANIEL
What?

CHARLES
Rassle me! Like two young pioneers out on the western prairie.

He pushes Nathaniel off the chair.

CHARLES
Come on. Let's go. You'll find that I'm stronger than a bear.

Charles begins to move like a wrestler around the room.

NATHANIEL
Too much poetry has gone to your head. Get out this room. At once!

CHARLES
I'm an American! Spawned of the Mississippi River and the Cumberland Mountains. I'm half-horse, half-alligator with a touch of snapping turtle.

He jumps onto the bed.

CHARLES
I can leap the Ohio, ride down a streak of lighting, and lick my weight in wild cats. Bring on those European poets. Shelley. Byron. Keats. I'll rassle 'em all.

Charles jumps onto the floor and chases Nathaniel.

NATHANIEL
I'm warning you, Mr. Newcomb!

CHARLES
Ummmmmmm. Uhhhhhhh.

Nathaniel hesitates, then lunges toward Charles. Charles sidesteps and Nathaniel falls on the floor.

Charles stands over Nathaniel. When Nathaniel tries to get up, Charles steps on his chest -- pushing him back onto the floor.

CHARLES
See? What did I tell you? I'm a swamper screamer. I'm a mountain goat. I'm a yelping, whelping, son of the plains.

NATHANIEL
That's it. You force me to use extreme methods.

CHARLES
Sorry, Nathaniel. You're a good
writer, but I bet you couldn't kick
a coon from a tree. I can out-rassle,
out-jump, out-drink, out-holler any
man who --

Very angry, Nathaniel jumps to his feet. He throws himself on
Charles and the two men wrestle, forcing each other back and
forth across the room.

Nathaniel kicks at Charles' legs. Charles tries to avoid him.
Both men push against the bed, and then fall on the floor.

They look at each other -- and start laughing.

NATHANIEL
I feel like I'm back in college.

CHARLES
There's nothing wrong with that.

NATHANIEL
Yelping, whelping...

CHARLES
Son of the plains. That's me.
Now, I let you sleep.

Charles stands up and begins to exit.

NATANIEL
Charles...

CHARLES
I need to know something important.

CHARLES
Go ahead and ask.

NATHANIEL
Where's the other privy? I only saw
the one about twenty yards from the
kitchen.

CHARLES
That's the only one we have, I'm afraid. I left my copy of Milton's *Prometheus Unbound* in there. You're welcome to read it at your leisure.

NATHANIEL
I need to use the out-building, but it's raining. And there doesn't seem to be a receptacle in the room.

Charles picks up the wash basin and gives it to Nathaniel.

CHARLES
I'd use the famous blue basin if I were you.

NATHANIEL
But I wash my face in that.

CHARLES
I won't tell anybody. In an emergency, I use my hollow bust of Aristotle.

NATHANIEL
But I can't--

CHARLES
Don't worry about your dignity, Nathaniel. We're all human. Read Shakespeare's sonnets. Even the immortal bard felt desire and fell in love. It's passion that elevates us. Passion for God or poetry or another. Passion is the only thing that's real.

Charles exits. Sound of thunder. Nathaniel sits on the bed with the blue wash basin on his lap. He contemplates urinating in the basin, and then shudders. He places the basin back on the floor.

Nathaniel walks upstage to one of the arches. He hesitates, then raises his nightgown and urinates out the "window." Nathaniel finishes just Kathleen enters.

KATHLEEN
Hello.

Nathaniel quickly lowers his nightgown.

NATHANIEL
Hello.

KATHLEEN
You're Mr. Hawthorne. Correct? I hope I got that right. I'm not always good with names. I saw the light beneath your door so I knew you were awake. I'm sorry to bother you, but...

NATHANIEL
No need to apologize. My bedroom seems to the meeting place for the Brook Farm Wrestling and Debating Society. So what do you want to discuss, Miss Boyle? Poetry? Mesmerism? The first step in the future reform of everything?

Kathleen sits on the bed.

KATHLEEN
I have pain. This awful pain. Right inside me head.
    (touches her forehead)
It comes at night. Usually. Sometimes, it hurts so much that it blinds me. Sometimes, I hear a hushing sound...like waves.

NATHANIEL
I don't have any medicine.

KATHLEEN
Talk to me. That's all. When I'm sick, a friend of mine talks to me. And often the pain goes away.

NATHANIEL
What shall be the topic of our **conversation**?

KATHLEEN
Anything you wish. A man like you must know a great many things.

Nathaniel sits at the writing table.

NATHANIEL
Actually, I know very little. After college, I went back to my family's house in Salem, **moved** my desk up to the attic, and stayed there for **eight** years. I want to write a Romance, an American Romance, but nothing romantic has ever happened to me.

Kathleen picks up the blue wash basin.

                    KATHLEEN
This blue wash basin is very romantic.

                    NATHANIEL
You mean...beautiful?

                    KATHLEEN
Oh, yes! If I had a basin like this where I lived in Boston, someone would have stolen it right away.

                    NATHANIEL
Where exactly do you live?

                    KATHLEEN
On Winfield Street. Three rooms. Two dollars for one week.

                    NATHANIEL
An excellent price for three rooms.

                    KATHLEEN
Fourteen people live in the rooms. Including children. There used to be twenty-three people there. So it's better now.

                    NATHANIEL
That is not a proper situation for a young woman.

                    KATHLEEN
Yes. There are poison vapors in the air. I'm sure of it.

                    NATHANIEL
I mean...it's not a *moral* situation.

                    KATHLEEN
Morals are for wealthy people. I can't afford them yet.

She lies down on the bed.

                    NATHANIEL
What are you doing?

                    KATHLEEN
Keep talking, Mr. Hawthorne. You have a very pleasant voice. It's sweet and rich and deep. Makes me sleepy.

Nathaniel stands and approaches the bed.

              NATHANIEL
Thank you for the compliment, Miss
Boyle. But you really can't stay here.

              KATHLEEN
I'll go. In a little while.

              NATHANIEL
This is most unusual for me.

Kathleen is asleep. Nathaniel stands beside the bed.

              NATHANIEL
Miss Boyle, I have no place to
sleep. I could go to Miss Fuller's
room and get her to come in here,
but she's already in her bed.
Everyone is asleep, but me!

He sits down on the bed.

              NATHANIEL
Miss Boyle...
           (no response)
These things don't happen in Salem!

Kathleen rolls over on her side, turning away from him.

              NATHANIEL
My father was a sea captain. And
although he died when I was young,
I've heard that he was a very
decisive man!

Nathaniel lies down beside her and pulls up the quilt.
Kathleen moves slight and places her hand on his chest.
Immediately, Nathaniel gets out of bed.

              NATHANIEL
Oh, my God.

He paces around the room, then stops and looks at her.
Kathleen rolls over slightly. Now, she's lying on her back.

Slowly, Nathaniel walks over to one end of the bed. Music.
He leans over, hesitates, and then kisses Kathleen.

His lips seem to burn. He crosses the room to the window
and picks up his black cloak. Wrapping it around his body,
he returns to the bed.

Nathaniel sits on the floor beside the bed. He rocks slightly back and forth.

Blackout.

                    End of Act One

II

Next morning. The barnyard. Music, then lights up. Looking tired, Nathaniel enters and sits down.

Charles enters. As he approaches Nathaniel, he cheerfully recites Miranda's lines from *The Tempest*.

CHARLES
Oh, wonder? How many goodly creatures are there here? How beauteous mankind is! Oh, brave new world That hath such people in it!

NATHANIEL
I would sell my soul for a cup of coffee.

CHARLES
What's wrong, Nathaniel? Did the thunder keep you awake?

NATHANIEL
Miss Boyle entered my room last night and slept in my bed.

CHARLES
Good heavens? What would the Peabody sisters say?

NATHANIEL
I slept on the floor.

CHARLES
That wasn't necessary. You could have stayed in my bedroom. On my horsehair couch.

NATHANIEL
I wanted to sleep in my own bed. With my own blankets.

CHARLES
Now, Margaret's bedroom is somewhat larger, but she doesn't have...

NATHANIEL
There are too many bedrooms in this community! And too many *theories*.

CHARLES
They have a way of intermingling with each other.

Sophia walks outside, carrying a china teacup and saucer.

SOPHIA
Good morning everyone! Wasn't it a lovely storm! Lovely thunder! Look at the trees, Nathaniel! The dew-drops cling to each leaf like diamonds!

CHARLES
A cup of hot coffee might aid Mr. Hawthorne's aesthetic sensibility.

SOPHIA
What about some tea?
     (offers cup)
I made this for someone.

NATHANIEL
Thank you, Sophia.

Nathaniel takes the teacup.

CHARLES
Oh! I see! You got the china cup!

NATHANIEL
What's wrong with it?

CHARLES
Nothing at all. It just happens to be the only cup and saucer owned by the community of Brook Farm.

SOPHIA
We had four others, but they all broke. Now we just have the brass mugs you used at dinner. George thinks they're more practical.

Nathaniel offers the cup to Charles.

NATHANIEL
You were up first, Charles. Why didn't you use this cup?

CHARLES
The floral design reminds me of my mother.

Nathaniel gives the cup back to Sophia.

NATHANIEL
Well, I don't need the cup either. You can give it to someone else.

George enters, carrying a pitchfork.

GEORGE
There's a hole in the roof of the cow barn. We better fix it before the next rain.

SOPHIA
Have some tea, George.

GEORGE
I'll drink tea, but not from that cup. Give it to Emerson and his timorous friends. I've just pitched two bales of hay.

CHARLES
You drink it, Sophia. Go ahead.

SOPHIA
But I made it for someone else!

Margaret strides out of the house.

MARGARET
Good morning everyone! The lightning has charged up the ether surrounding us. Can't you feel it?
(glances at Nathaniel)
Animal magnetism abounds.

SOPHIA
Have some tea.

CHARLES
Please do.

NATHANIEL
Go ahead, Margaret.

Margaret immediately recognizes the cup.

                    MARGARET
          Look, I've stated several times that
          I'm not going to use the teacup. Only
          one person can drink from it while the
          rest have to use the brass mugs. It's
          not fair.

                    SOPHIA
          I'm going to get a hammer and smash
          this cup into pieces. You all make
          me feel like I've brought a snake
          into the Garden of Eden.

                    CHARLES
          Don't get angry, Sophia.

                    NATHANIEL
          Don't destroy something just because --

                    GEORGE
          Perhaps we should all take turns --

Kathleen enters and Nathaniel stands up immediately.

                    KATHLEEN
          Good morning. I hope I'm not
          interrupting anything.

                    SOPHIA
          Have a cup of tea.

                    KATHLEEN
          Thank you, Mrs. Ripley.
                    (takes the cup)
          Oh...what a romantic cup.

                    NATHANIEL
          She means beautiful when she says
          romantic.

                    MARGARET
          Really? How would you know?

                    KATHLEEN
          I spent the night in Mr. Hawthorne's room.

Everyone glances at each other. George drops the pitchfork.

                    NATHANIEL
          I didn't...I wasn't...

CHARLES
Nathaniel slept on the floor.

MARGARET
I see. And where did Miss Boyle sleep?

KATHLEEN
In the bed...I'm afraid to say.

Nathaniel sits on the ground. Sipping the tea, Kathleen moves around them.

KATHLEEN
I suffer from terrible headaches. It's like a hot piece of wire is burning through my skull. Last night, the pain came again and I went into Mr. Hawthorne's room for comfort. He was the only person who had a lamp burning.

GEORGE
And did he give you...comfort?

KATHLEEN
Oh, yes. He has a lovely voice. Very calm and relaxing. We talked for awhile and then I fell asleep.
        (approaching Nathaniel)
I'm terribly sorry, Mr. Hawthorne. It won't happen again.

Margaret walks up to Kathleen and touches her arm.

MARGARET
It doesn't need to happen again. Are you familiar with mesmerism?

KATHLEEN
Mesmer...what-is-it?

MARGARET
It's a method of healing. A way to conquer your pain. We'll have a séance tonight and you'll be cured. Forever.

KATHLEEN
How wonderful! Oh, you're all such kind people. I'm so glad I found my way here.

GEORGE
In exchange, we'll ask just one favor. Please call us by our first names. We're all equal here at Brook Farm.

KATHLEEN
All right...George.

Elated, she moves among them.

KATHLEEN
Sophia. Margaret. Nathaniel. Charles. Aren't we all happy? It's such a *romantic* morning.

NATHANIEL
She means "beautiful."

MARGARET
Stop correcting her, Nathaniel.

GEORGE
I agree. This is America. People are free to choose their own words.

NATHANIEL
Of course. Choose whatever word you want. But what about the meaning? You can't just...

Michael James appears in the distance.

MICHAEL JAMES
Don't run, Kathleen! You're not getting away from me again!

He enters.

MICHAEL JAMES
I've been walking all night through the rain and muck...knocking on a hundred doors...asking every fool if they've seen a wet scrap of a girl in a brown dress walking west to some place called Brook Farm!
   (approaches Kathleen)
And there you are...drinking from a teacup with some strangers.

KATHLEEN
As you can see, they're not whoremongers.

GEORGE
What?

KATHLEEN
That's what he thought you were...
whoremongers...luring poor girls
into a life of sin.

GEORGE
(to Michael James)
I happen to be a former
Unitarian minister who...

MICHAEL JAMES
I don't give a pig's arse who you
are! That's me wife and she's
coming back to Boston with me.

NATHANIEL
Your wife?

KATHLEEN
(to Michael James)
Oh, you're a liar!

MICHAEL JAMES
Don't deny it. We've been sharing the
same blanket for the last two years.
When she got the bedbugs, I pinched
them off with these two fingers.

Michael James approaches the women, but they avoid him.

CHARLES
That's was very kind of you, but
I question its legal validity.

KATHLEEN
We're not married at all. He
called me his wife, but I never
said he was my husband.

MICHAEL JAMES
At night you did, sweetheart.
Don't forget at night.

GEORGE
Why don't you two go off somewhere and
discuss this problem.

KATHLEEN
I'm not going anywhere with him. I
want to stay at Brook Farm.

GEORGE
We're trying to preserve a harmonious community that...

MARGARET
That's nonsense, George. This community becomes nothing but a collection of leaky farm buildings if we don't defend Kathleen's right to be here. She came to us from some desperate situation. We must offer her shelter.

MICHAEL JAMES
What are you chattering about? We're saving money to go to Ohio. Don't forget that, Kathleen. Don't forget how we planned. If I lose you, I've got no plans. I'm just another poor lad killing pigs at the slaughterhouse.

KATHLEEN
I told you that I couldn't stay in Boston, Michael James. You wouldn't listen to me.

Margaret approaches Michael James.

MARGARET
Kathleen has chosen to come here. She does not consider herself your wife so please leave.

MICHAEL JAMES
Don't talk to me like that. I'm not some stray dog you can chase away.

Margaret turns to the three men.

MARGARET
Do what is fair and just and decent and remove him from this farm!

CHARLES
Can't we have breakfast first?

Margaret returns to Sophia and Kathleen.

MARGARET
Do it at once.

George approaches Michael James.

GEORGE
All right, young man. I guess you'll have to leave Perhaps you can write a letter from Boston.

MICHAEL JAMES
I don't read and I don't write. I'm taking Kathleen and we're walking home.

The two men stand face to face.

GEORGE
No.

MICHAEL JAMES
You think you're going to stop me?

Charles steps forward.

CHARLES
We're all going to stop you.

Nathaniel steps forward.

NATHANIEL
You better go.

MICHAEL JAMES
(to Charles)
When I first started working at the slaughterhouse, they put me at the place where the hogs came in from the outside pen. Me and the other lads would lift them up, kicking and squealing, then hitch their legs to a chain and I'd cut their throats with my knife.
(to Nathaniel)
I did that for two years. Two years of stink and shit and the blood splattering on my arms. Two years of killing.
(to George)
So don't think I'm going to be scared by some gentlemen farmers!

GEORGE
You'll be punished. I'm warning you.

MICHAEL JAMES
Out of my way or I'll crack your skulls together!

Michael James raises his fist. Everyone shouts.

                    SOPHIA
          Stop this! All of you! You should
          be ashamed!

Sophia darts forward and faces Michael James. George is
pointing the pitchfork at the younger man.

                    SOPHIA
          George, what do you think you're
          doing with that ridiculous
          pitchfork? This is supposed to be a
          community of faith and goodwill.

                    GEORGE
              (lowers pitchfork)
          I was defending the young lady.

                    SOPHIA
          That's not necessary. I'll solve the
          problem.

She extends her hand to Michael James.

                    SOPHIA
          I'm Sophia Ripley. Glad to make your
          acquaintance.

                    MICHAEL JAMES
          Out of me way.

                    SOPHIA
          Are you too frightened to tell me
          your name?

                    MICHAEL JAMES
          Michael James Connor. Now, step aside.

                    SOPHIA
          I'm inviting you to breakfast, Mr.
          Connor.

                    MICHAEL JAMES
          What?

                    SOPHIA
          Breakfast. The first meal of the day.
          Porridge. Corn bread with butter.
          Wild raspberries. Fresh cream.

MICHAEL JAMES
You're as crazy as a moon calf! I didn't walk all the way from Boston for raspberries and cream!

SOPHIA
Half of the problems in this world are caused by the lack of a decent breakfast. Come inside with me. Sit down. Fill your stomach. And then we'll talk about the problem.

Michael James pulls away from her.

SOPHIA
Even if you dragged Kathleen back to Boston, she'd run away the first time you turned your back.

KATHLEEN
That's true, Michael James. Listen to what she's saying.

MICHAEL JAMES
(to Sophia)
You'll probably poison me.

SOPHIA
Don't insult my cooking.

MICHAEL JAMES
I'm not. I'm...

SOPHIA
Charles, chop some wood. George and Nathaniel...fill the water barrel. Margaret, Kathleen...go milk the cows. Hurry up. All of you. Don't dawdle.

She exits with Michael James. Kathleen, Nathaniel and Margaret exit. George looks surprised.

CHARLES
You heard what she said, George.

He slaps George on the back.

CHARLES
Let's get to work.

Sound. Blackout. Later that morning. Lights up on Michael James and Kathleen.

KATHLEEN
So? How did you like the breakfast?

MICHAEL JAMES
I've had better.

KATHLEEN
Now that's a surprise. You ate most of the bread and half the butter.

MICHAEL JAMES
I was hungry. Had nothing to eat since I left Boston.

KATHLEEN
And what about the people here? They're not whoremongers, are they?

MICHAEL JAMES
No. But they do like to air their vocabulary. That Margaret woman could argue the leg off an iron pot.

KATHLEEN
They're kind, and generous.

MICHAEL JAMES
Mrs. Ripley has a good heart.

KATHLEEN
They all have good hearts. I'll swear to that. And most of them have written books and poems. It's nothing to them. Like sewing a button on a shirt.

MICHAEL JAMES
And now they're going to be farmers.

KATHLEEN
That's right. Just look around you. Walk anywhere you want. They've got cows and chickens and a field of corn.

MICHAEL JAMES
Remember when Mr. Feely gave me the dollar and we went to that theatre on Grand Street? Remember the play?

KATHLEEN
"The Queen of Hearts or Her Honor Defended." She was a brave girl. Even in the opium den.

MICHAEL JAMES
It wasn't a real opium den. Nothing was real. The canvas walls flapped like sails every time someone slammed the door.

KATHLEEN
What of it?

MICHAEL JAMES
This place is the same thing, Kathleen. It isn't a real farm and these aren't real farmers...they're playing at being farmers. Standing around with shovels like they know how to use them.

KATHLEEN
That was real porridge you were shoveling down your throat.

MICHAEL JAMES
Whenever I turn around here I half expect to find a ticket collector or a butcher boy selling candy.

KATHLEEN
What's wrong with that? That's why I like it here. You can be whoever you want at Brook Farm. Go ahead, Michael James. Change yourself. You might enjoy it.

She exits. Michael James exits. Carrying shovels, Nathaniel and Charles enter.

CHARLES
Back to the gold mine! I just knew that George would send us here this morning. Maybe this is a subtle commentary on my poetry.

Lost in thought, Nathaniel looks downstage.

CHARLES
Nathaniel?

NATHANIEL
They were lovers.

CHARLES
Are you talking about Kathleen and Michael James? Yes, that does appear to be the situation.

NATHANIEL
She allowed him to...to --

CHARLES
Quite frequently, I imagine.

NATHANIEL
This is common practice among the poor.

CHARLES
It's also a common practice among
the rich. As far as I can see, it's
only the genteel souls in the middle
that suffer cold feet at night.

The light softens on the two men while they sit together.
(Note: during this sequence of scenes, three separate groups
will be on the stage.) Spotlight on Kathleen and Sophia as
they enter the farmyard. They carry towels and a washtub.

SOPHIA
In the summer, we bathe out here in
the farmyard. It keeps water from
getting all over the kitchen floor.

Kathleen reaches into the tub and touches the water.

KATHLEEN
It's warm!

SOPHIA
Yes. I thought it would be more
comfortable for you. George believes
in cold-water baths.
        (half-whisper)
I don't.

Kathleen starts to unbutton her dress.

KATHLEEN
I haven't had a hot bath in four or
five years. It takes too much coal to
heat the water.

SOPHIA
What are you --

Sophia tries to conceal Kathleen with the skirts of her dress.

SOPHIA
Margaret!

Kathleen begins to removes her dress. She wears a long petticoat and cotton camisole.

> KATHLEEN
> What's the problem?

> SOPHIA
> The men. They might see you.

> KATHLEEN
> You didn't say anything about men.

> SOPHIA
> I told George. And he was supposed to tell the others. But sometimes they forget.
> (calling)
> Margaret!

Margaret enters, carrying a sheet.

> MARGARET
> Sorry. I couldn't find a...
> (sees Kathleen)
> Oh.

> SOPHIA
> Hurry...Hurry up. Stand over by the tub, Kathleen.

She takes one corner of the sheet. Margaret and Sophia hold up the sheet so only Kathleen's head is revealed.

> SOPHIA
> We'll just have to hold it up like this and --

> MARGARET
> Instant modesty.

Kathleen continues to get undressed.

> KATHLEEN
> Is this what the men do for each other?

> SOPHIA
> Heavens no. They bathe in the duck pond.

> KATHLEEN
> But that's out in the open.

                    SOPHIA
          We just don't walk over there during
          those times.

                    MARGARET
               (smiling at Sophia)
          Except on one occasion...

                    SOPHIA
          Oh, I never should have told you that!

                    KATHLEEN
          What happened? Tell me.

                    MARGARET
          Three young Harvard students came
          here one weekend. After an afternoon
          of pitching hay, they all went down
          to the pond. Sophia saw them lying
          on the rocks.

                    KATHLEEN
          Were they handsome?

                    SOPHIA
          I didn't look...very long. It
          reminded me of a fresco of some
          young Greeks in a classical pose.

                    MARGARET
          Especially Mr. Darlington.

                    KATHLEEN
          Oh! What was he like?

                    SOPHIA
          Mr. Darlington had a...he was
          very...It was...I think and...
               (decisively)
          It showed the beauty that God has
          created in the world.

                    KATHLEEN
          You mean he wasn't some greasy old
          slab of lard with a hairy back?

Naked, Kathleen moves to get the soap lying on the ground.
Sophia and Margaret are startled. They scurry back and forth
with the sheet -- trying to shield her.

                    SOPHIA
          Don't! Wait!

                    KATHLEEN
          I'm sorry. Just wanted to get the soap.

                    SOPHIA
          I'll get it.

                    KATHLEEN
          Oh, don't worry. So what if they
          saw me?

Kathleen gets the soap and sits down in the tub.

                    MARGARET
          I agree. Brook Farm is supposed
          to start a new way of living.
          We're not in Boston anymore.

The two women drape the sheet around Kathleen as she sits in the tub.

                    SOPHIA
          People leave Boston and try to
          pretend that it doesn't exist.
          They do things, scandalous things,
          and hope that no one will ever
          know. People always find out. And
          Boston is always there. It never
          leaves us. Unfortunately.

The lights soften on the women. Spotlight on Michael James and George in a downstage area. They set up a wooden frame that holds a log.

                    GEORGE
          I hope you don't mind cutting a
          few logs, Michael James. Everyone
          has to work at Brook Farm. Even
          young men who have come here
          looking for young women.

                    MICHAEL JAMES
          I don't mind. I've worked all my
          life. It's the way of the world.

                    GEORGE
          I don't know if you want advice
          about matters of the heart.

                    MICHAEL JAMES
          I don't want any advice.

GEORGE
Nevertheless, you and Kathleen are
here, in this community, and all of
us have an interest in resolving
your disagreement.

MICHAEL JAMES
Could you say that in plain words?

Using a two-man crosscut saw, they get ready to cut the log.

GEORGE
I think you should get married.
Legally. That's probably what she
wants.

MICHAEL JAMES
I asked her to tie the knot. Many a time.

GEORGE
And she refused?

MICHAEL JAMES
Wouldn't even talk about it. I met
Kathleen about two weeks after her
father had gone to Albany, looking for
work. I wasn't saving my wages then
so I had enough to buy her a new
shawl and some rosewood combs for
her hair. After we got together, I
couldn't do that anymore. Didn't
have the money. Or the time.

GEORGE
In a perfect society, courtship would
wither and die like a useless weed.

MICHAEL JAMES
You're dreaming, Mr. Ripley.

GEORGE
In the perfect society, romance will
be unnecessary.

The light rises on Charles and Nathaniel.

CHARLES
Everyone is too damn practical in
this country. Even our idealists
want to be practical. That's what
Brook Farm is all about.

Charles puts down his shovel and sits beside Nathaniel.

                      NATHANIEL
There's nothing wrong with that.

                      CHARLES
I admire the fact that Michael James walked through the rain, trying to find Kathleen. Don't you wish that someone was trying to find *you*?

                      NATHANIEL
I wouldn't know what to do with them when they arrived.

                      CHARLES
Your heart would tell you.

                      NATHANIEL
My heart whispers. It doesn't shout. I can't change the way I am.

                      CHARLES
You can change anything you want, Nathaniel. That's the one thing I've learned here at Brook Farm. The problem with America is that the ghosts of the Puritans still drift through our bedrooms at night. If I were elected President, I would try to establish a more romantic country.

                      NATHANIEL
And how would you do that? Build Gothic castles on the Concord River?

                      CHARLES
Better than that! I would immediately organize a public lottery. A lottery... of romance.

                      NATHANIEL
What if people didn't want to be romantic?

                      CHARLES
They wouldn't have to. The lottery would be strictly voluntary. But after awhile, it would be so attractive, everyone would want to join.
(MORE)

CHARLES
First, you'd subscribe, giving your name, age and full particulars. Then once a month you'd receive a letter, sealed with red wax.

NATHANIEL
Go on.

CHARLES
It would offer you the name of some stranger and you would have to send them love poems, toss roses through their bedroom windows, things like that. The following month, someone might be throwing roses at you.

The light rises on the three women. Kathleen sits in the tub with the sheet covering her. Sophia is combing her hair. Margaret paces back and forth.

MARGARET
The problem with Boston is the men.

KATHLEEN
That's right. We should put them on a boat and send them back to where they came from.

SOPHIA
Oh, no! We should keep a few.

KATHLEEN
Your Mr. Darlington. On a rock. With his very large --

SOPHIA
Kathleen! Please!

MARGARET
I don't think we should send the men away. I think we should educate them. In the 14th century, Queen Isabeau of France established a School of Love.

KATHLEEN
I hope they taught the men to wash their feet before they got into bed.

SOPHIA
And not to discuss machinery.

The lights soften on the women. It rises on Michael James and George as they saw the log.

> MICHAEL JAMES
> Women want flowers and fine words. I'd bet my life on that.

> GEORGE
> It's only a consequence of our economic system.

The two men stop working.

> GEORGE
> Romantic ballads first appeared during the Renaissance when poor troubadours attempted to woo aristocratic women. Because they didn't have enough money, they had to invent love poems as a substitute for economic status. If we were all equal, this foolishness would disappear.

> MICHAEL JAMES
> You're forgetting one thing, Mr. Ripley. Men got a roaring Jack in their trousers.

> GEORGE
> A what?

> MICHAEL JAMES
> (points to his groin)
> A lad's third leg. His --

> GEORGE
> That problem will be solved in government-run brothels.

> MICHAEL JAMES
> I'll be damned! You really are a whoremonger!

> GEORGE
> They'd be scientific brothels with a rational use of labor. Everything would be organized in a fair and decent manner.

The light rises on Charles and Nathaniel.

CHARLES
After awhile, everything would be organized. The lottery would be in every city and village. And each month, you would wait for your letter. Alone in your room, away from all mothers in whale-bone corsets, you would crack the red seal. Instructions: You must dress up as a Renaissance cardinal, mount a black stallion, and appear at someone's door at midnight. Instructions: you must connive to have a gold necklace slipped beneath a virgin's pillow before she wakes.

NATHANIEL
You're joking.

CHARLES
Not at all! Down in New Haven, they're making guns with utmost efficiency. Why can't this country forget about guns and manufacture unexpected passion and desire. Instead of the United States of America, we'll become the United States of Romance!

Blackout on Charles and Nathaniel. Light rises on the women. Margaret and Sophia help Kathleen bathe.

MARGARET
Men learn the Art of War at West Point. Why can't they study the Art of Love at Brook Farm?

KATHLEEN
That's a good idea.

SOPHIA
Every wife I know would send her husband.

MARGARET
And we'd be the three instructors. I teach poetry and ethics.

KATHLEEN
I'd tell them what to wear.

SOPHIA
And I'd teach them what to eat. Wild strawberries. Musk melon. Chocolate. Rare liqueurs and cold champagne. Candles flickering above a white linen table cloth. The moonlight making the crystal glitter and gleam and oh...
(sighs)
I think I'm back in Boston again.

Blackout on the women. The light rises on Michael James and George sawing the log.

GEORGE
Brook Farm is just the beginning, Mr. Connor. An experiment to prove the practicality of our ideals.

George stops working and sits down.

MICHAEL JAMES
Come on. Let's keep sawing.

GEORGE
In the New America, men and women will meet freely, instead of luring each other with romantic snares. There will be no need for perfume, low-cut bodices, books of poems, secret letters, fancy dress balls, the waltz, flirting, fondling, general lying and deceit!

MICHAEL JAMES
Not much fun.

GEORGE
What?

MICHAEL JAMES
Not much fun. Don't you think?

Music. Everyone exits. Standing mirrors are placed on stage. A chair is placed in the middle.

Kathleen enters and sits downstage. Margaret, Charles, Nathaniel and the Ripleys enter. Margaret carries a candelabra. Everyone else carries candles. They stand upstage with their backs to the audience.

The music fades as Michael James approaches Kathleen.

                    MICHAEL JAMES
          They're waiting for you in the parlor,
          Kathleen. The men brought all these
          mirrors into the room. Miss Fuller says
          that mirrors "increase the magnetism"
          ...whatever that means.

                    KATHLEEN
          I'll Join them. In a minute. I'm
          just looking at the summer moon.

                    MICHAEL JAMES
          Looks the same as the winter moon
          to me.

                    KATHLEEN
          No. It's different. It's dark gold
          color like an old coin that you've
          polished up for good luck. And the
          light shines down and it touches
          the world. And it changes every-
          thing, can't you see? That grass
          looks like a lady's cape I once
          embroidered. Green velvet lying on
          the ground.

Michael James sits beside her.

                    MICHAEL JAMES
          You talk more since you've come
          here, Kathleen. It must be these
          people with all *their* talking. They
          rattle on like me old gran. She
          kept talking just to prove she was
          still alive.

                    KATHLEEN
          They're kind people, Michael James. You
          said that yourself.

                    MICHAEL JAMES
          That doesn't mean that you've got to
          enter that parlor and let them have a
          go at you with their "magnetism."

                    KATHLEEN
          They're going to help me stop the
          pain in me skull.

MICHAEL JAMES
Maybe...maybe I was the one that was causing the pain with all me bluster. I'm a different man, Kathleen. I swear to that. Let's just walk down that road and keep walking *in* the moonlight. I'll say yes and amen to anything you want *in* the world.

KATHLEEN
I want to be here.

MICHAEL JAMES
We're not like these people. You can see that.

Margaret moves upstage --- as if she was stepping out onto the porch.

MARGARET
Kathleen? We're ready!

KATHLEEN
They're calling me.

Kathleen stands and moves away from Michael James.

MICHAEL JAMES
You can work, eat with them -- even sleep with them. But it won't change things. These people have never been hungry. They talk about changing the world, but they don't know what the world is.

KATHLEEN
They see what the world can be, Michael James. Don't you understand?

MARGARET
Kathleen!

KATHLEEN
I better go.

Music. Lights change. Kathleen walks upstage and enters the parlor with Margaret. Michael James follows slowly.

Kathleen sits *in* the chair surrounded by the mirrors and the members of Brook Farm.

Music. As Margaret holds the candelabra close to Kathleen, then slowly draws it away from her.

The music fades. Margaret places the candelabra on the floor in front of Kathleen.

Margaret stands behind Kathleen and begins to make mesmeric "passes." She lightly strokes the girl's forehead, then her neck, shoulders, and arms.

> MARGARET
> Energy surrounds us. It pulses through the universe. Feel its power, moving through my blood and bones and tissue, melting through my skin. It touches you like a warm wind on summer's day. It pushes you forward, faster and faster, until your spirit is lifted into the sky.

Kathleen closes her eyes. Her head -- which has dropped slightly -- goes up on this last line. (Note: this "mesmeric sleep" would now be called a hypnotic trance.)

> MARGARET
> Can you hear me, Kathleen?

> KATHLEEN
> Yes.

> MARGARET
> Are you asleep?

> KATHLEEN
> Yes.

> MARGARET
> But you can hear my voice?

> KATHLEEN
> I can.

Margaret turns to the others.

> MARGARET
> She is now in a mesmeric state.

> MICHAEL JAMES
> It looks like she's dreaming.

> MARGARET
> In a way, she is. But it's a special condition. Separated from the senses, the mind is able to have a new sense of spiritual things.

(MORE)

MARGARET
Kathleen has been lifted closer to the fountain of all good and of all truth. She is incapable of deceit, vanity, and hate.

GEORGE
Admirable. What if all Americans could be this way?

MICHAEL JAMES
We are. When we're asleep.

MARGARET
Please, Mr. Connor, you must try to --

KATHLEEN
Don't go away! Don't!

MARGARET
Don't worry. I'm here.

KATHLEEN
I don't want you to go away.

MARGARET
We are connected, you and I. It is an attraction stronger than any affair of the senses. Now, we shall remove your pain...forever.

KATHLEEN
Yes.

MARGARET
How long have you had these headaches?

KATHLEEN
Ten years.

MARGARET
(to the others)
This pain is probably the consequence of an old injury. This is a common problem.
(to Kathleen)
Tell me, Kathleen. Do you remember when you first experienced these headaches?

KATHLEEN
Yes.

MARGARET
Where were you?

KATHLEEN
In my father's home. In Boston.

MARGARET
The pain is in a room at the top of the stairs. Let's go there and see what happened.

KATHLEEN
I will.

MARGARET
Walk up the stairs, Kathleen. Don't be scared. I'll be with you. Go on. Tell me what you see.

KATHLEEN
The old stairs. Mud smeared on the walls. Smell of onions. Cooked cabbage.

MICHAEL JAMES
That's most of South Boston.

MARGARET
(to Kathleen)
Go ahead. Keep going.

KATHLEEN
Going higher now. Last step. Down the hallway. There's a door. A light. Don't want to go in.

MARGARET
You must walk inside. Go ahead.

KATHLEEN
The door creaks open. A room. My mother. Lamp on the floor. Burning its light.

MARGARET
Yes. And how did you injure yourself?

KATHLEEN
My mother washing the shirts. Two wood tubs. The lamp. She's laughing. Talking. Her dress. The dark blue petticoats. Touching the lamp. Knocking it over. Fire on her dress. Spreading. She screams --

SOPHIA
My god!

MARGARET
No. Go away from there. You mustn't see this. You...

KATHLEEN
Her dress in flames. Shouting. Rolling on the floor. My hands touching the fire. Hurt. Burning. Help! Someone help me!

She opens her eyes and sees the burning candelabra.

KATHLEEN
No!

Kathleen staggers out of the room.

CHARLES
Stop her! Don't let her get away!

Kathleen runs away. Michael James is surprised, then he follows after her. Blackout. The mirrors are removed. Everyone exits. Lights up on Charles and Nathaniel as they enter.

NATHANIEL
Kathleen! Kathleen!

CHARLES
I don't see her anywhere.

NATHANIEL
This is all Margaret's fault.

CHARLES
She was trying to help Kathleen. How could she know about this horrible tragedy?

NATHANIEL
Some secrets are best kept hidden.

CHARLES
I'm a Catholic. Remember? I see the virtue in confession.

NATHANIEL
All this touching and stroking and candles and mirrors is like an amateur magician performing a parlor trick.

CHARLES
On the contrary. No stroking ever occurred in my family's parlor.

Charles sits down on the ground.

NATHANIEL
You know what I'm saying! This mesmerism is simply a shabby form of entertainment. Now someone's been hurt because of it.

CHARLES
There's a bit of Puritan in you, Nathaniel. Perhaps it's the blood of that ancestor you told us about... the whip-cracking Judge Hawthorne.

NATHANIEL
This has nothing to do with my ancestors. I'm simply condemning irresponsible behavior. One must have values.

CHARLES
Values are not as interesting as motives. What did Judge Hawthorne feel when they stripped that Quaker woman and bound her wrists? Was he proud? Ashamed? Excited?

NATHANIEL
I can't imagine.

CHARLES
There seems to be an intimate connection between the censors and the sinners.

NATHANIEL
Oh, for God's sake! Spare me any more Brook Farm philosophizing! What you're talking about has nothing to do with this lost woman, wandering around in the night.

CHARLES
I just wonder why you're so passionate about a girl you met for the first time yesterday.

Nathaniel approaches Charles.

                    NATHANIEL
          Please withdraw your insinuation.

Charles stands up.

                    CHARLES
          I never withdraw insinuations. It's
          so tiring to run around and catch them.

                    NATHANIEL
          As you know, I am engaged to Miss
          Sophia Peabody.

                    CHARLES
          If I were in love with someone, I
          would be by their side. You declare
          your love to this woman and promptly
          leave Salem.

                    NATHANIEL
          We need a place to live.

                    CHARLES
          You wear Miss Peabody around your
          neck like a fragment of the true
          cross. It protects you from all the
          demons in the world.

                    NATHANIEL
          That is enough, Mr. Newcomb! I do not
          wish to continue our intercourse. Good
          evening.

                    CHARLES
          Don't resist this darkness, Nathaniel.
          It's not a negation of daylight. It's
          simply another aspect of our own hearts.

Approaching Nathaniel, Charles quotes a passage from *A Midsummer Night's Dream*:

                    CHARLES
          Now it is the time of night
          That the graves, all gaping wide
          every one lets forth its sprite
          In the church-way paths to glide.

                    NATHANIEL
          I'm really not interested in sprites.

                    CHARLES
          What about a friend?

NATHANIEL
You must eradicate your European mannerisms and your constant impulse to be cynical about everything.

CHARLES
Does this mean we have to wrestle again?

Charles gets ready to wrestle.

CHARLES
All right. Get ready. Here I come!

NATHANIEL
No wrestling. Please! If you want friendship, then we must meet on the highest level. Both our hearts displaying manly strength and virtue.

CHARLES
Manly virtue. Got it.

NATHANIEL
We are Americans. Men.

CHARLES
Manly men.

NATHANIEL
We're building a new country. A new literature.

The two men face each other.

CHARLES
Free. Passionate. Without the constraints of the past.

A Beat. Then Charles leans forward to kiss Nathaniel. At the last moment, Nathaniel pulls away. Flustered, he starts to exit.

NATHANIEL
I...don't...think...

CHARLES
Come back. Please. You can blame it on the moonlight.

NATHANIEL
I will search alone!

Nathaniel exits. Charles shakes his head and follows him.

Kathleen enters. Exhausted, she lies on the ground. George enters.

> GEORGE
> Kathleen! Where are you! Kathleen!

George sees Kathleen lying on the ground.

> GEORGE
> Oh, my God.

He hurries over to Kathleen and helps her sit up.

> GEORGE
> Are you all right? Can you hear me? Wake up. Try to wake up. Please.

Kathleen opens her eyes.

> KATHLEEN
> What happened?

> GEORGE
> How do you feel? Is anything broken?

> KATHLEEN
> I don't think so.

> GEORGE
> We've all been searching for you. Running around in the dark.

> KATHLEEN
> Sorry.

> GEORGE
> There's nothing to be sorry about. Absolutely nothing. Margaret was experimenting rashly. It will never happen again.

> KATHLEEN
> I was sleeping. But not really asleep. I could hear Margaret's voice.

> GEORGE
> Yes...

> KATHLEEN
> I was walking up some stairs. It was very dark. Then I came into a room and I saw my mother.

                    GEORGE
          It's horrible what happened. Try
          to forget about it as quickly as
          possible.

                    KATHLEEN
          I tried to forget about it. But
          it was still there. Like a door
          you have to open.

George takes her hand.

                    GEORGE
          You're a young girl. You've strayed,
          perhaps, but you're still innocent
          in your heart. I'm sure of it.

                    KATHLEEN
          What are you talking about?

                    GEORGE
          This night is the start of a new
          journey in your life. You must put
          the past behind you and move on.

                    KATHLEEN
          I guess so. I don't want to be
          a seamstress anymore.

                    GEORGE
          I'll be here to help you. Every
          step of the way.

                    KATHLEEN
          Thank you -

                    GEORGE
          George.

                    KATHLEEN
          George.

                    GEORGE
          Sometimes, I'll have to be firm
          with you. You don't mind a
          little firmness? Do you?

                    KATHLEEN
          Maybe...Maybe we should go back
          to the farmhouse.

George stands and approaches her.

GEORGE
Oh, no! That's the worst thing you can do. The outdoors helps dissipate excess animal magnetism. Rooms capture it. Concentrate it. Your body begins to swell. Your clothes feel tight.

KATHLEEN
I want to go back.

She starts to move away.

GEORGE
Do you think I'm old?

KATHLEEN
A little. Just...a little.

GEORGE
Brook Farm drains me. All the tasks to be done. All the responsibilities. I wake up in the morning and feel tired and fearful. But I go on.

KATHLEEN
It's a beautiful place here. The work will get easier. You'll see.

GEORGE
I need to be revitalized. Like a plant that pushes its root down and draws up nourishment from the earth. Do you understand?

KATHLEEN
No.

George approaches her.

GEORGE
Sometimes two people have a common soul. They can help each other grow.

He touches Kathleen's breasts and she pulls back.

KATHLEEN
Mr. Ripley!

She pulls away from him.

GEORGE
I respect you deeply. My affections are on the highest level.

                    KATHLEEN
          I don't want any level. High or low.

Kathleen begins to exit.

                    GEORGE
          We're a member of the same
          community. Like brothers
          and sisters or...

                    KATHLEEN
          No!

Kathleen exits.

                    GEORGE
          Kathleen!

George exits. Blackout. Lights up on Sophia in the kitchen. Michael James enters. His clothes are wet.

                    SOPHIA
          Did you find her?

                    MICHAEL JAMES
          I found the duck pond instead.

                    SOPHIA
          Good heavens, you're soaked to the
          bone. Sit down and take off your
          shirt. You can borrow some of my
          husband's clothes.

Sophia puts a stool in front of Michael James, then hands him a towel.

                    MICHAEL JAMES
          I don't need any favors.

                    SOPHIA
          It's not a favor, Mr. Connor.
          It's just common decency to help
          someone who's had an accident.

                    MICHAEL JAMES
          I don't need your decency either.

                    SOPHIA
          Why are you so angry? It such a
          waste. Angry people remind me of
          a hornet, trapped in a house,
          bashing his head against the
          window pane again and again. He
          doesn't see that there are dozen
          different ways to freedom.

MICHAEL JAMES
You and your friends hurt Kathleen tonight. Made her run out into the darkness. God knows where she is right now.

SOPHIA
It was an accident, Michael James. No one wanted that to happen. It was terrible to hear about her mother.

Michael James places a wash tub in front of the stool.

MICHAEL JAMES
I never knew about it.

SOPHIA
People keep tigers locked in their hearts because it's too frightening to set them free.

Michael James sits down in front of the wash tub.

MICHAEL JAMES
She shouldn't have come here. I shouldn't have followed her.

SOPHIA
But you're here and you're wet...so take off your shirt.

Michael James takes off his shirt. Blackout. Lights up on Kathleen sitting on the grass. Nathaniel enters, then slowly approaches her.

NATHANIEL
Kathleen?

He touches her. Startled, she stands up.

KATHLEEN
It's you.

NATHANIEL
I beg your pardon. Are you all right?

KATHLEEN
Yes, I'm fine. A little tired.

NATHANIEL
We've been searching for you.

KATHLEEN
I know. I already met Mr. Ripley.

NATHANIEL
Why didn't you go back to the farmhouse?

KATHLEEN
I wanted to stay out here in the moonlight for awhile. All my thoughts are jumping around like a bagful of cats.

NATHANIEL
I understand.

KATHLEEN
Yes. I see that in your eyes. You understand most things.

Neither of them wants to look at each other. Kathleen moves away from Nathaniel.

KATHLEEN
Tell me something. Why do people always want to...to...

NATHANIEL
Yes?

KATHLEEN
I know a common word for it. But not a word to use with you.

NATHANIEL
You mean...be lovers?

KATHLEEN
Yes. That's it.

NATHANIEL
Perhaps we are only animals wearing trousers and petticoats. Or perhaps each one of us is a ruined image of God, searching for another soul to make us perfect again.

KATHLEEN
So which do you believe? That we're like animals or God?

NATHANIEL
It depends on the weather.

KATHLEEN
Don't joke. Please.

NATHANIEL
I'm not joking at all. When I'm with my sisters, I feel pure and rational. Then at night, I put on my cloak and go to the taverns in Salem. I drink ale and watch the women approach me and others. And different sensations appear.

KATHLEEN
Do you sleep with them?

Nathaniel looks surprised.

KATHLEEN
I'm...sorry.

NATHANIEL
I smile and I speak to them, but one part of me is always watching. It is my strength and my damnation that I'm always the audience and never the actor. God knows how I'll ever be able to write a Romance.

KATHLEEN
I'm sure you could write anything.

NATHANIEL
You're very kind.

KATHLEEN
Just think up some people and give them names...that's important...and have them talk to each other.

NATHANIEL
That's not always easy to do.

KATHLEEN
Try it out first. See if it works.

She sits on the ground.

KATHLEEN
I'm a lady that you've always loved from afar. I'm sitting alone in the moonlight and you try to talk to me.

She folds her hands and waits. Nathaniel hesitates.

                    KATHLEEN
          I'm waiting.

He approaches her and bows.

                    NATHANIEL
          Madam.

She reacts in an exaggerated fashion.

                    KATHLEEN
          Oh!
               (smiles)
          Do you like that? I saw an actress
          do that in a play. It was called
          "The Queen of Hearts or Her Honor
          Defended.".

                    NATHANIEL
          So, ahhh --

                    KATHLEEN
          Oh! I was trapped in an opium den.
          Thank you for rescuing me.

                    NATHANIEL
          It's getting cold. Could I bring
          you a shawl?

                    KATHLEEN
          Don't talk about shawls. They're
          not very romantic.

                    NATHANIEL
          I...admire you.

                    KATHLEEN
          "Admire?" What kind of word is that?

                    NATHANIEL
          I adore you.

                              KATHLEEN
          Much better.

He sits beside her.

                    NATHANIEL
          There are dead plants in every parlor
          in Salem. Dead flowers pressed in a
          memory book. You are not in the parlor.
                              (MORE)

                    NATHANIEL
          You are a hawk cutting through a
          dawn sky. The pale green leaves
          on an elm tree in spring. You are
          a snake, a cat, a young horse
          kicking up the snow on a winter's
          morning. You are everything I
          dream about, but can never call
          my own.

A Beat, then he kisses Kathleen. She responds and touches him. Nathaniel stands up quickly. Kathleen stands and approaches him.

                    KATHLEEN
          See? You can be romantic.

                    NATHANIEL
          No. It's impossible. While I was
          kissing you, one part of my mind was
          distant, noticing the scar near your
          lip, the mud on your hem, the faint
          odor of onions on your breath.

Nathaniel approaches Kathleen and she slaps him -- hard.

                    NATHANIEL
          My apologies.

                    KATHLEEN
          Don't want them.

She exits. Blackout. Nathaniel exits. Lights up on Michael James and Sophia in the kitchen.

Michael James is bare-chested. He sits on the stool, bent over the washtub. Sophia pours in a teapot of hot water.

                    SOPHIA
          There. That should make it a
          little warmer.

Michael James begins to splash water on his face.

                    SOPHIA
          There's a bar of soap floating in there.

                    MICHAEL JAMES
          I see it.

                    SOPHIA
          You could use it, too.

MICHAEL JAMES
I'm old enough to wash me self, Mrs. Ripley.

SOPHIA
But not old enough to do it well.

She sees something *in* his hair and steps back.

SOPHIA
Oh, my god!

MICHAEL JAMES
What's wrong?

SOPHIA
You have lice on the roots of your hair.

MICHAEL JAMES
It's common where I live.

Sophia picks up a small cooking pan.

SOPHIA
Well, you're living here now. At Brook Farm.

MICHAEL JAMES
No. I'm just a visitor.

SOPHIA
Close your eyes, Mr. Connor.

MICHAEL JAMES
What for?

SOPHIA
Close your eyes and lean over the tub. I'm going to scrub those awful things out of your hair.

Michael James hesitates, and then obeys her. Sophia scoops up some water *in* the pan.

SOPHIA
I don't think I've ever met a man so resistant to having people help him.

She pours the water over his head, then soaps her hands.

SOPHIA
Everybody else I know is eager for help. Appreciative. Whereas you seem to think accepting help is the biggest insult in the world.

MICHAEL JAMES
People help you if they're strong and you're weak. It makes me feel like a beggar on the street.

She starts to wash his hair.

SOPHIA
You're not a beggar, Mr. Connor. You're a hard-working, intelligent young man who, I'm sure, will be very successful in America.

MICHAEL JAMES
You think so?

SOPHIA
Close your eyes.

He closes his eyes and she pours water on his head.

MICHAEL JAMES
You think I'll be rich?

SOPHIA
If that's what you want. People usually get what they want. Unfortunately, it never turns out the way they planned.

MICHAEL JAMES
I'm going to like being rich.

SOPHIA
I thought I'd enjoy being a minister's wife, sitting in the front pew, listening to my husband's sermon and leading the ladies missionary society. It didn't work out that way. Eyes tight.

She fills the pan and pours it over his head.

MICHAEL JAMES
Sorry about the lice.

SOPHIA
One more time.

She pours some more water on his hair.

                    SOPHIA
      There. Now let's see if we were successful.

Michael James remains on the chair. Sophia starts to look through his hair.

                    MICHAEL JAMES
      I can't remember anyone ever washing me hair. Not even me mother.

                    SOPHIA
      You can do it yourself, Mr. Connor. With a penny's worth of soap.

                    MICHAEL JAMES
      Didn't seem to be much of a reason. I always had to go to the slaughter-house the next morning. Put on me work clothes. Still stiff with yesterday's blood.

                    SOPHIA
      Got one!

She pulls a nit out of his hair and flicks it away.

                    MICHAEL JAMES
      Maybe it's wrong to be clean...too clean. It might change you somehow. You might never want to get dirty again.

                    SOPHIA
      Your neck is filthy.

Sophia takes a rag out of the washtub and begins to scrub Michael James's neck.

                    MICHAEL JAMES
      Did you hear what I said?

                    SOPHIA
      Yes. And I'm ignoring it. Don't get too philosophical about everyday matters, Mr. Connor. Many of the people here have that problem.

She begins to wash his arms and back.

                    SOPHIA
          This isn't going to change your
          life. It's just soap and water.
          And the result *is* clean skin.

                    MICHAEL JAMES
          Thank you, Mrs. Ripley.

Michael James reaches out and takes her hand. He leans
forward and kisses her knuckles. Sophia gasps, but she
doesn't pull her hand away.

                    SOPHIA
          I'm a married woman.

                    MICHAEL JAMES
          Yes.

He stands up suddenly. Sophia doesn't step away.

                    SOPHIA
          What's more, I'm older than you.
          And plain. Very plain. Kathleen *is*
          a beautiful girl.

                    MICHAEL JAMES
          She doesn't love me. She never has.

                    SOPHIA
          But you love her. You walked all the
          way from Boston when you realized
          she was gone.

                    MICHAEL JAMES
          Kathleen was my future. I took all my
          dreams and put them on her shoulders.

                    SOPHIA
          That wasn't fair, Michael James. We
          all have our own dreams. Our own
          desires.

Michael James leans forward and kisses her lightly on the
lips. He pulls away. Sophia leans forward, then kisses him.

                    MICHAEL JAMES
          Let's go outside.

                    SOPHIA
          Whatever for?

Michael James picks up Sophia and holds her *in* his arms.

MICHAEL JAMES
We'll look at the moon. The summer moon. It's different than the one that shines on a winter night.

Blackout as Sophia and Michael James exit. Lights up on Margaret sitting in the meadow. Kathleen enters and approaches her.

KATHLEEN
Margaret?

MARGARET
Kathleen! Where did you go! We were all so worried.

Margaret stands quickly and approaches Kathleen.

KATHLEEN
I've been floating around like the fluff from a dandelion. It's the animal magnetism. I'm quite sure of it.

MARGARET
Are you all right? Do you remember what happened?

The two women sit together.

KATHLEEN
Yes. It was like I was asleep...half-asleep...and then I saw my mother and the lantern.

MARGARET
I'm very sorry, Kathleen. That's never happened before.

KATHLEEN
I feel better. If that means anything. Does the magnetism inside you act like a real magnet?

MARGARET
Why do you ask?

KATHLEEN
Tonight, everything *is* different. I seem to be pulling men toward me as if they were little pieces of steel.

MARGARET
How lucky for you.

KATHLEEN
Oh, no. It hasn't been lucky. I'm afraid I've caused a lot of confusion.

MARGARET
I've always had the opposite reaction on men. Maybe my magnetic poles are reversed.

KATHLEEN
I don't believe that, Margaret. You're so clever. And you speak so well.

MARGARET
I argue well.

KATHLEEN
It's wonderful to watch you. All those gears and wheels moving in your brain. You're like a new clock with a shiny brass face, ticking away and telling us all the time.

MARGARET
Why don't people ever compare me to a tiger. I'd like that. Creeping through the jungle. My soft paws crushing the dark green grass.

KATHLEEN
Go on.

MARGARET
Sorry. That's all. The clock has chimed.

KATHLEEN
Are you angry with me? Don't be that way. Please.

MARGARET
I'm not angry, Kathleen. Just impatient. I want an adventure. A grand adventure. I don't want to spend the rest of my life waiting for something to happen.

KATHLEEN
You'll have adventures. I'm sure of that.

MARGARET
Tell me something, Kathleen. Do I seem different to you?

KATHLEEN
Oh, yes! I've never met a woman like you before.

MARGARET
Different...in a physical way.

KATHLEEN
What do you mean?

MARGARET
Do you sense...Can you perceive...
    (gives up)
Look at me. I'm a virgin. Does it show?

KATHLEEN
What are the signs of being a virgin? Is it the way a girl walks or wears her dress? You do look like a lady.

MARGARET
I would like to have a lover. Someone like your Michael James. Does that surprise you?

KATHLEEN
Oh, don't do that! It just makes problems! They either boss you around or follow you around.

MARGARET
I have a friend in Concord. A philosopher named Ralph Emerson. He's one of most intelligent, sensitive men I know and yet he keeps his wife out of the study while we're having our conversations. If he's that way, then how would an ordinary man act?

KATHLEEN
Ordinary, I expect. You'll have to cook his food and wash his clothes and pull off his boots when he passes out drunk on the bed.

MARGARET
You make it sound so appealing.

KATHLEEN
There are good men, too. Michael James is a good man. It's just that he wants to put me on a wagon bound for Ohio.

MARGARET
And what do you want to do?

KATHLEEN
My mother taught me how to read and cipher before she died. But I've always wanted to study it proper in a school.

MARGARET
I could arrange that for you. But you'd have to go back to Boston.

KATHLEEN
Really? Are you sure? Oh, that would be wonderful!

MARGARET
I think you'd be very good student.

KATHLEEN
You don't think it would be a waste of money?

MARGARET
Not at all. Women must be self-reliant. It is our only salvation.

KATHLEEN
You make it sound so easy.

Margaret coaxes Kathleen to stand up.

MARGARET
Come with me. Right now. We'll sneak back to the farmhouse, grab our belongings, and walk to Roxbury. We can leave on the morning train.

KATHLEEN
Walk in the dark?

MARGARET
Why not? There's a lovely moon.

They start to cross the stage together.

KATHLEEN
And I'll go to school? And read?

MARGARET
Of course. Education is one of the
most important things in the world.

KATHLEEN
What about animal magnetism?
How does that come into it?

Margaret stops walking for a moment.

MARGARET
From what I've seen in the last
few days, animal magnetism can
take care of itself.

Blackout. The women exit. It's early the next morning.
Lights up as Charles and Nathaniel walk across the pasture.

CHARLES
Once more, the gold mine. A critic might
say this has become a recurrent theme in
my work.

NATHANIEL
We shouldn't be working at all.
Everyone's exhausted from running
around last night.

CHARLES
I had a wonderful time. It was
much more fun than debating the
rational use of labor.

Nathaniel turns and looks at Charles.

NATHANIEL
You won't tell anyone.

CHARLES
About what?

NATHANIEL
Our...conversation.

CHARLES
I'd like to tell everyone about it,
Nathaniel, but the mood seems to
have disappeared in the cold dawn
light.

Charles approaches the dung pile.

CHARLES
Once again, you have your Miss
Peabody and I have my poetry
...and the gold mine.

NATHANIEL
It's not only the mood that's
vanished. Margaret and Kathleen
have fled like a pair of wood nymphs.

CHARLES
The wood nymphs took the six o'clock
train to Boston.

Sophia and George enter. Sophia carries a rake.

GEORGE
Well, this is a pleasant surprise!
You're both up early...ready to work!

SOPHIA
Did you find Margaret's note?

CHARLES
Yes. We read it.

GEORGE
All this is really for the best.
I'm sure that Margaret will find
a good school for Kathleen.

CHARLES
Is Michael James still asleep? Does
he know what happened?

SOPHIA
He and I were searching
together. When we came back to
the farmhouse we found the note
on the kitchen table.

NATHANIEL
Was he angry?

SOPHIA
He seemed rather exhausted. Spent.

Charles looks downstage and sees Michael James.

CHARLES
Well, here he comes right now,
marching up the hill like a
soldier off to war.

                    GEORGE
          Apparently he marched Sophia all
          over the farm last night. Her dress
          was covered with dew.

                    SOPHIA
          Yes. It was quite a vigorous...hike.

Michael James enters.

                    MICHAEL JAMES
          I took some bread and cheese from
          the kitchen. I'll be glad to pay
          you for it.

                    GEORGE
          Nonsense, Michael James. You worked
          hard yesterday. For a short period
          of time you were a member of Brook Farm.

Michael James shakes George's hand.

                    MICHAEL JAMES
          I'll consider that an honor, Mr.
          Ripley. Kathleen was right. This is a
          wonderful place. You can be any-
          thing you want here...for a time.

                    GEORGE
          If you meet other working men and
          women of good moral character,
          please send them here.

                    MICHAEL JAMES
          I'll do what I can.

Michael James shakes Charles' hand.

                    CHARLES
          Where are you going, Michael James?
          Off to Boston in search of the fair
          Kathleen?

                    MICHAEL JAMES
          No. She's got to go her own way.
          I'm traveling west to work on the
          railroad. I'll keep saving my
          money. Try to buy some land.

                    NATHANIEL
          Good luck.

Michael James shakes Nathaniel's hand.

                    MICHAEL JAMES
          Thank you. Thanks to all of you.

He glances at Sophia, hesitates, then turns and walks away.

                    GEORGE
          A fine young man. When he arrived, he
          wanted to crack our skulls. Remember?

                    CHARLES
          And you were going to skewer him
          with your pitchfork.

                    SOPHIA
          Oh, I...I should tell him which
          way to get back to the main road.

                    GEORGE
          He knows, Sophia. He found his way here.

                    SOPHIA
          I better make sure. We don't want
          him tramping across someone else's
          pasture.

Sophia crosses the stage while Charles and George remain by the manure pile. Nathaniel walks upstage.

                    SOPHIA
          Mr. Connor! Mr. Connor!

Michael James stops walking as Sophia approaches him.

                    SOPHIA
          I don't suppose we'll see each
          other again.

                    MICHAEL JAMES
          Not unless you want to come along
          with me.

                    SOPHIA
          Don't make a joke, Michael James.

                    MICHAEL JAMES
          I'm not joking at all. Take my hand
          and we'll walk down the road together.

                    SOPHIA
          That would destroy my husband.

MICHAEL JAMES
Maybe. But he's got the farm and all his dreams. Believe me, I know about dreams. They can give you comfort.

SOPHIA
I can't go.

MICHAEL JAMES
Talk to your husband. Tell him what happened.

SOPHIA
It's not just George. It's me, too. I like Brook Farm. I'm happy here. I really am a minister's wife. But now I have one small secret in my heart. It's a passionate secret. Luxurious. I think I'll like having it there.

George shouts to his wife.

GEORGE
Tell him to take the canal road! It's faster!

Sophia reaches out and shakes Michael James's hand.

SOPHIA
Farewell. Have a good journey.

MICHAEL JAMES
Every time I see the moon, I'm going to think of you.

SOPHIA
Good.

She turns and walks back to her husband. Michael James exits. Nathaniel remains standing upstage.

GEORGE
All right. We're finished with animal magnetism and young seamstresses and love. It's time to improve the soil. That's what this country really needs.

CHARLES
Isn't there some other issue we can debate? Preferably in the shade.

GEORGE
No more debates. Let's get to work.

Sophia moves toward the garden area with her rake, then she stops and faces her husband.

SOPHIA
Could I have your shovel, George?

GEORGE
Whatever for?

SOPHIA
I would like your shovel.

She walks over to her husband, pulls the shovel from his hand and gives him the rake.

GEORGE
If there's a stone or something, I'll get it.

SOPHIA
Please.

GEORGE
Sophia! What are you doing? We already discussed this. The men shovel. The women rake.

CHARLES
Margaret didn't accept that idea.

GEORGE
Margaret...is Margaret. Sophia is a more practical woman.

SOPHIA
I'll rake tomorrow, George. We'll take turns.

GEORGE
That's not the plan.

SOPHIA
Yes, it is.

Sophia exits. George follows after her. Nathaniel sits downstage.

GEORGE
That's not the plan!

CHARLES
I think I'm going to go look for eggs.

Charles approaches Nathaniel and sits beside him.

CHARLES
What are you thinking, Nathaniel? Whatever it is, it makes you look very poetical.

NATHANIEL
Look at the horizon. You can see the mountains in the distance.

CHARLES
Yes. I can see them.

NATHANIEL
I've been in Salem too long. Hiding upstairs in my little room. This country of ours is vast and unrestrained. There are unknown rivers and grasslands. A wilderness that has never been surveyed. All is possible here. All is possible. But only if we discover a New World in our hearts...

Nathaniel glances at Charles, then looks back at the horizon. Music. The lights fade.

www.ingramcontent.com/pod-product-compliance
Lightning Source LLC
Chambersburg PA
CBHW051751100526
44591CB00017B/2657